ONE PIECE:
PIRATE RECIPES
By Sanji

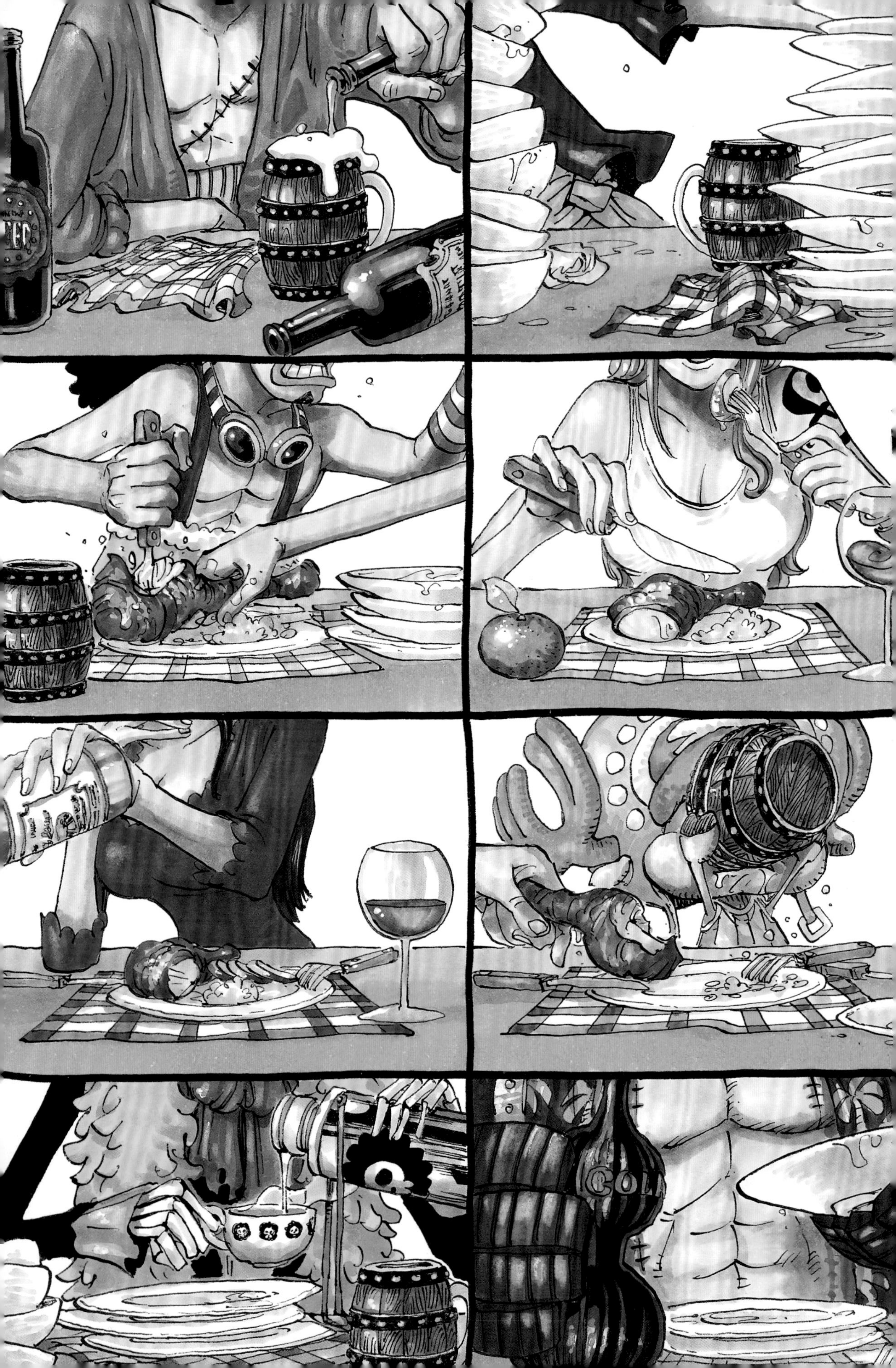

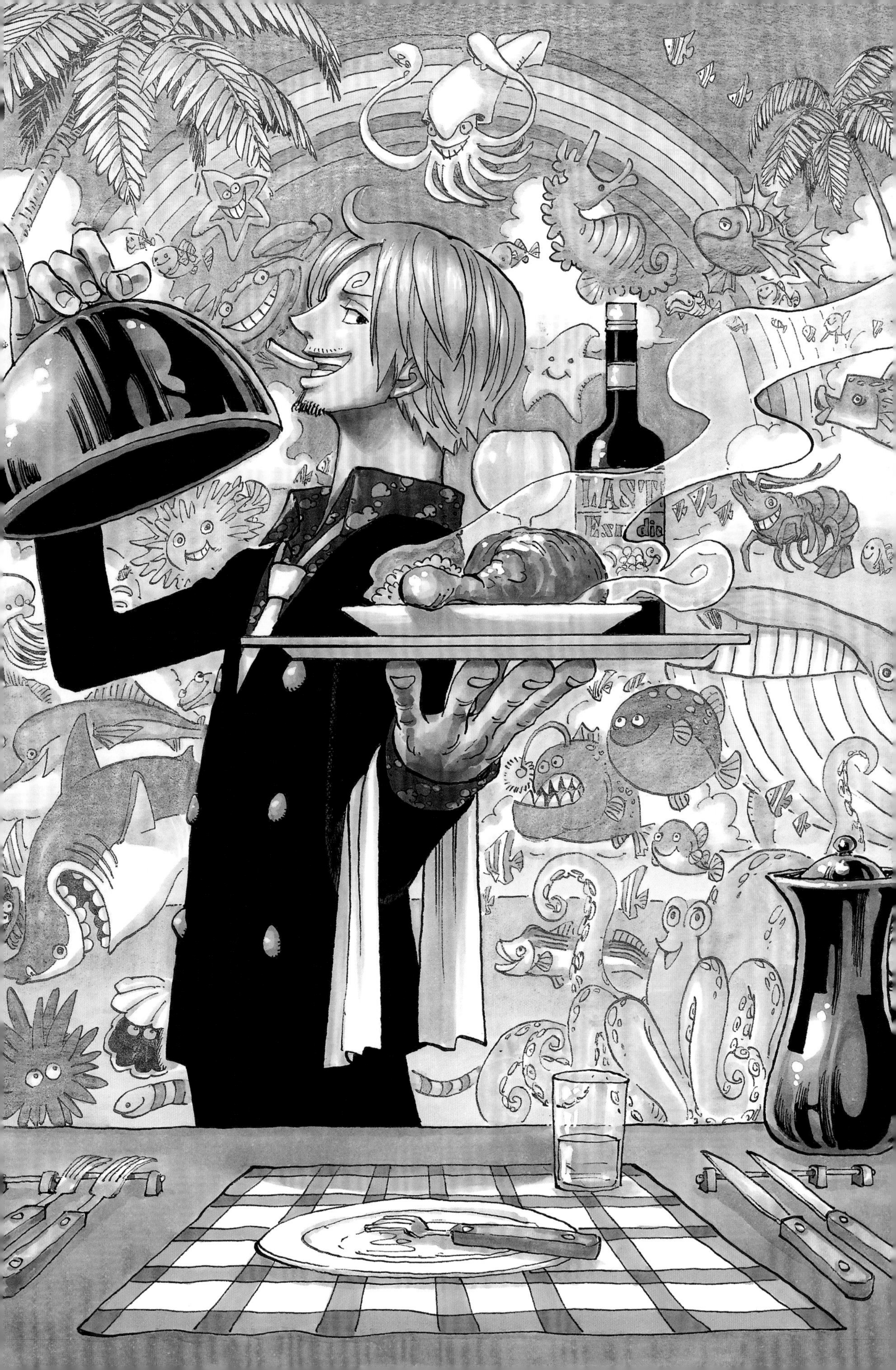

Sanji

A first-rate cook of the sea who mans the kitchen for the Straw Hat Crew. His keen eye for selecting ingredients of all kinds is second to none. He's also an expert kicker, having learned from his master, Red-Leg Zeff. But he has a fondness (weakness) for women.

Hey! You ever eaten my cooking?

I've been a cook for many years and have spent my time cooking dishes at sea. My crew and I have come across all kinds of ingredients on our adventures. In this book, I'm going to teach you the secrets of how to prepare them.

You might find certain things in these recipes that aren't available in your world, so just substitute with something a bit more familiar if you need to.

And I can guarantee the taste of these dishes. I've simplified the directions so you can whip them up just as fast as I do on the ship.

Finally...cooking is love.

If even the mere peeling of the onion is performed without love...the dish will be ruined.

Good luck in the kitchen!

BEFORE YOU START

Each recipe is proportioned for ease of preparation.

The steps to making a basic **dashi broth** like a first-class cook are on pages 94 and 95. However, you may substitute a store-bought instant concentrate diluted in water too.

A tablespoon (tbsp.) is 15 ml, and a teaspoon (tsp.) is 5 ml.

Sea Chicken is a trademarked product of Hagoromo Foods.

CONTENTS

Instantl

If a man is hungry, I feed him!

You can't do nothin' on an empty stomach! When you're starving, what's better than a power meal to replenish your stamina? Rice, bread, and pasta will fill you up and give you the strength to bust out of any trouble! You eat your fill? Feelin' better? Then let's get moving.

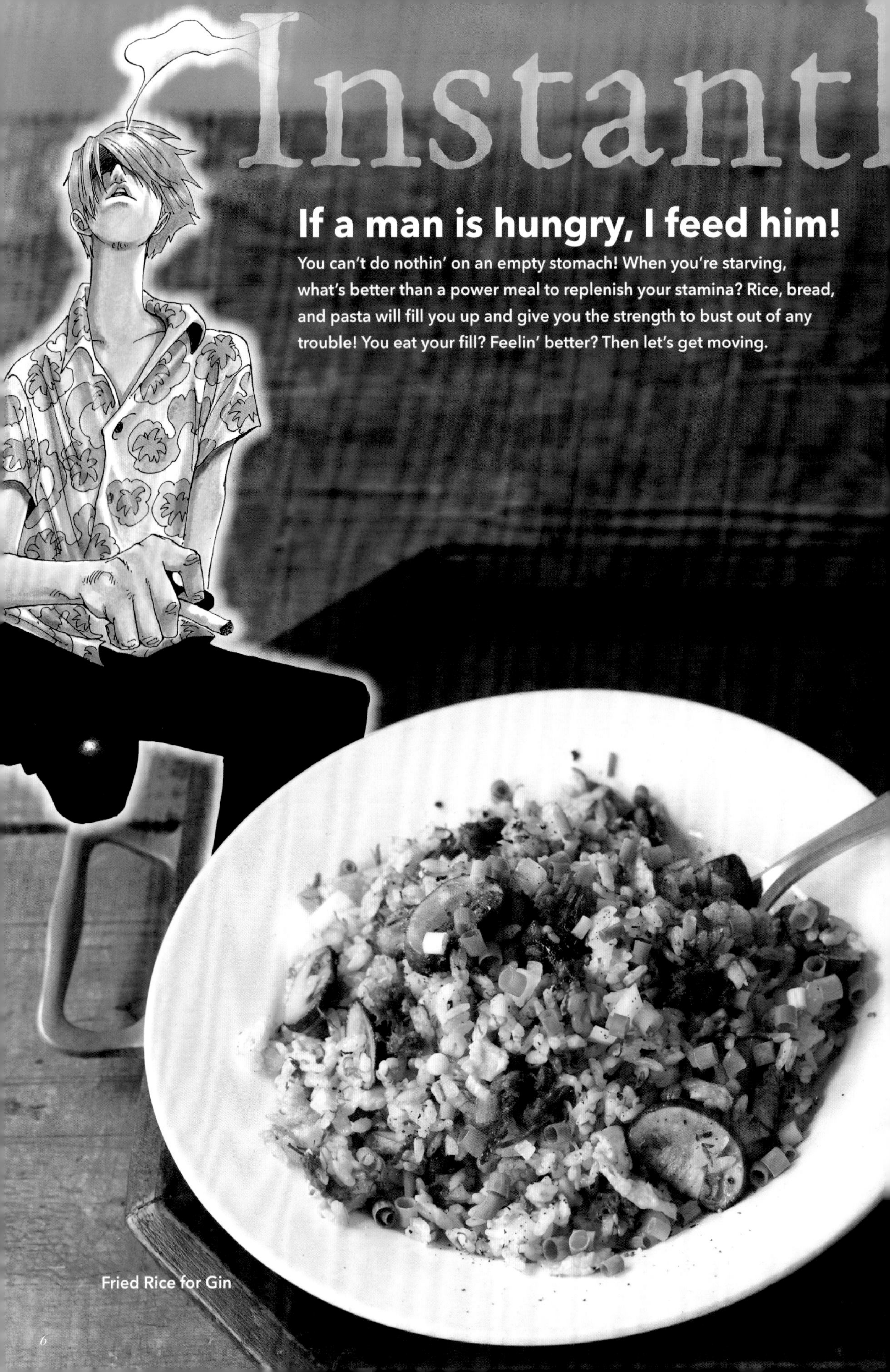

Fried Rice for Gin

Filling Meals

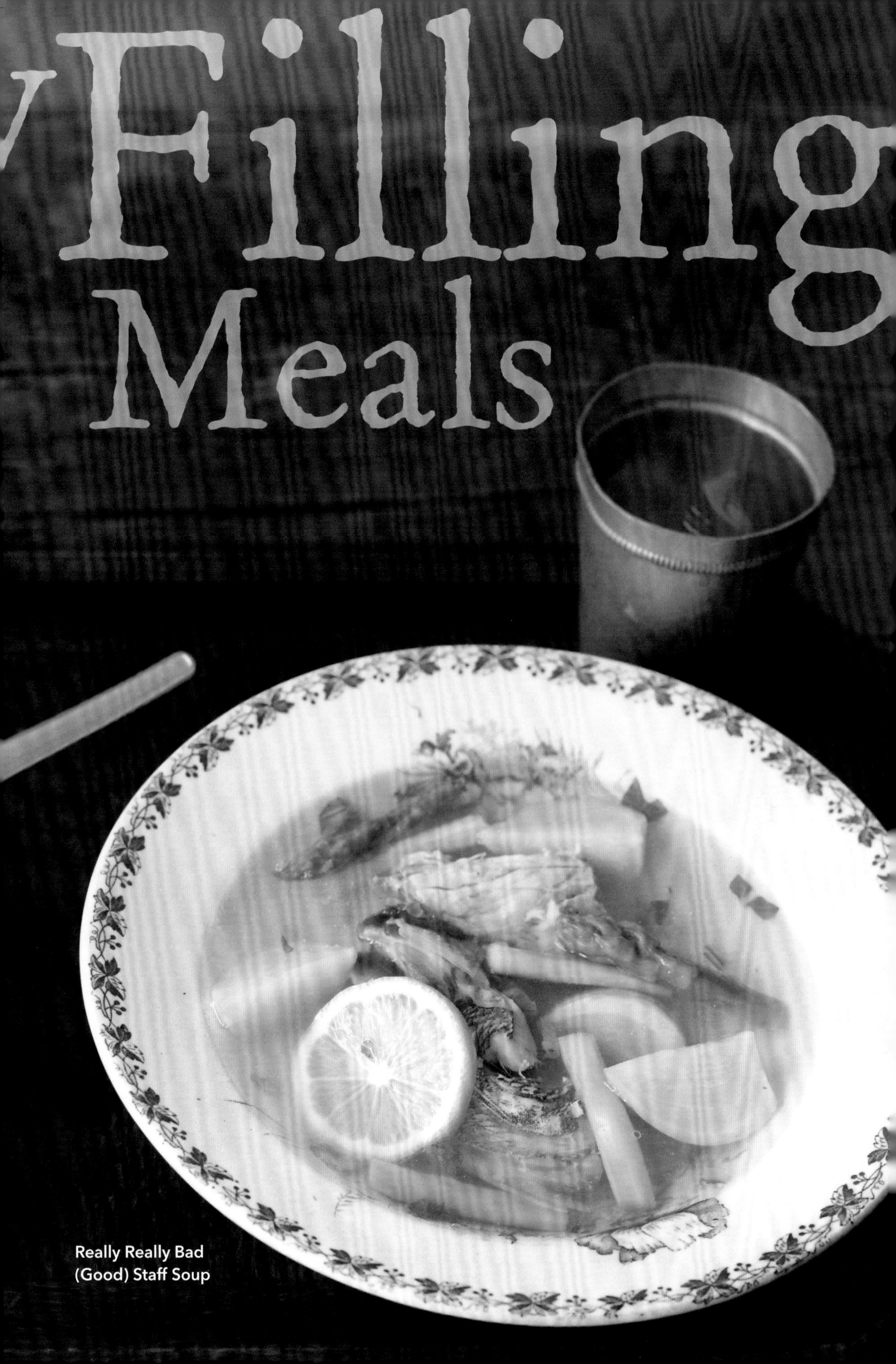

Really Really Bad
(Good) Staff Soup

Fried Rice
for Gin

Fried rice with corned beef you can cook in one frying pan!

INGREDIENTS Serves 2

2 cups (360 g) cooked rice
2 large eggs, beaten
about 2 oz. (50 g) corned beef
¼ onion
4 small brown mushrooms
1 tbsp. vegetable oil
½ tsp. salt
black pepper to taste
1 ½ tsp. soy sauce
1–2 green onions to taste

STEPS

① Mince the onion, finely slice the mushrooms, and chop the green onions.

② Oil the frying pan and fry half the minced onion and all the mushrooms, then add the corned beef.

③ Push the fried ingredients to one side of the pan and apply more oil to the empty space, then pour in the beaten eggs **(A)**. Add the rice before the egg firms up and mix everything in the pan. Sprinkle salt and pepper, and then add the remaining onion. Drizzle in soy sauce from the side of the pan **(B)** and mix briefly. When cooked, divide between plates and scatter the chopped green onions on top.

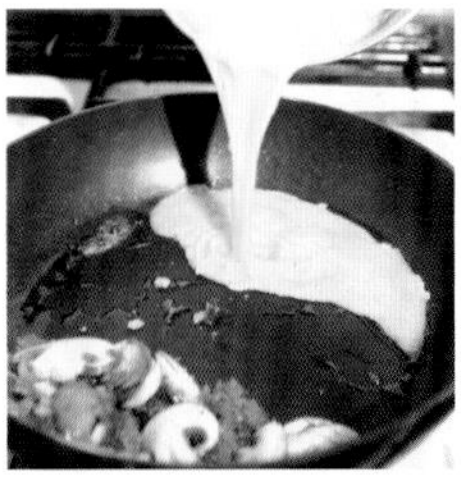
A

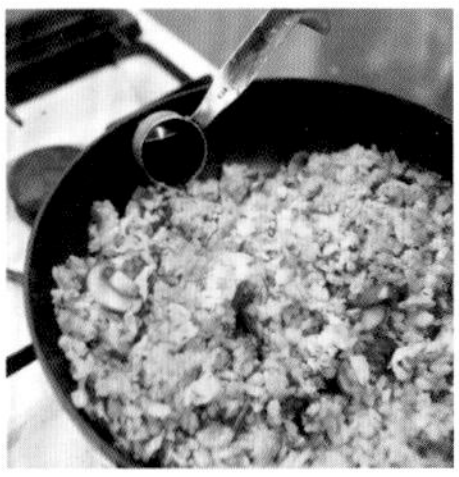
B

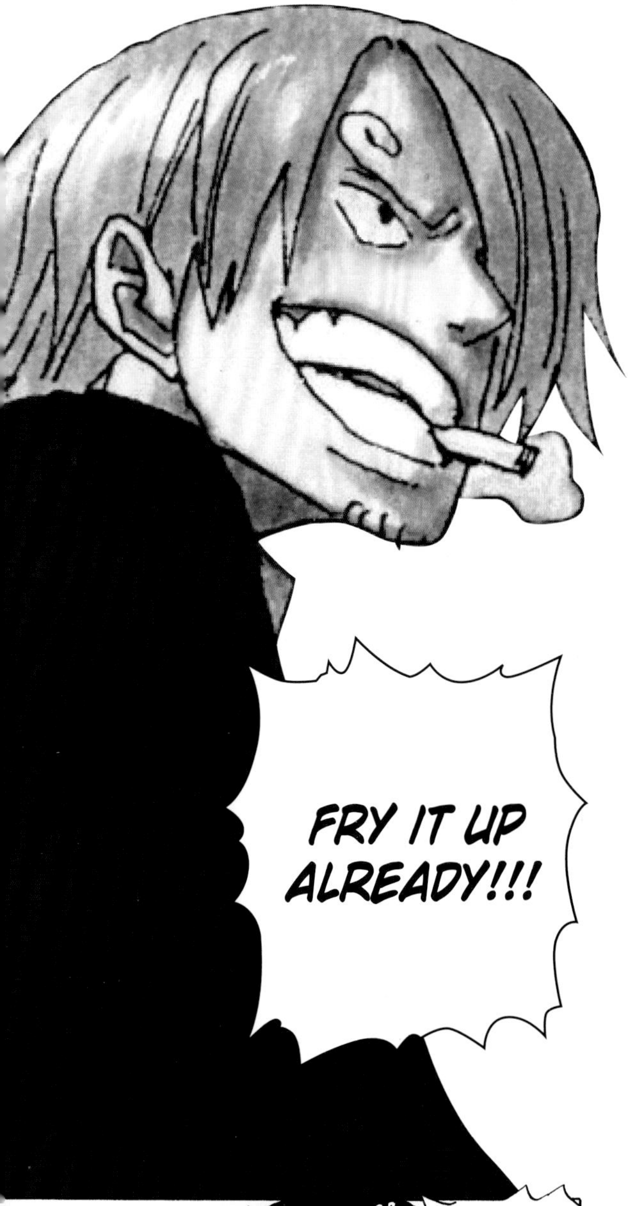
FRY IT UP ALREADY!!!

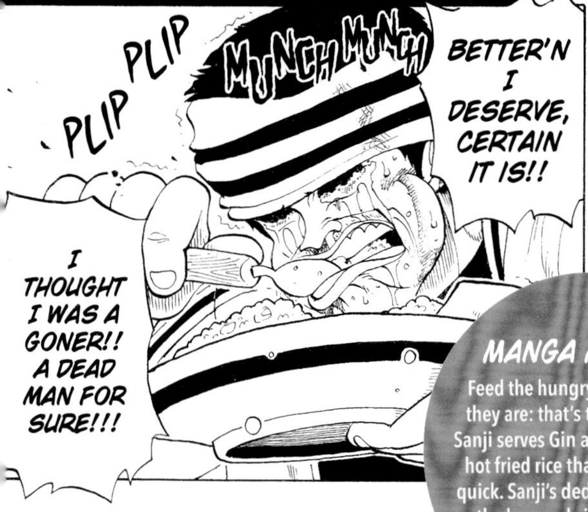
BETTER'N I DESERVE, CERTAIN IT IS!!
MUNCH MUNCH
PLIP PLIP
PLIP
I THOUGHT I WAS A GONER!! A DEAD MAN FOR SURE!!!

MANGA MOMENT

Feed the hungry, no matter who they are: that's the job of a cook. Sanji serves Gin a plate of steaming hot fried rice that he whipped up quick. Sanji's dedication to feeding the hungry brings tears to the eyes of this demon man.
(FROM VOL. 5, CH. 44)

Really Really Bad (Good)

Staff Soup

A Western-style clear soup made with sea bream and kombu kelp

INGREDIENTS Serves 2-3

1 sea bream head (about 11 oz./300 g, Japanese name "madai")
1 sheet kombu (4x4 in.)
2 turnips
6 asparagus pencil spears
½ lemon
5 cups (1,200 ml) water, plus more to boil
2 tsp. salt
a little soy sauce

STEPS

① Soak kombu in water for at least 30 minutes. Slice the sea bream head into pieces if necessary and place in a separate pot of boiling water deep enough to cover fish head. When the surface becomes white, remove and place in another bowl of cold water, then scrub clean to remove blood and stains **(C)**.

② Cut turnips into wedges and slice greens finely. Peel the bottom third of asparagus and slice into 2 inch (5 cm) pieces. Slice lemon into wheels.

③ Pour water from ① and sea bream into same pot and bring to boil. Skim the scum off the top and lower heat to medium. Add turnip wedges **(D)** and let simmer, skimming regularly.

④ After 10 minutes, add asparagus and simmer for 5 minutes. Add salt, and soy sauce to taste. Transfer to bowls, add lemon slices, and scatter turnip greens on top.

C

D

HEY, WHO MADE THIS CRAP-AWFUL MUCK !!?
WE CAN'T SERVE A MESS LIKE THIS TO OUR CUSTOMERS !!!
BUT THIS SOUP IS REALLY GOOD!!
!
GLUG GLUG GLUG

MANGA MOMENT

A soup Sanji served to the restaurant staff just after the battle against Krieg. The *Baratie* cooks all made a show of saying it was bad, but of course, it was perfect. It was Sanji's final piece of work on the *Baratie*, and the start of his send-off.

(FROM VOL. 8, CH. 67)

THE SECRET IS THE KOMBU BROTH!!

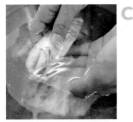

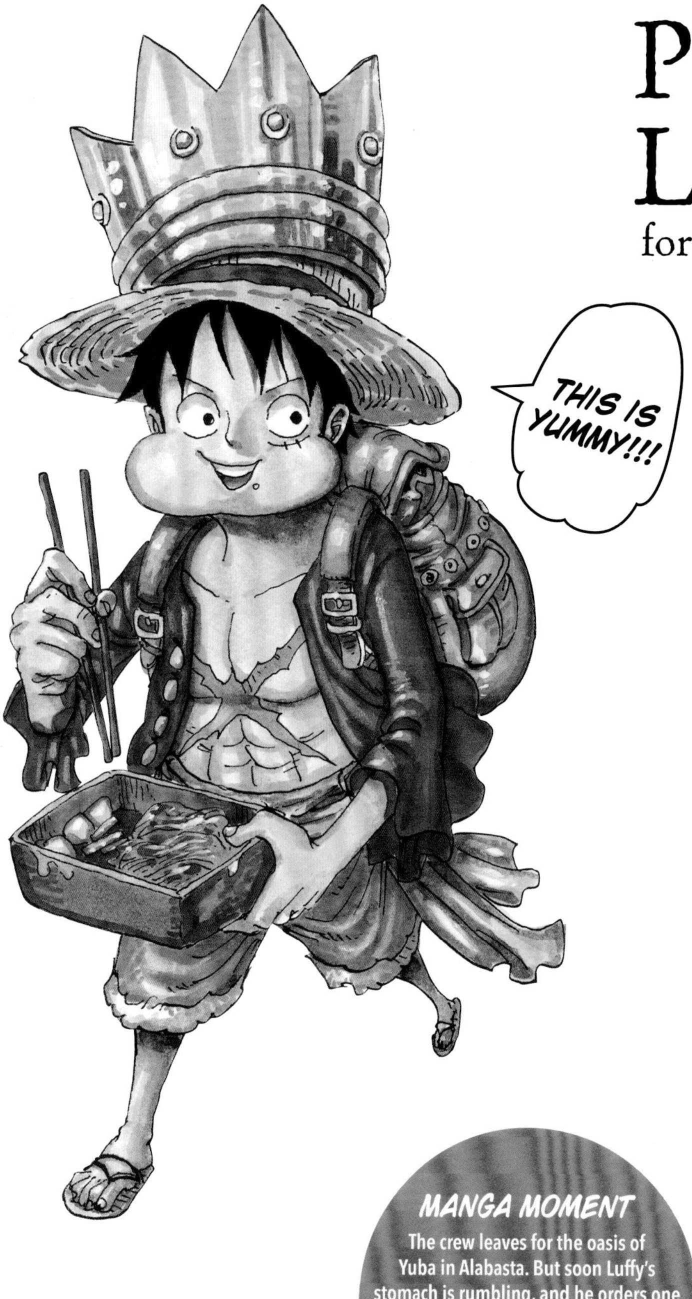
THIS IS YUMMY!!!

Pirate Box Lunches for Crossing the Desert

Lightly breaded fried chicken

INGREDIENTS Serves 4

2 boneless, skinless chicken thighs (about 18 oz./500 g)

Mix (a.)

- **1 clove garlic, grated**
- **1 tsp. salt**
- **1 tbsp. saké**
- **a bit of black pepper**

about 4 tbsp. all-purpose flour
about 4 tbsp. of vegetable oil
***Sausages and hard-boiled eggs optional.**

STEPS

① Trim fat and sinew from chicken thighs and cut into bite-size pieces. Grate garlic. Put chicken into a bowl, add mix **(a.)**, and marinate for 20–30 minutes.

② Sprinkle flour over ①. Heat up vegetable oil in a pan on medium heat, then fry chicken in batches for 4–5 minutes undisturbed each side.

Tomato and roe spaghetti

INGREDIENTS Serves 2

about 6 ½ oz. (180 g) spaghetti
8 cups (2,000 ml) water
1 sheet kombu (4x4 in./10x10 cm)
⅓ oz. (10 g) salt

Sauce

- **1 strip (about 60 g) pollock roe**
- **3–4 tbsp. grated tomato**
- **⅓ oz. (10 g) butter**
- **chopped nori seaweed to taste**

STEPS

① Heat water, kombu, and salt in a pot. Separate pollock roe from outer membrane **(A)** and grate tomato. Place roe, tomato, and butter in a bowl.

② Boil spaghetti according to package instructions, then remove from water and add to ① bowl and mix **(B)**. If sauce is too thin, add a small amount of liquid from the pot. Transfer to container and add chopped nori on top.

MANGA MOMENT

The crew leaves for the oasis of Yuba in Alabasta. But soon Luffy's stomach is rumbling, and he orders one of Sanji's pirate box lunches. It's meant for refueling energy, so it gets Luffy's seal of approval. This is stamina food for explosive power!!

(FROM VOL. 18, CH. 162)

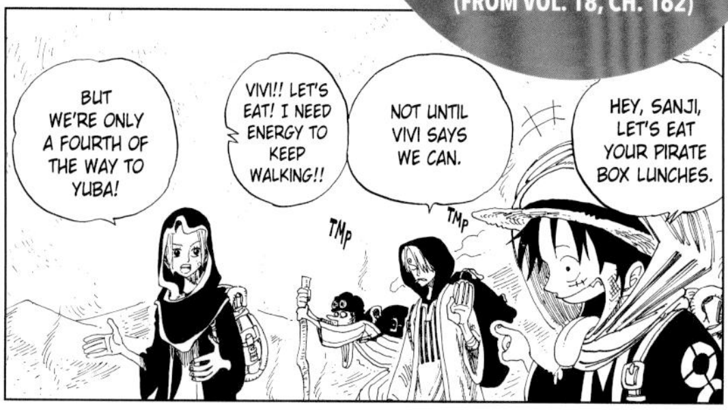
HEY, SANJI, LET'S EAT YOUR PIRATE BOX LUNCHES.
NOT UNTIL VIVI SAYS WE CAN.
TMP
VIVI!! LET'S EAT! I NEED ENERGY TO KEEP WALKING!!
TMP
BUT WE'RE ONLY A FOURTH OF THE WAY TO YUBA!

A

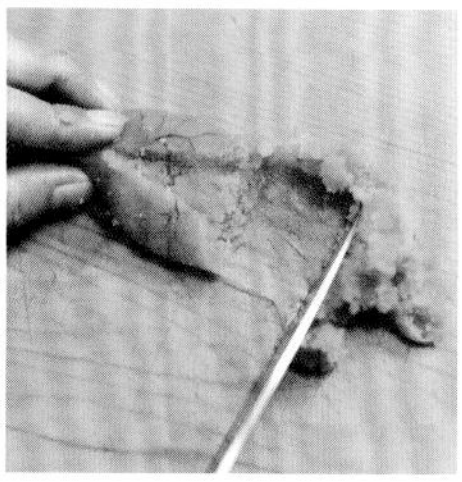

B

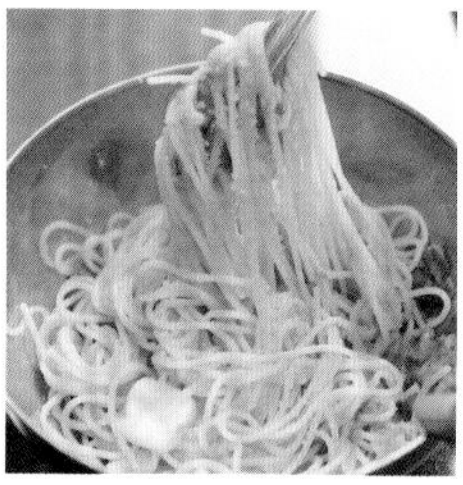

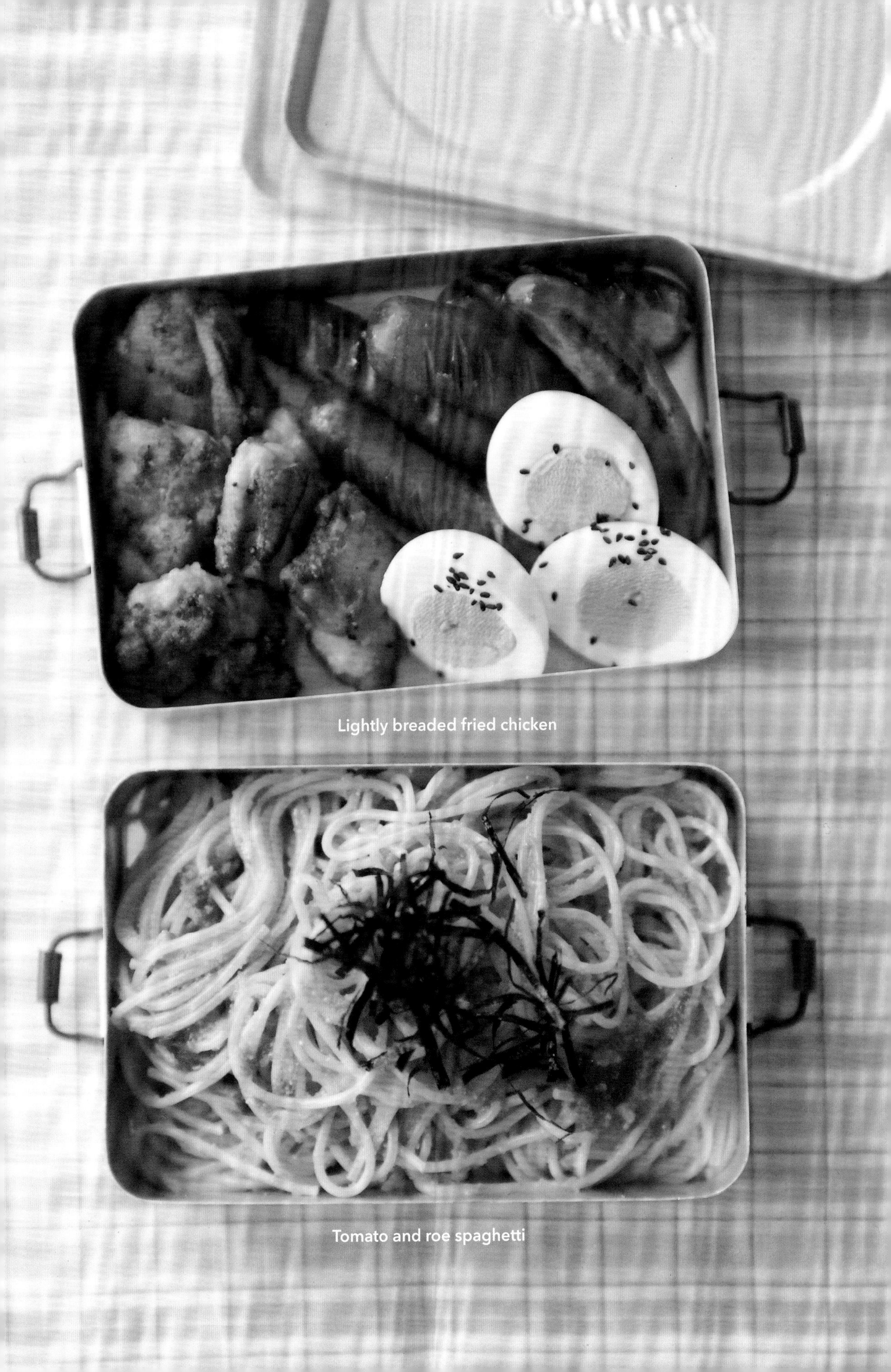

Lightly breaded fried chicken

Tomato and roe spaghetti

Treasure-splitting

Sandwiches

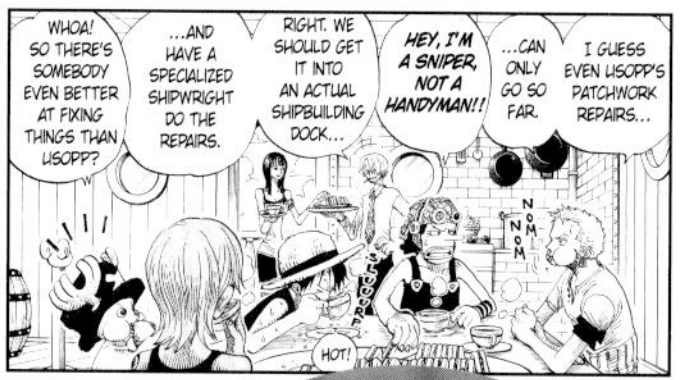
I GUESS EVEN USOPP'S PATCHWORK REPAIRS...
...CAN ONLY GO SO FAR.
HEY, I'M A SNIPER, NOT A HANDYMAN!!
RIGHT. WE SHOULD GET IT INTO AN ACTUAL SHIPBUILDING DOCK...
...AND HAVE A SPECIALIZED SHIPWRIGHT DO THE REPAIRS.
WHOA! SO THERE'S SOMEBODY EVEN BETTER AT FIXING THINGS THAN USOPP?
NOM NOM
HOT!

Full of ingredients from the sea! Three flavors of sandwich

MANGA MOMENT

Upon returning to the Blue Sea from Skypiea, the crew has a meeting to decide their next destination. The accompaniment to their discussion is Sanji's special sandwiches. The more they eat, the more they discuss. Usopp just brought up a good idea!!

(FROM VOL. 32, CH. 303)

INGREDIENTS

Egg and Crab 3 sandwiches

- 6 slices of bread
- 3 eggs
- 2 oz. (60 g) boiled crab meat (or imitation crab)
- 2 tbsp. onion, minced
- 2 tbsp. mayonnaise
- room temperature butter

Tuna 3 sandwiches

- 6 slices of bread
- about 4 oz. (120 g) raw tuna, roughly chopped
- salt to taste
- garlic power or grated garlic to taste
- white pepper to taste
- 1 tsp. olive oil
- 2-3 basil leaves
- butter
- mayonnaise

Potato and Canned Tuna 2 sandwiches

- 4 slices of bread
- 2.8 oz. (80 g) Sea Chicken® canned tuna
- 1 potato (5 oz./150 g)
- 1 ¾ tsp. (10 g) butter
- a little salt
- a little black pepper
- Worcestershire sauce to taste
- 1 tbsp. mayonnaise

STEPS

① **Egg and Crab:** Boil eggs whole for 12 minutes until hard-boiled. Let cool. Peel off shells and cut into thick slices. Tear crab meat by hand. Mince onion, then soak in water, remove, and press liquid out. Put egg, crab, and onion into a bowl, then mix with mayonnaise **(A)**. Spread butter on bread slices, then divide mix to make three sandwiches.

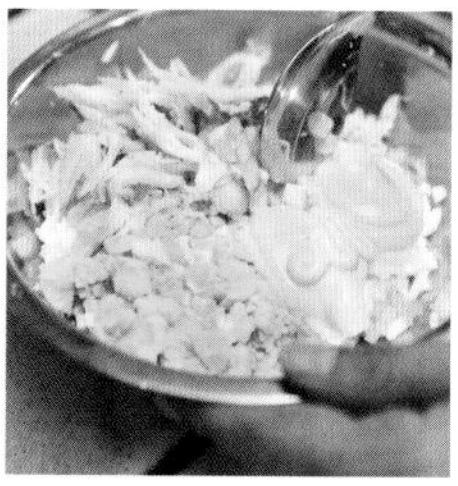
A

② **Tuna:** Put tuna into a bowl and mix with salt, garlic powder, white pepper, and olive oil. Tear up basil leaves and add to bowl **(B)**, then split contents into three equal parts. Spread butter on one piece of bread and mayonnaise on the other, then add contents to make sandwiches.

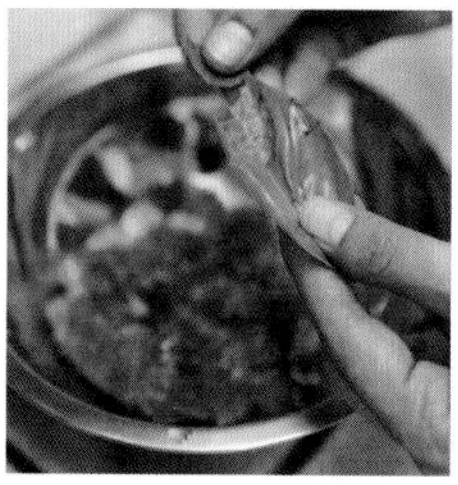
B

③ **Potato and Canned Tuna:** Drain oil from tuna can. Peel potato, cut into pieces ⅖ inch (1 cm) thick, boil for 10–12 minutes, then place in bowl with butter and mash lightly **(C)**. Mix in tuna, salt, black pepper, Worcestershire sauce, and mayonnaise. Split contents in half and make into sandwiches.

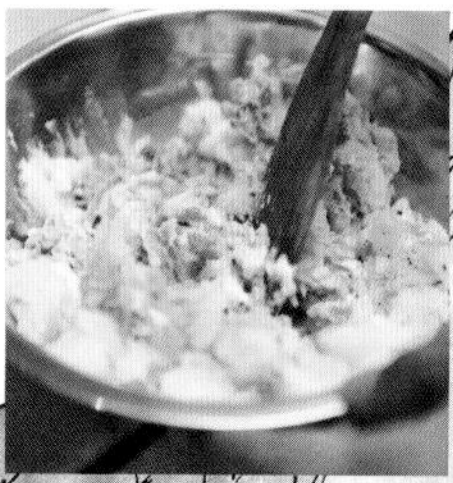
C

④ Remove crusts and slice sandwiches into into easy-to-eat pieces.

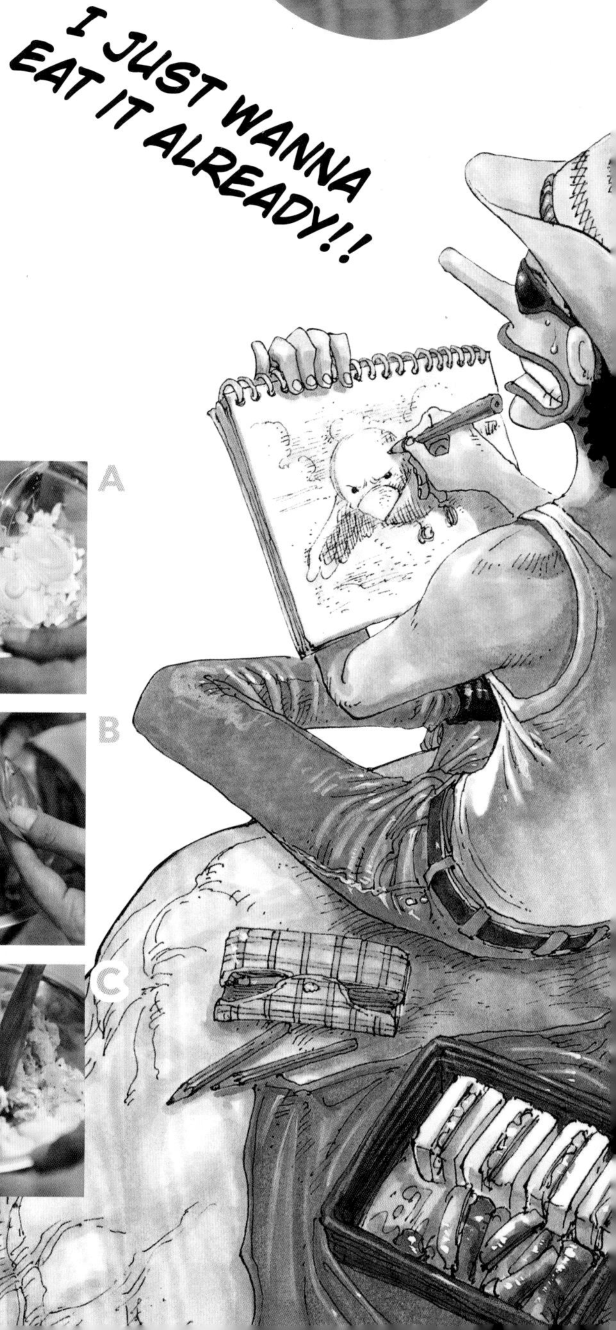
I JUST WANNA EAT IT ALREADY!!

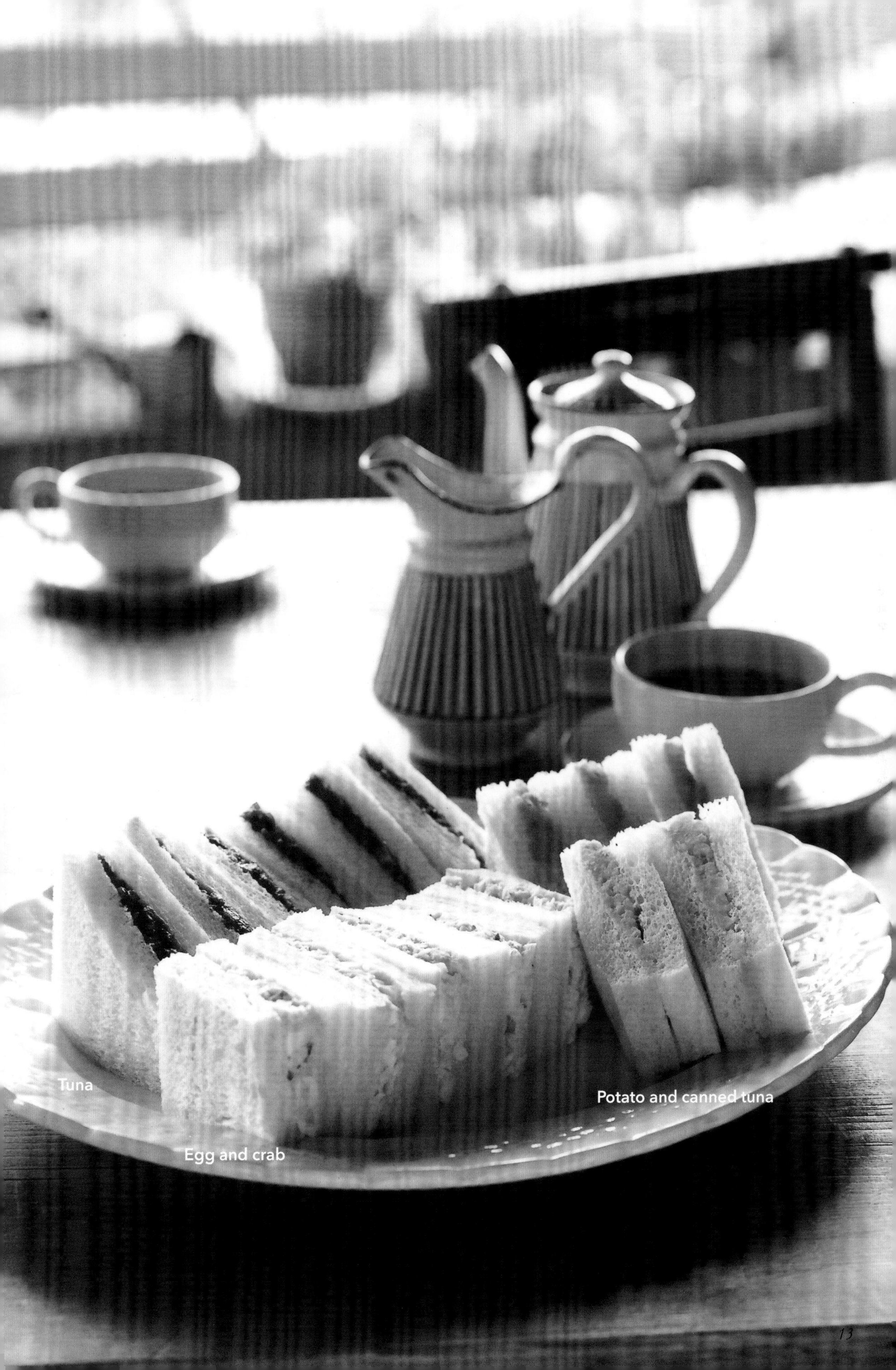
Tuna
Potato and canned tuna
Egg and crab

Hearty

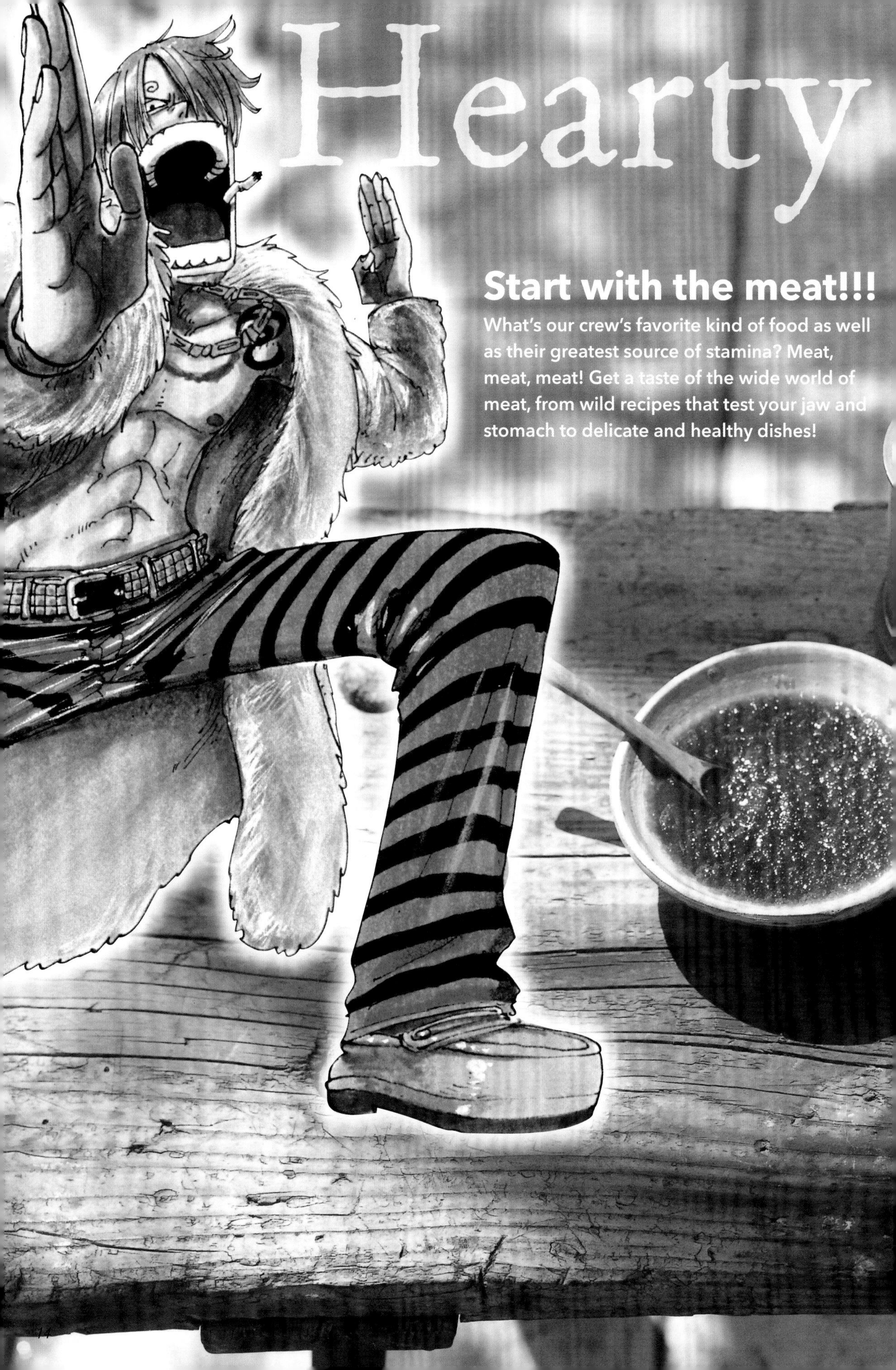

Start with the meat!!!

What's our crew's favorite kind of food as well as their greatest source of stamina? Meat, meat, meat! Get a taste of the wide world of meat, from wild recipes that test your jaw and stomach to delicate and healthy dishes!

Meat Recipes

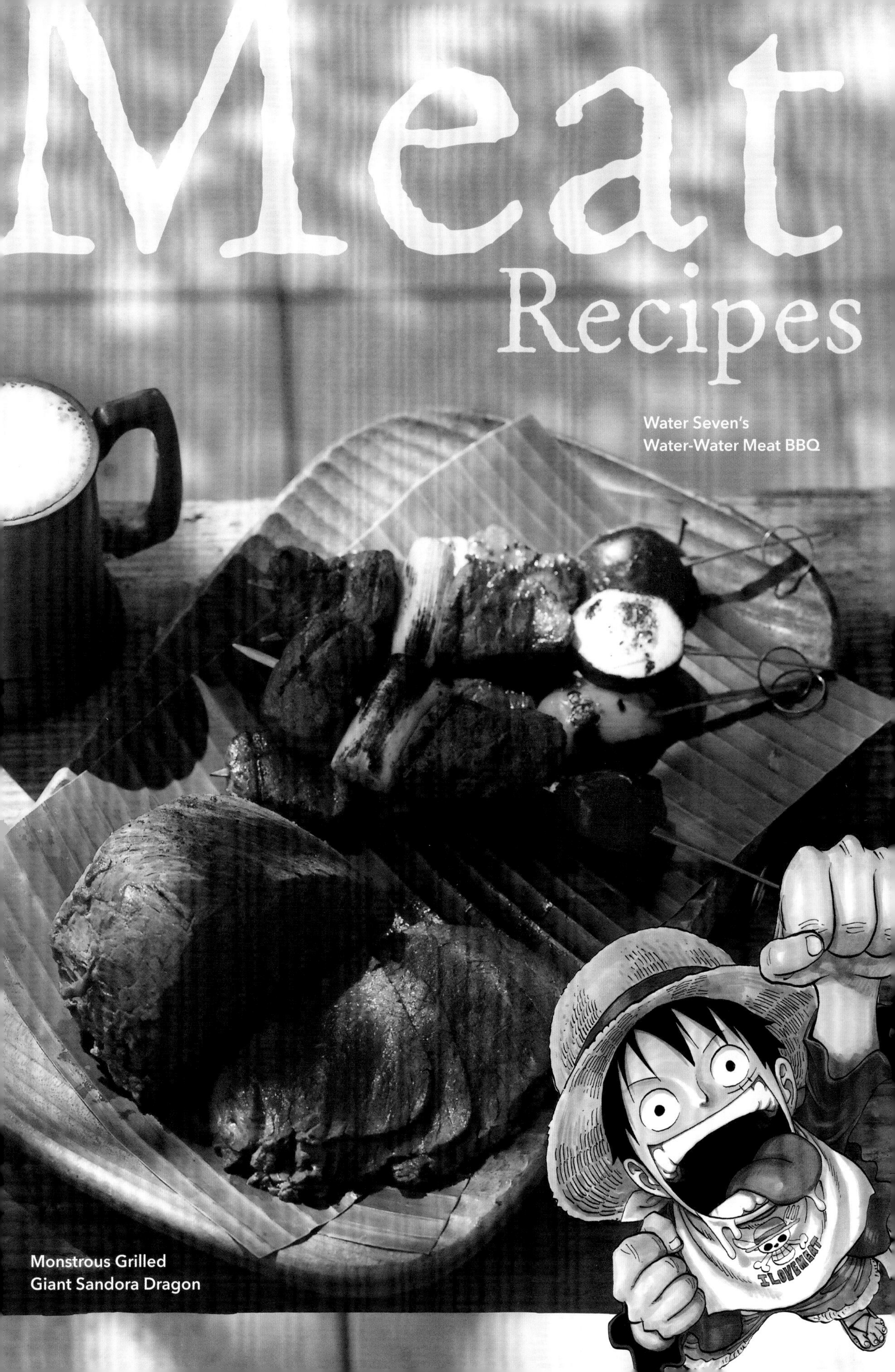

Water Seven's
Water-Water Meat BBQ

Monstrous Grilled
Giant Sandora Dragon

Monstrous
Grilled Giant Sandora Dragon

Roast beef cooked in the frying pan

INGREDIENTS

Portioned for easy preparation

14–18 oz. (400–500 g) prime or choice round steak, whole
½ clove garlic
1 tsp. salt
a little black pepper
1 tbsp. vegetable oil

Sauce

- **½ onion**
- **½ clove garlic**
- **3 tbsp. saké**
- **2 tbsp. soy sauce**
- **½ tbsp. butter**
- **½–1 tsp. vinegar**

STEPS

① Let beef sit at room temperature for 30 minutes, and grate onion and garlic for sauce. Just before cooking, rub the other garlic half against meat **(C)**, then rub on salt and pepper. Pour oil on a heated frying pan and cook the meat surface on medium heat **(D)**. Cover and heat on low for 6–8 minutes, then turn over and heat for another 4–5 minutes.

② Remove from pan, wrap in aluminum foil, and let sit for 15 minutes to heat through **(E)**.

③ Add onions, garlic and saké to the meat juice in the frying pan. Once bubbling, mix in soy sauce and butter. Once mixed in, turn off heat, add vinegar and mix again.

④ Slice meat thinly and transfer to plate, then drizzle sauce from pan. Add mustard or wasabi as desired.

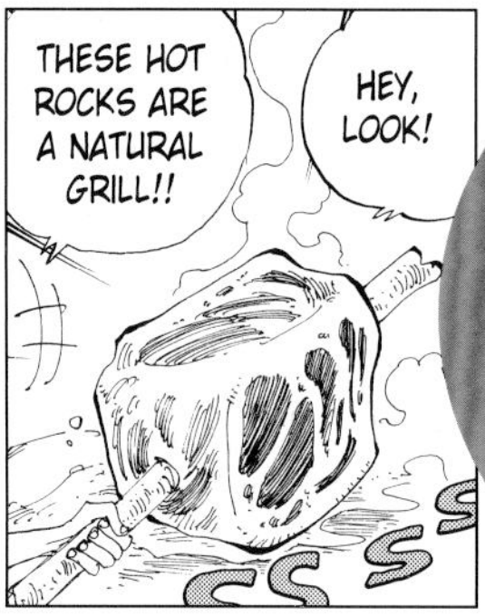
HEY, LOOK!
THESE HOT ROCKS ARE A NATURAL GRILL!!

MANGA MOMENT

The largest reptile found on Sandy Island, the desert home of the Kingdom of Alabasta. It's a fearsome beast with tough hide and muscular flesh, but to the Straw Hats, it's a feast!! Cook whole cuts of it on burning rocks and chow down!!
(FROM VOL. 18, CH. 162)

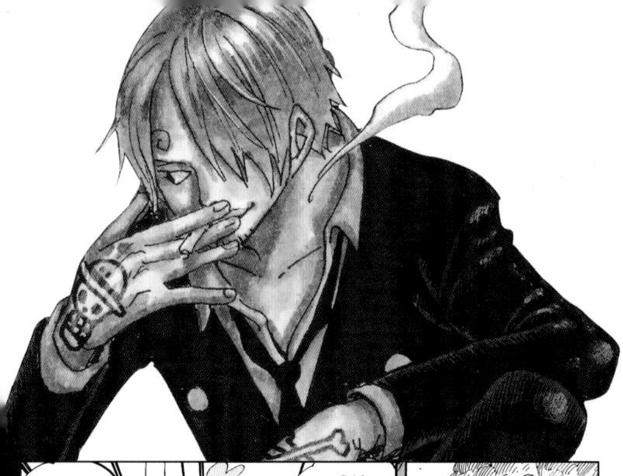

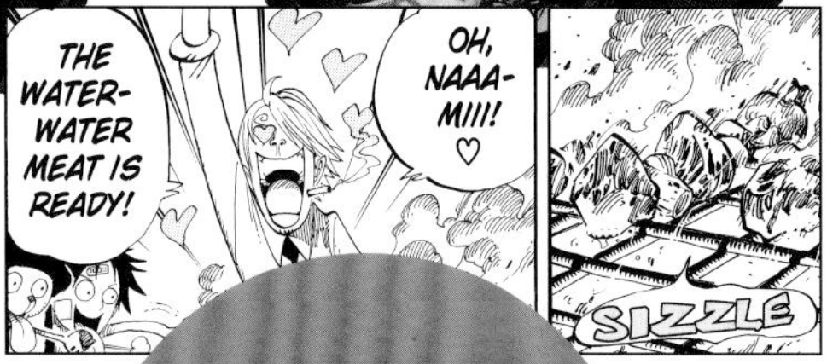
SIZZLE
OH, NAAA-MI!!! ♡
THE WATER-WATER MEAT IS READY!

MANGA MOMENT

On the day Luffy wakes up again, there's a huge feast at Water Seven with the crew, headlined by some Water-Water Meat BBQ!! Under Sanji's expert eye, it's grilled just right until the fat is dripping off!!
(FROM VOL. 45, CH. 433)

Water Seven's
Water-Water Meat BBQ

Just marinate the beef first

INGREDIENTS Serves 4

16 oz. beef, made into 1inch cubes
1 spring onion stalk
¼ each of red and yellow bell peppers
½ zucchini

Mix (a.)

- **¼ cup (50 ml) water**
- **1 ½ tsp. salt**
- **½ lemon**
- **1 clove garlic**
- **¼ onion**
- **a little black pepper**
- **½ tbsp. vegetable oil**

STEPS

① Slice lemon, garlic and onion. Put beef and marinade **(a.)** into a large plastic bag and knead well, then let sit for one hour **(A)**.

② Cut spring onion into 1 inch (3 cm) pieces. Cut bell peppers into bite-sized pieces. Slice zucchini into thin pieces.

③ Skewer meat ① and vegetables ② alternately, then place on grill on high heat and turn over until cooked evenly on both sides, roughly 1-2 minutes **(B)**.

A

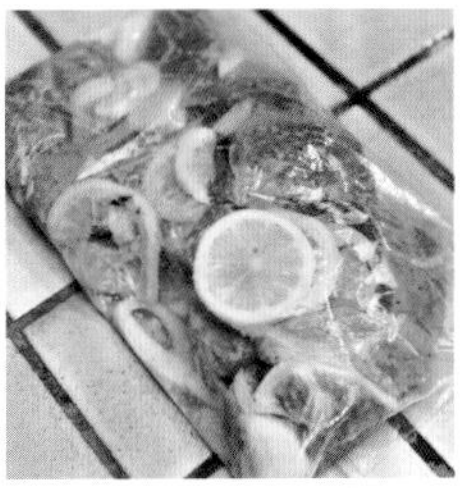

B

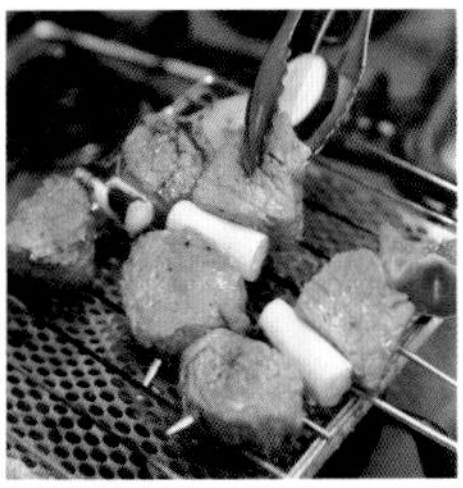

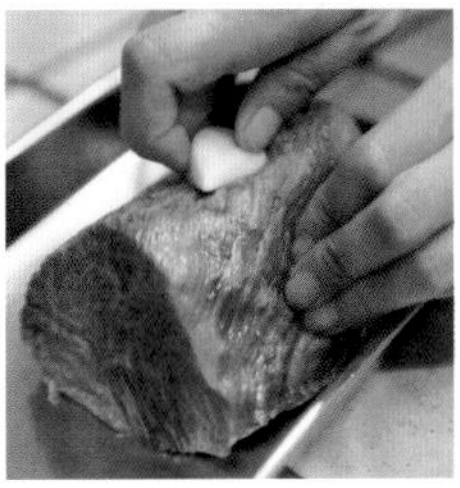

C

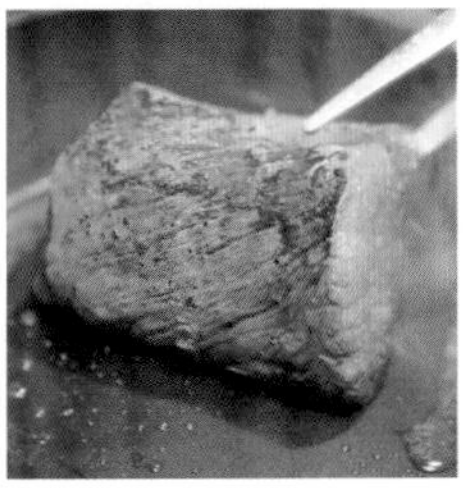

D

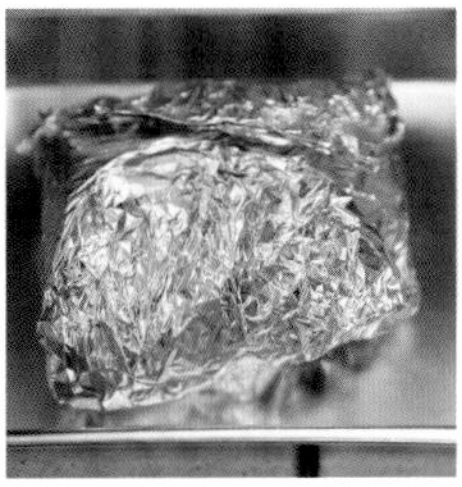

E

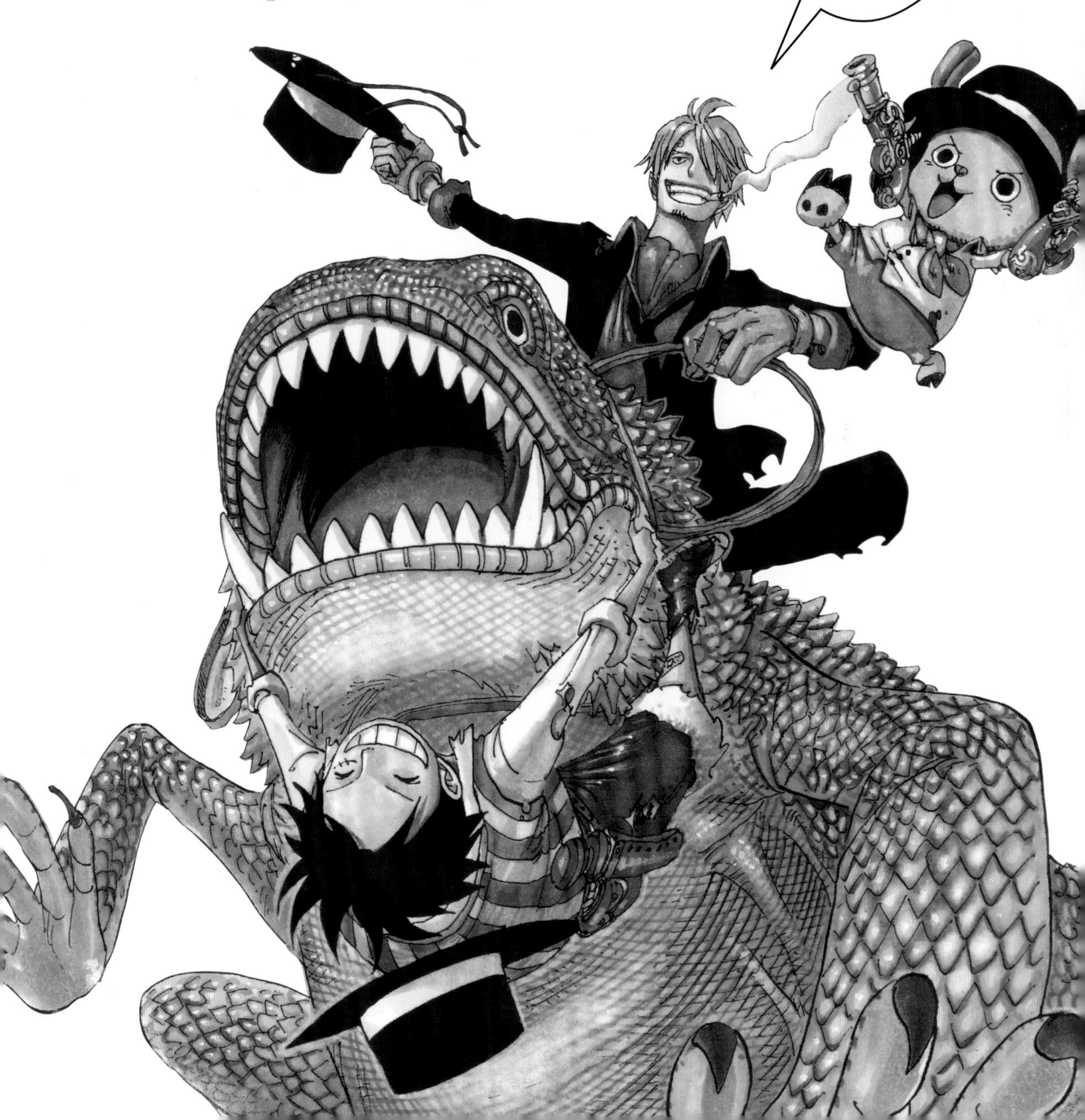
USE THAT RESIDUAL HEAT!!!

Luffy's Favorite

Meat on the Bone

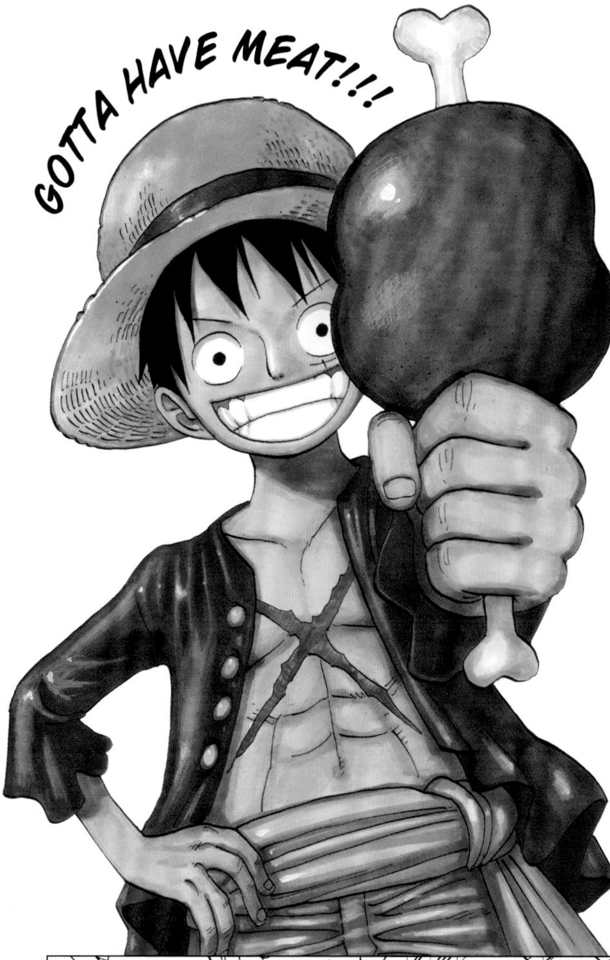
GOTTA HAVE MEAT!!!

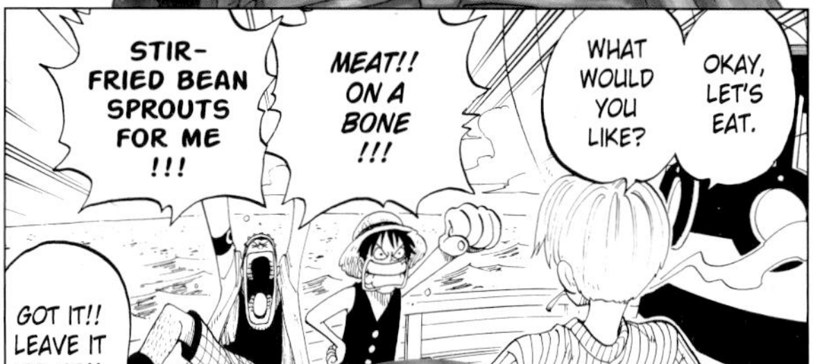
OKAY, LET'S EAT.
WHAT WOULD YOU LIKE?
MEAT!! ON A BONE !!!
STIR-FRIED BEAN SPROUTS FOR ME !!!
GOT IT!! LEAVE IT TO ME!!

MANGA MOMENT

The first thing Sanji cooked once he left the *Baratie*. Luffy's order was "Meat!! On a bone!!!" The classic chunk of meat on the bone is an indispensable part of Luffy's adventures!!

(FROM VOL. 8, CH. 69)

A Scotch egg made with chicken

INGREDIENTS Serves 4

4 chicken drumsticks
4 hard-boiled eggs
¼ cup breadcrumbs
3 tbsp. milk

Mix (a.)

- **18 oz. (500 g) ground chicken**
- **1 tsp. salt**
- **a little black pepper**
- **1 egg**

vegetable oil

STEPS

① Make chicken drumstick "tulips." Use kitchen scissors to cut the meat loose from the handle end of the drumstick **(A)**. Roll the meat down the bone until it is fully inside-out at the end.

② Soak the breadcrumbs in milk. Knead mix **(a.)** in a bowl, then add breadcrumbs and knead again.

③ Fold the meaty end of the drumstick around a hard-boiled egg **(B)**. If the meat doesn't cover well enough, add cuts to loosen it up. Oil hands lightly and cover drumstick and egg with step ② breadcrumb mixture **(C)**.

④ Bake at 400°F (200°C) for 15–20 minutes, watching carefully.

A

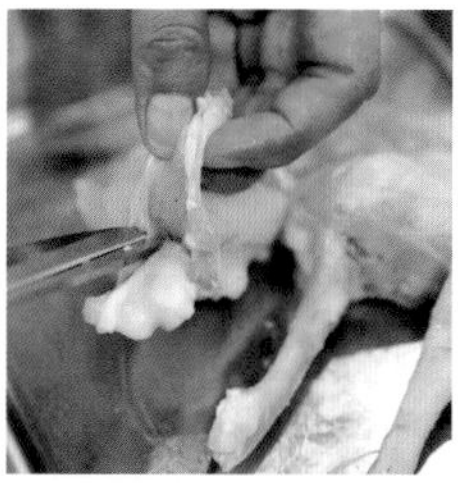

B

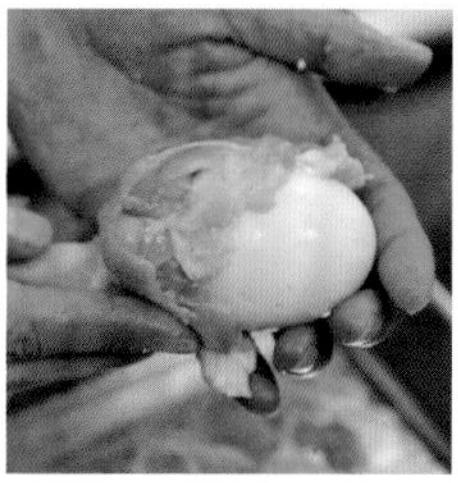

C

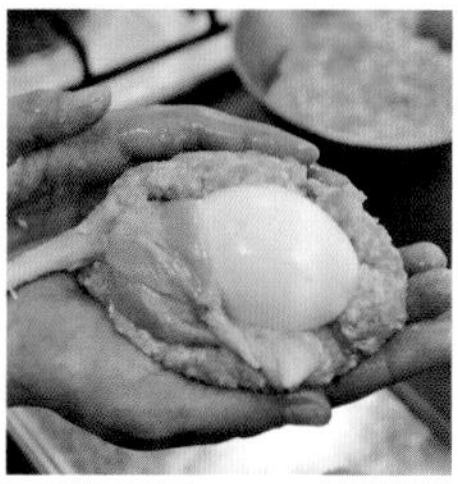

The inside looks like this!

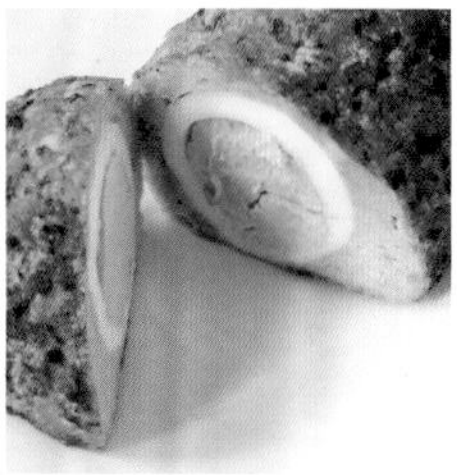

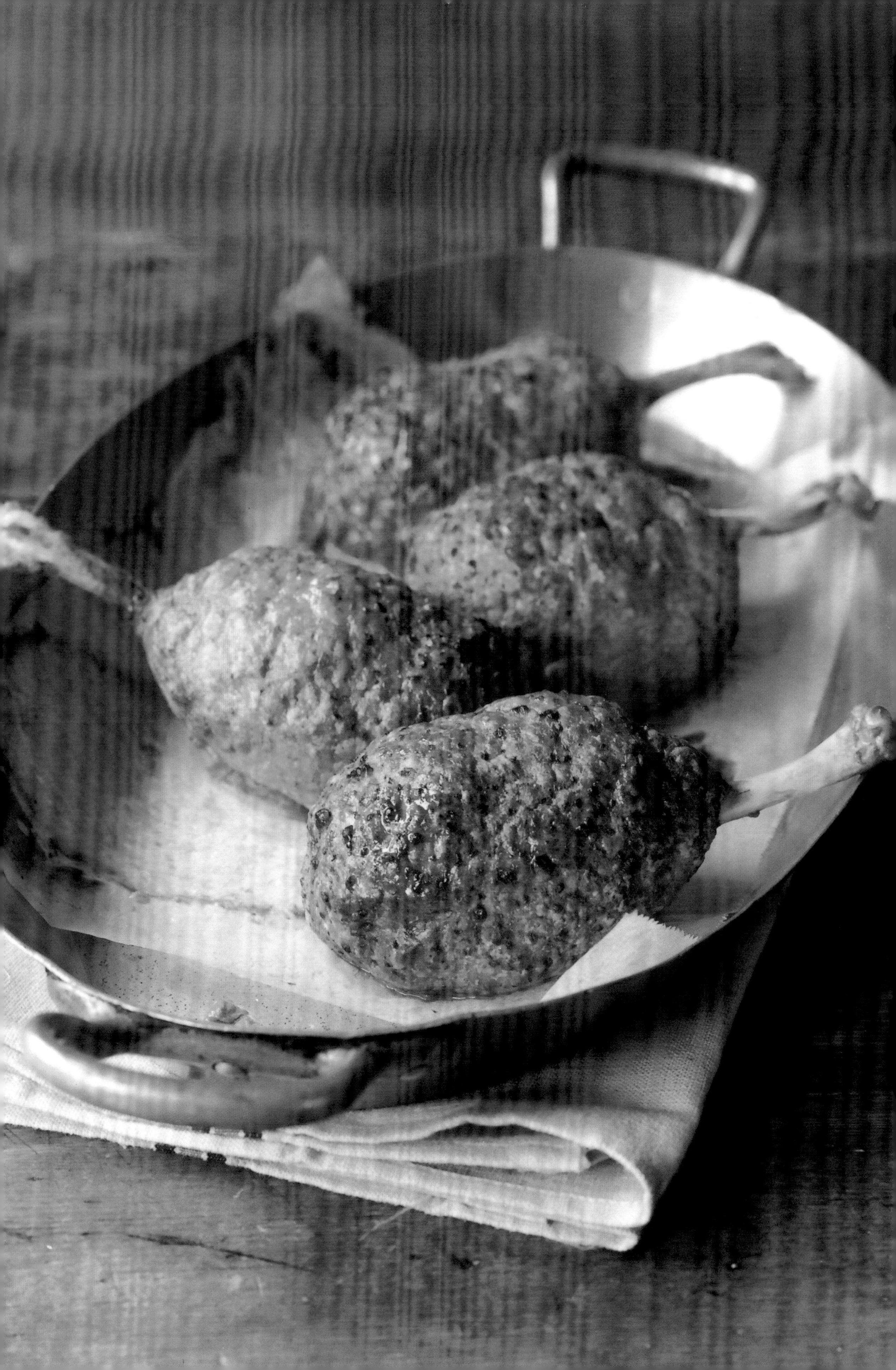

Yagara Bull's Favorite

Steamed Water-Water Meat

A steamed spare rib dish

INGREDIENTS Serves 4

18 oz. (500 g) pork spare ribs
½ tsp. salt
a little black pepper
1 celery stalk
½ carrot
¼ daikon radish cut lengthwise
½ head of lettuce

Tare sauce

½ green onion
1 tbsp. sesame oil
6–7 tbsp. (100 ml) ponzu
grated garlic to taste

STEPS

① Put spare ribs, salt, and pepper into a plastic bag, knead well, and let sit for one hour **(A)**. Peel celery, carrot, and daikon into ribbons **(B)**. Tear lettuce into reasonably sized pieces.

② Mince green onion for the tare sauce. Heat sesame oil in a frying pan, then pour over spring onion in a heat-resistant bowl, add ponzu, and mix.

③ Place spare ribs into a steam cooker and steam for 20 minutes. When the meat is tender, add vegetables to steamer **(C)**, and once heated, remove and serve. Drizzle tare sauce as you eat and add grated garlic as desired.

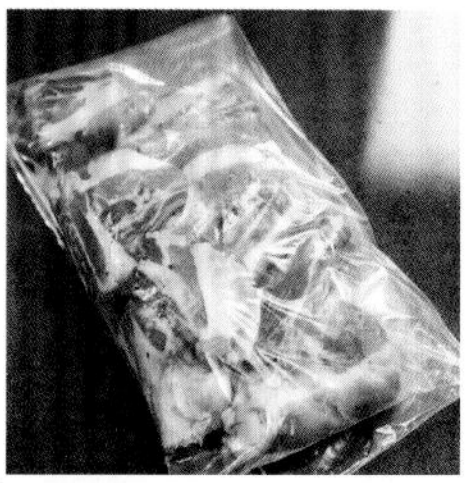

A

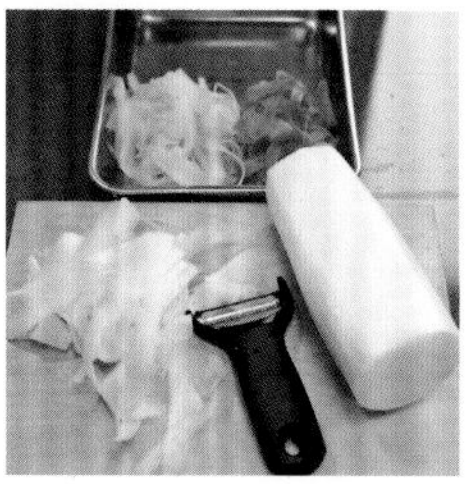

B

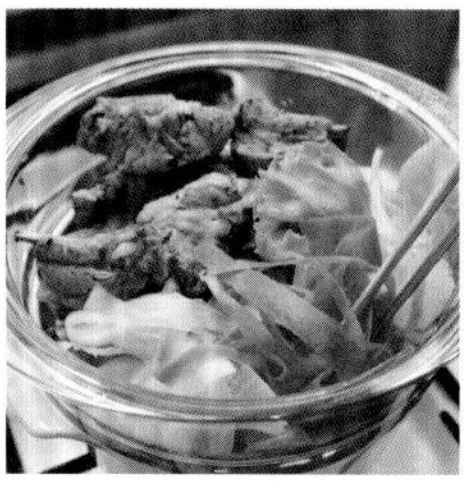

C

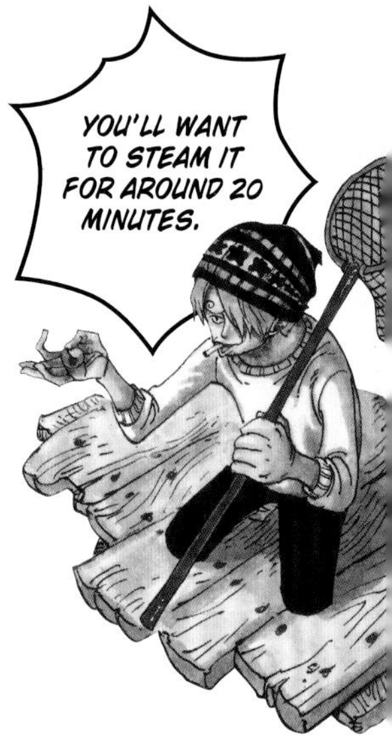
YOU'LL WANT TO STEAM IT FOR AROUND 20 MINUTES.

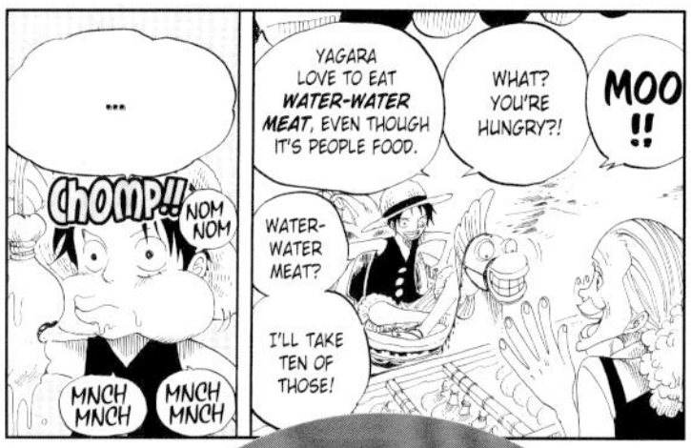
MOO !!
WHAT? YOU'RE HUNGRY?!
YAGARA LOVE TO EAT WATER-WATER MEAT, EVEN THOUGH IT'S PEOPLE FOOD.
WATER-WATER MEAT?
I'LL TAKE TEN OF THOSE!
...
CHOMP!!
NOM NOM
MNCH MNCH
MNCH MNCH

MANGA MOMENT

Water Seven is renowned as the "City of Water." The meat there is marinated in their crystal-clear water, making it melt in your mouth!! It's world-famous for being unbelievably juicy.
(FROM VOL. 34, CH. 324)

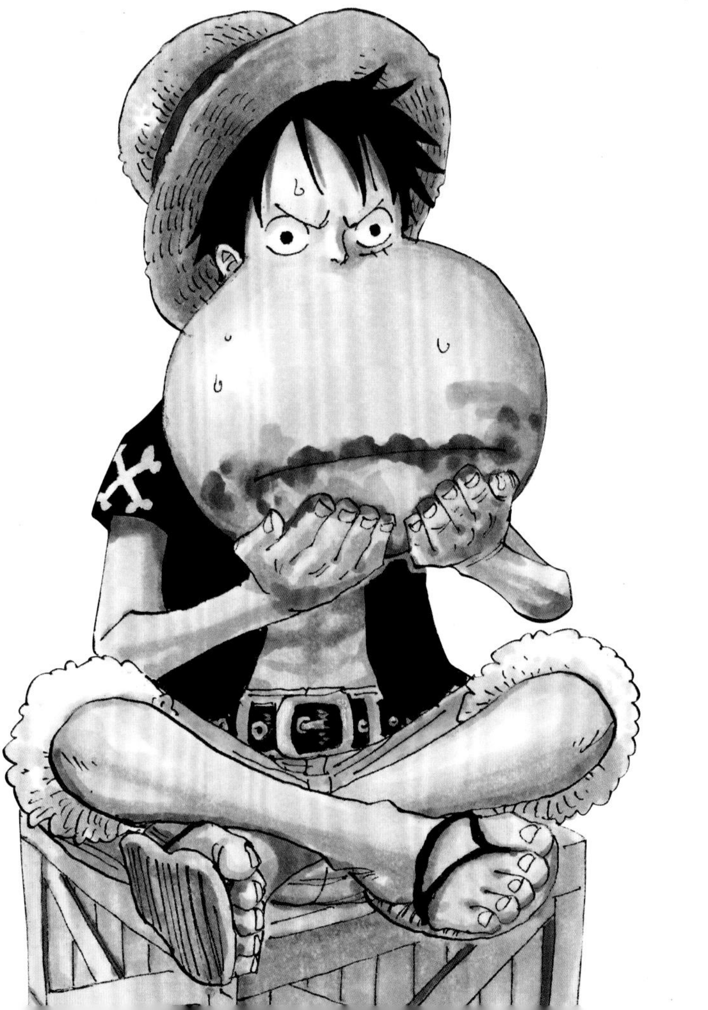

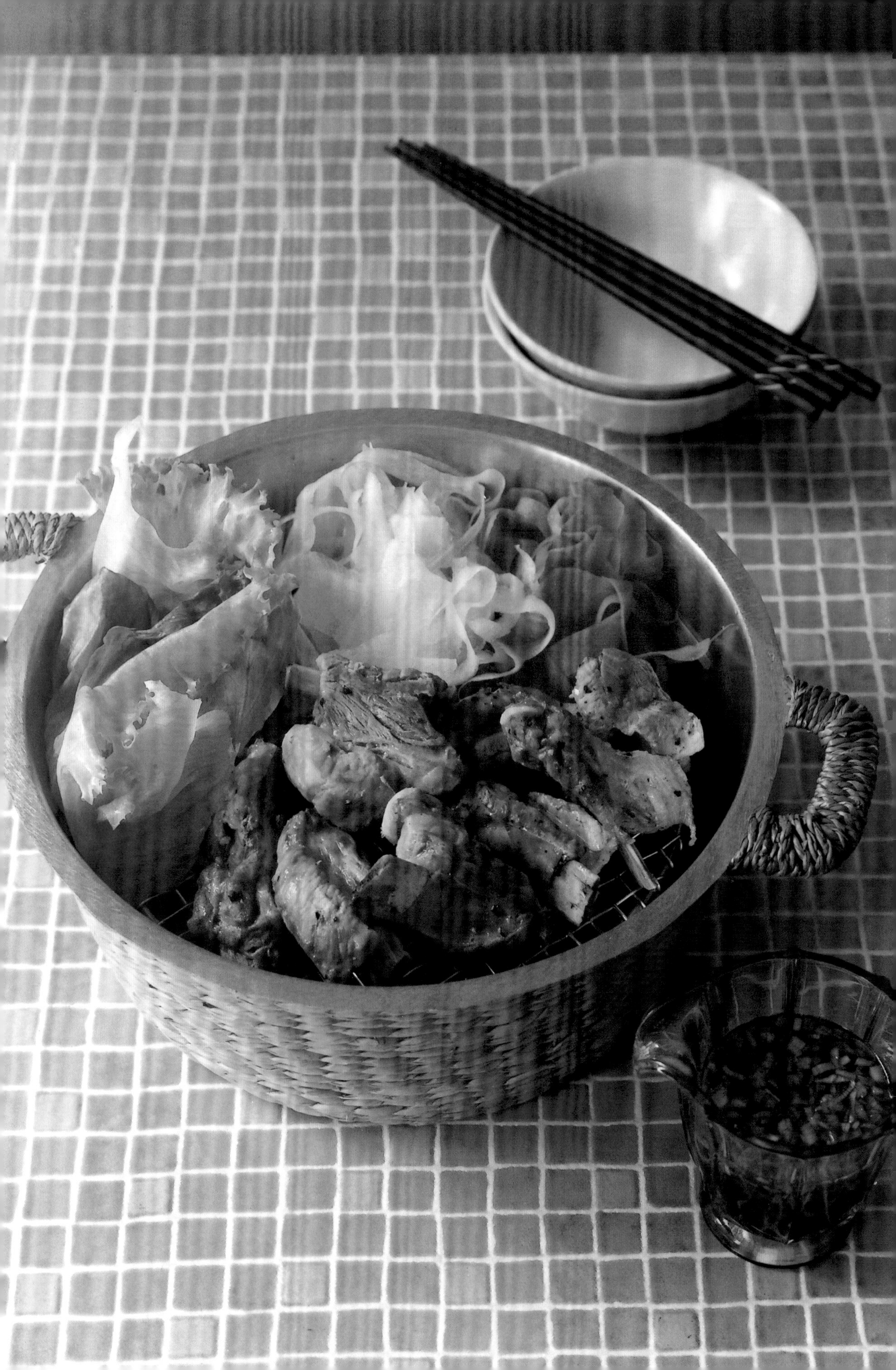

Impel Down's

Roast Hummingbird

Roasted chicken stuffed with special rice pilaf

WHOA!! I JUST THOUGHT OF ANOTHER INGENIOUS RECIPE!!!

INGREDIENTS Serves 4-5

1 chicken (about 4-5 lb./2 kg)
1 tsp. salt
a little black pepper
½ onion
1 tbsp. vegetable oil
¼ cup (50 ml) water

Mix (a.)

- **1 ½ cups (300 g) cooked rice**
- **½ tomato**
- **1 tbsp. chopped parsley**
- **½ tsp. salt**
- **a little black pepper**

STEPS

① Remove neck and organs if present, and rinse chicken clean. Dry excess liquid and rub salt and pepper onto exterior and interior.

② Slice onion thinly and cube tomato for mix **(a.)**. Mix **(a.)** ingredients and stuff chicken **(A)**. Use large toothpick to pin rear shut so stuffing doesn't spill out **(B)**. Rub vegetable oil onto exterior of chicken.

③ Spread out onion onto a large oven tray and rest chicken on top **(C)**. Add water and chicken neck, split in two. Put into the oven at 400°F (200°C) for 40–50 minutes, rotating tray partway and occasionally scooping juices back onto the chicken. Once cooked to an internal termperature of 165°F (74°C), extending cook time as needed, turn off heat and leave in the oven for another 10–15 minutes.

④ Strain juice from the tray and use as gravy. If the onions are dry and there is little juice, transfer to a small pot, add water (2–3 oz./50–80 ml) and boil, then strain. Cut the chicken into servings, then add gravy and sprinkle salt and pepper to taste.

MANGA MOMENT

A hummingbird in hell?! Luffy and Buggy discover a hummingbird that fell into the Level 3 inferno of Impel Down and then baked in the heat. The crispy roasted bird was the perfect snack.
(FROM VOL. 54, CH. 530)

A

B

C

CHUNK!!
HEY, A BARBECUED BIRD!
NO WAY.
SSS~
SZZT
SZZT...

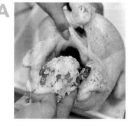

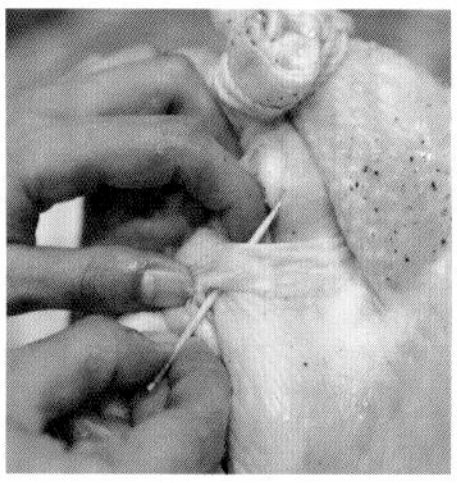

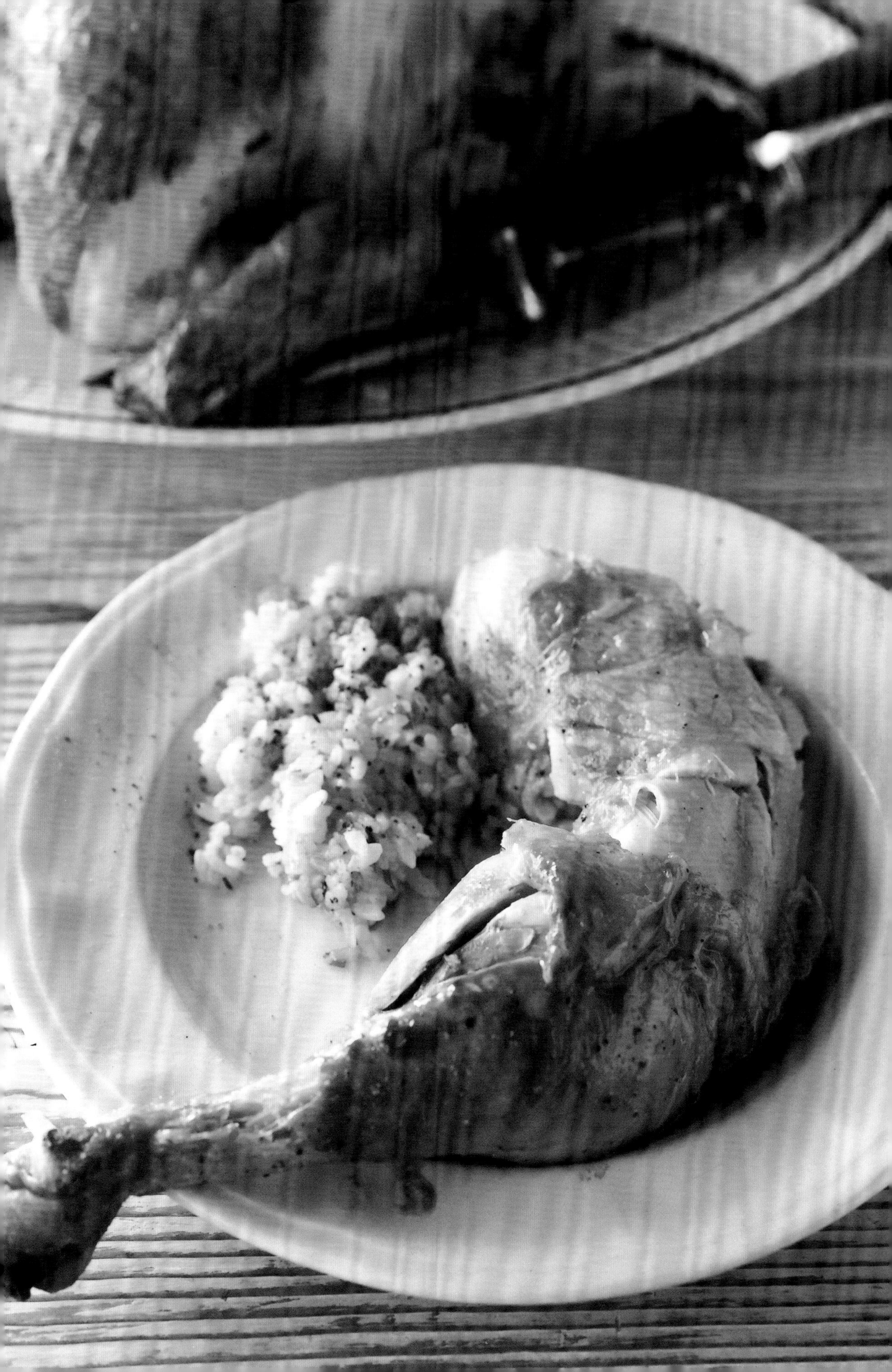

Lakeside Campsite

Hot Rock Stew

A rich pork stew,
no roux required

INGREDIENTS Serves 4

- **21 oz. (600 g) pork butt, whole, or pork shoulder with the fat cap removed**
- **½ tsp. salt**
- **a little black pepper**
- **1 clove garlic**
- **6 mushrooms**
- **½ peeled yellow or white onion**
- **1 tbsp. vegetable oil**
- **2 tbsp. butter**
- **¼ cup flour**
- **1 ⅔ cup (400 ml) red wine**
- **1 ⅔ cup (400 ml) chicken stock (see p. 95)**
- **2 bay leaves**
- **1 oz. (30 g) raisins**
- **5 tbsp. ketchup**

STEPS

① Cut pork into ½ inch (1.5 cm) pieces and place on a tray, then coat with salt, pepper, and flour **(A)**. Cut garlic in half, remove germ, and crush with the flat of your knife. Halve mushrooms and cut onion into 4 wedges.

② Put vegetable oil and garlic into a pot and cook on medium heat. When fragrant, remove garlic and add half of butter. When butter is melted, add meat and all the flour from the tray. Cook both sides until you see it start to sear.

③ Add red wine. Once the alcohol has been brought to a boil, add chicken stock **(B)**, cooked garlic from ②, and bay leaves. When it boils again and a froth starts to build, remove bay leaves and skim the top **(C)**. Add raisins and ketchup. Cover with pot lid ajar and simmer on low heat for 40 minutes.

④ Place the other half of the butter into a heated frying pan. Once melted, add mushrooms and onions to fry until browned, then add to main pot ③ and cook for another 20 minutes. Add salt to taste.

HUH?! WE'RE EATING ROCKS TOO?!
IS IT TASTY?
AS IF! THIS IS "HOT ROCK STEW"!
THE HEAT FROM THE HOT ROCKS COOKS THE STEW.
SIZZLE...!
WHEN YOU COOK THIS WAY, THE INGREDIENTS KEEP MORE OF THEIR NUTRIENTS.

MANGA MOMENT

The greatest cook is also a master of survival!! While undergoing the survival game on Skypiea, the crew eats a stew packed with meat and vegetables. Adding hot rocks to the stew ensures the ingredients get fully cooked, adding umami and nutrients to the stew!!

(FROM VOL. 27, CH. 253)

A

B

C

THE RED WINE AND RAISINS ARE THE KEY!!

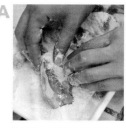

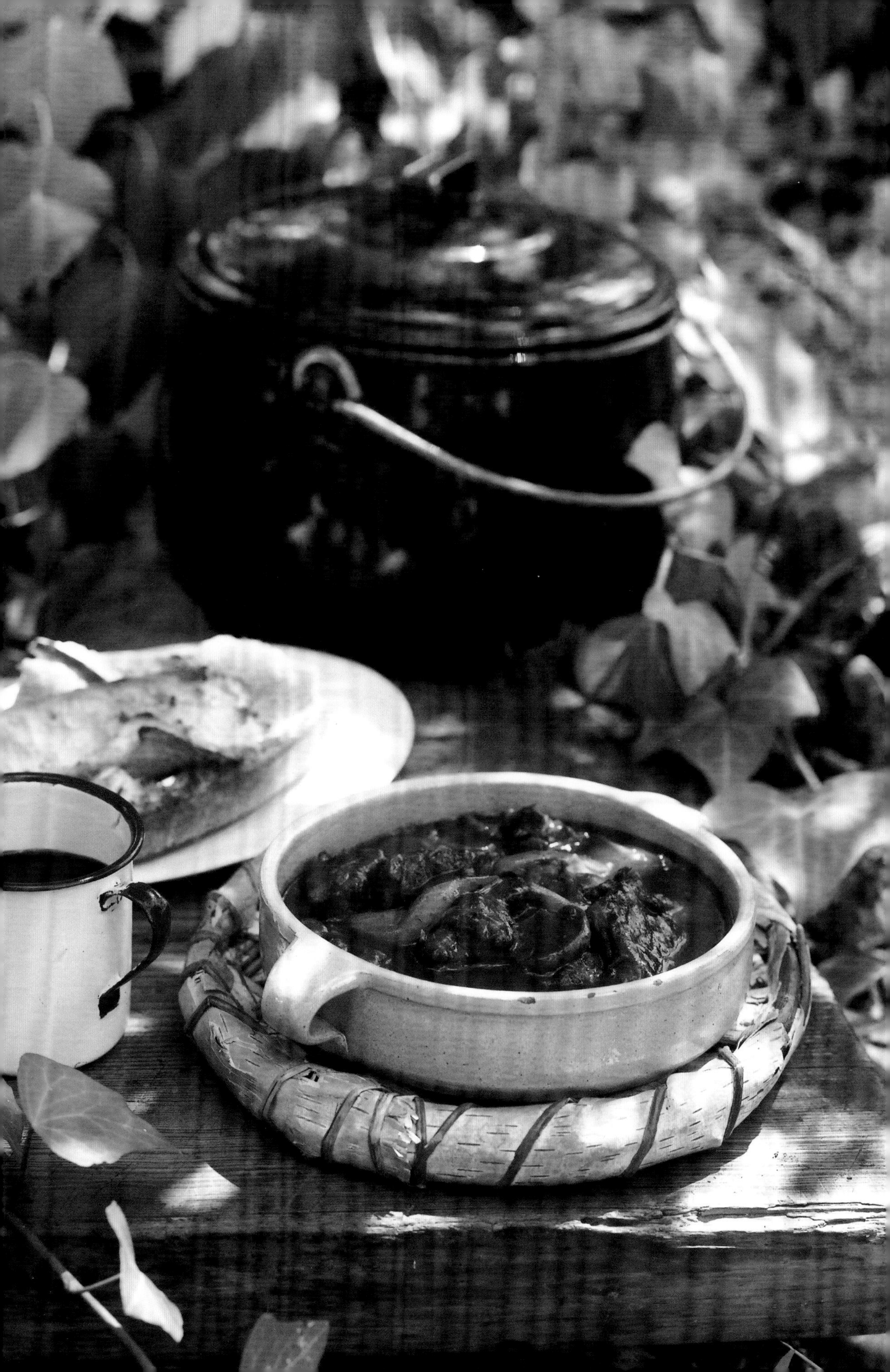

Absalom's (?!)

Croquettes

Potato croquettes, packed with beef!

INGREDIENTS Makes 10

4 small potatoes (21 oz./600 g)
7 oz. (200 g) mixed beef
½ onion
1 cup vegetable oil for frying, plus 1 ½ tsp., divided
1 tsp. salt
a little black pepper
1 tbsp. butter
up to ½ cup flour
1–2 large eggs
1 ½ cups panko
julienne-cut cabbage
Worcestershire sauce to taste

STEPS

① Steam potatoes in a steam cooker for about 40 minutes until they soften. Cut beef into ¾ inch (2 cm) strips **(A)** and mince onion.

② Pour vegetable oil into a heated frying pan and cook beef on medium heat. Once adequately heated, add onions and cook for 3–4 minutes until translucent, then flavor with salt (½ tsp.) and black pepper. Transfer food to a tray to cool.

③ While potatoes from ① are still hot, peel and place in a bowl. Mash with a ladle or spatula, add butter and salt (½ tsp.) and mix **(B)**. Add beef and onions from ② and mix, then transfer to tray to cool.

④ Separate ③ mixture into 10 equal parts and mold into oval shape **(C)**. Dip into flour, beaten egg yolks, and panko in that order, then fry in oil heated to 360°F (180°C) for three minutes, turning over partway.

⑤ Remove and place on cooling rack over baking sheet with paper towels beneath to catch oil. Transfer to serving plate with cabbage and drizzle sauce over.

A
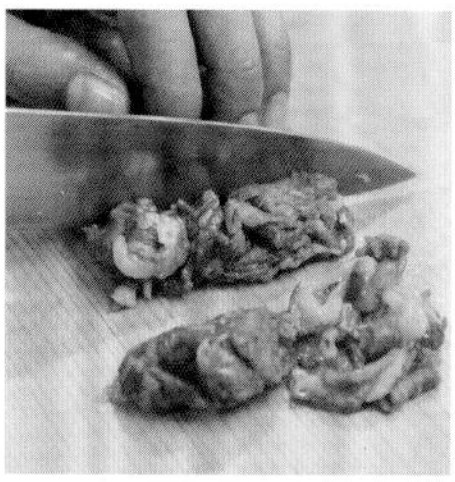

B
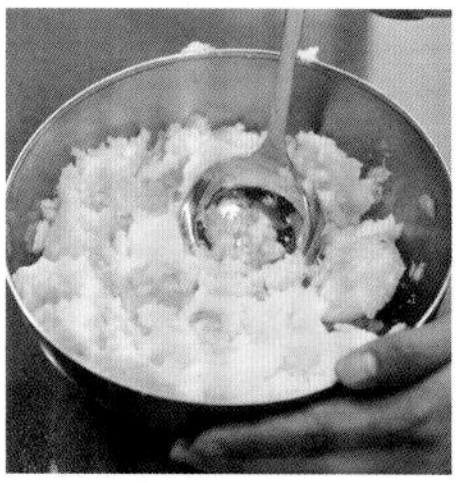

C
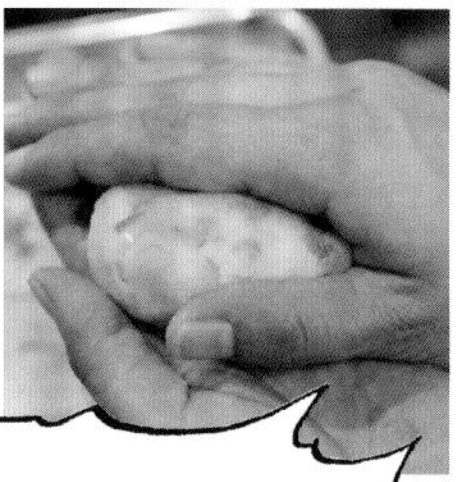

MANGA MOMENT

Sanji's dream was to have the powers of the Clear-Clear Fruit. But Absalom got it first and tried to steal Nami away!! Furious, Sanji swore to turn him into a croquette, and devastated his foe with a Veau Vengeance kick!!
(FROM VOL. 48, CH. 463)

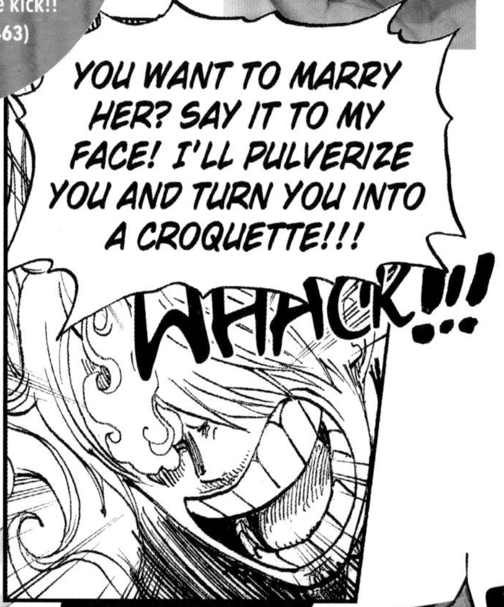
YOU WANT TO MARRY HER? SAY IT TO MY FACE! I'LL PULVERIZE YOU AND TURN YOU INTO A CROQUETTE!!!
WHACK!!!

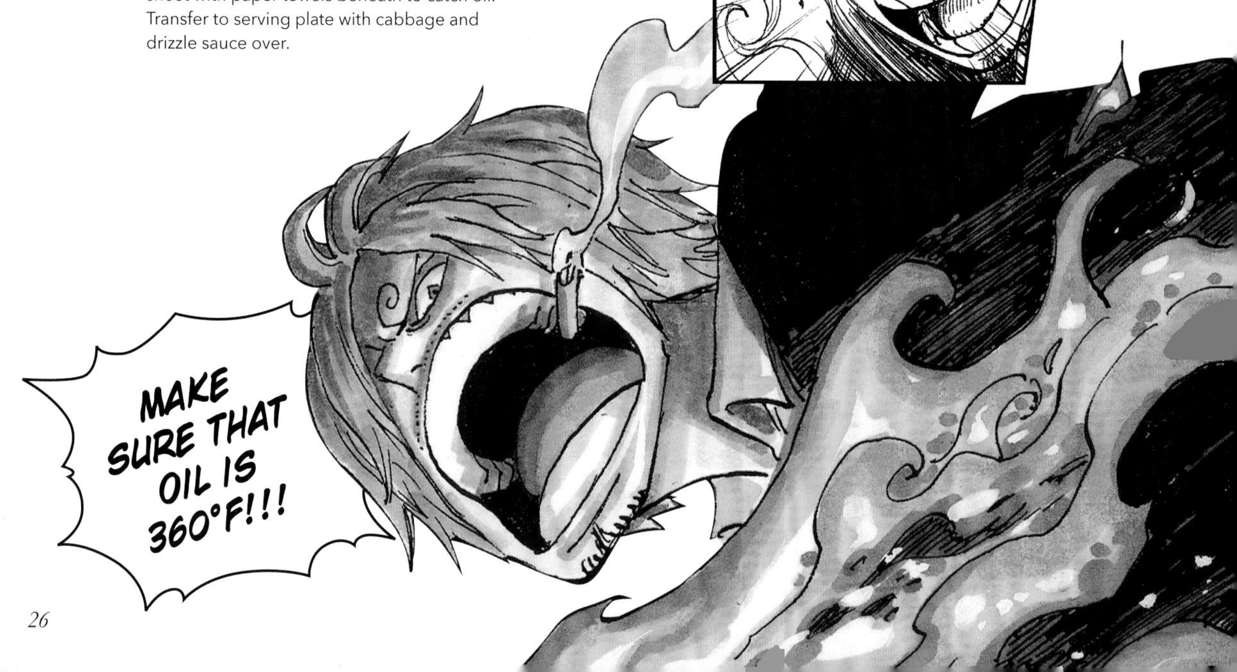
MAKE SURE THAT OIL IS 360°F!!!

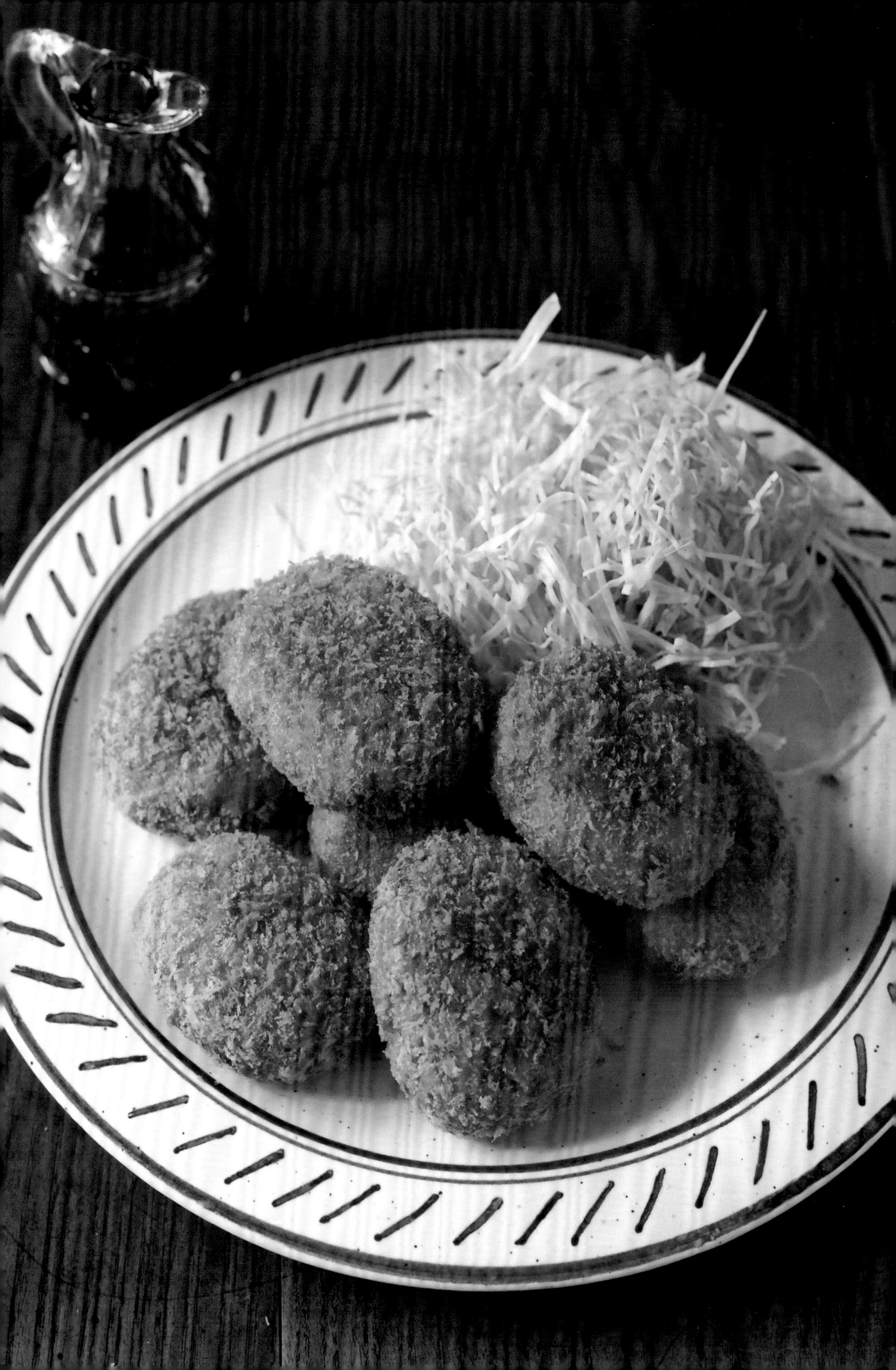

MANGA MOMENT

The pirate game Davy Back Fight puts crew and pride on the line. There you can buy the perfect festival food: frankfurters! They also sell lamb, cheese, biscuits, and salted meat!! (FROM VOL. 33, CH. 306)

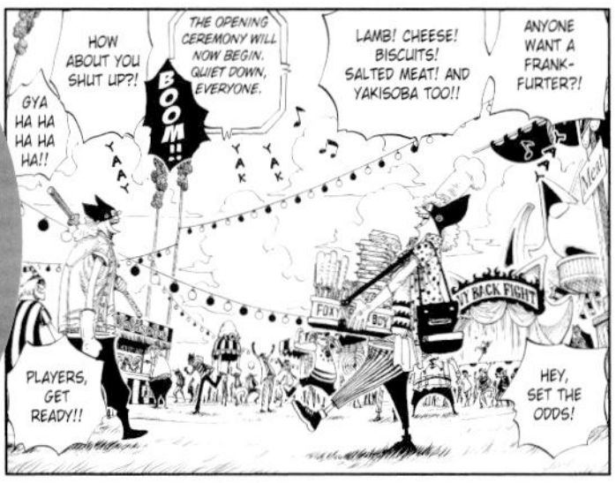
ANYONE WANT A FRANK-FURTER?!
LAMB! CHEESE! BISCUITS! SALTED MEAT! AND YAKISOBA TOO!!
THE OPENING CEREMONY WILL NOW BEGIN. QUIET DOWN, EVERYONE.
BOOM!!
HOW ABOUT YOU SHUT UP?!
GYA HA HA HA HA HA!!
HEY, SET THE ODDS!
PLAYERS, GET READY!!

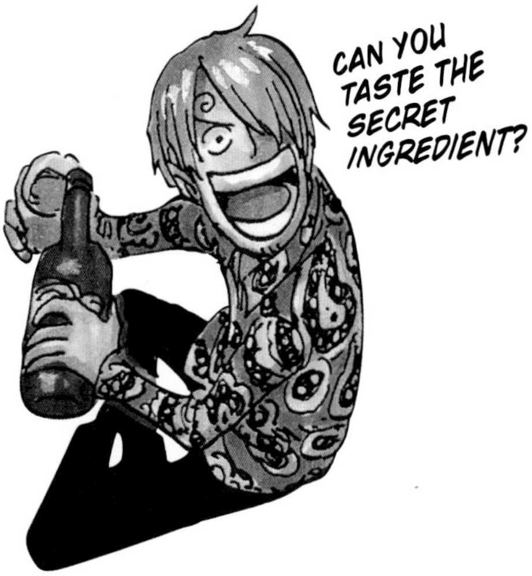
CAN YOU TASTE THE SECRET INGREDIENT?

Davy Back Fight Frankfurters

A rich pot-au-feu where the infused oil is the key

A

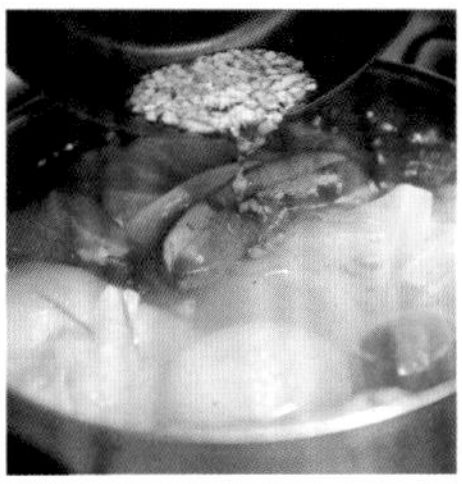

INGREDIENTS Serves 4

- 8 frankfurters
- 2 large Idaho potatoes
- 1 carrot
- ½ head of cabbage
- 2 small onions
- about 8 cups (2,000 ml) chicken stock (see p. 95)
- 2 tsp. salt

Mix (a.)
- 1 clove garlic
- 1 tbsp. olive oil

- Parmesan cheese
- black pepper

STEPS

① Lightly split frankfurters to allow flavor to blend. Peel potatoes and cut in half. Peel carrot and cut into bite-size quarters. Cut cabbage into four equal wedges and use toothpicks or skewers to hold in place. Peel onions and use whole. Mince garlic for mix **(A)**.

② Heat up chicken stock, salt, carrots, and onions in a pot. Bring to a boil, then reduce heat to low and let simmer for 20 minutes. Add cabbage and potatoes and simmer for 20 more minutes. When vegetables are soft, add frankfurters and simmer for 10 more minutes.

③ Cook mix **(a.)** in a frying pan on medium heat. When garlic begins to brown, add to pot **(A)**. If flavor is lacking, add extra salt, Parmesan cheese, and black pepper to taste. Once served, remove toothpicks from cabbage and enjoy.

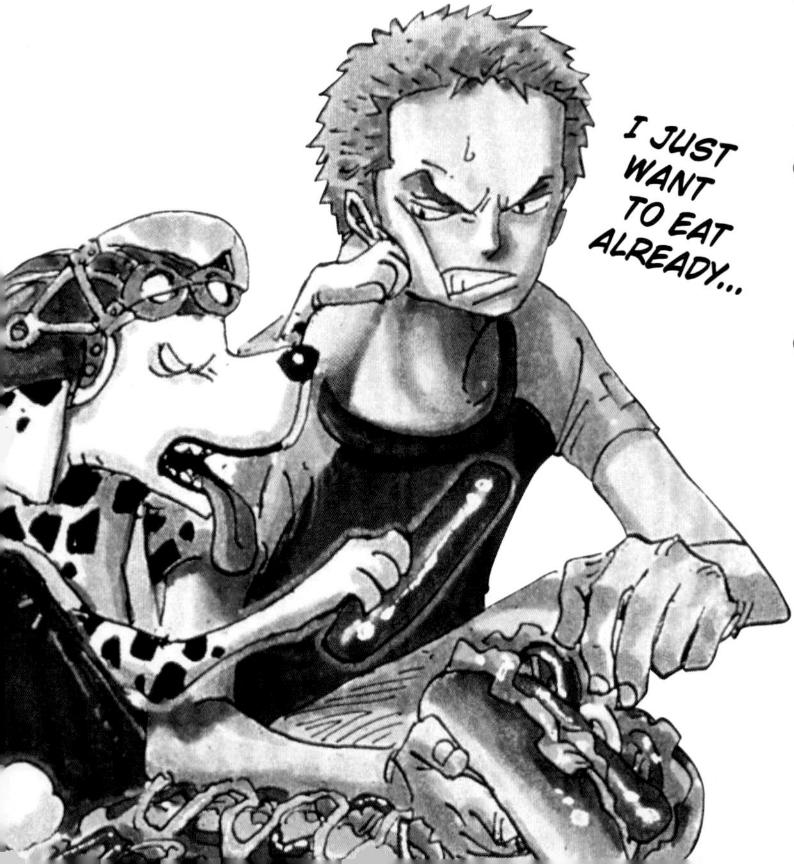
I JUST WANT TO EAT ALREADY...

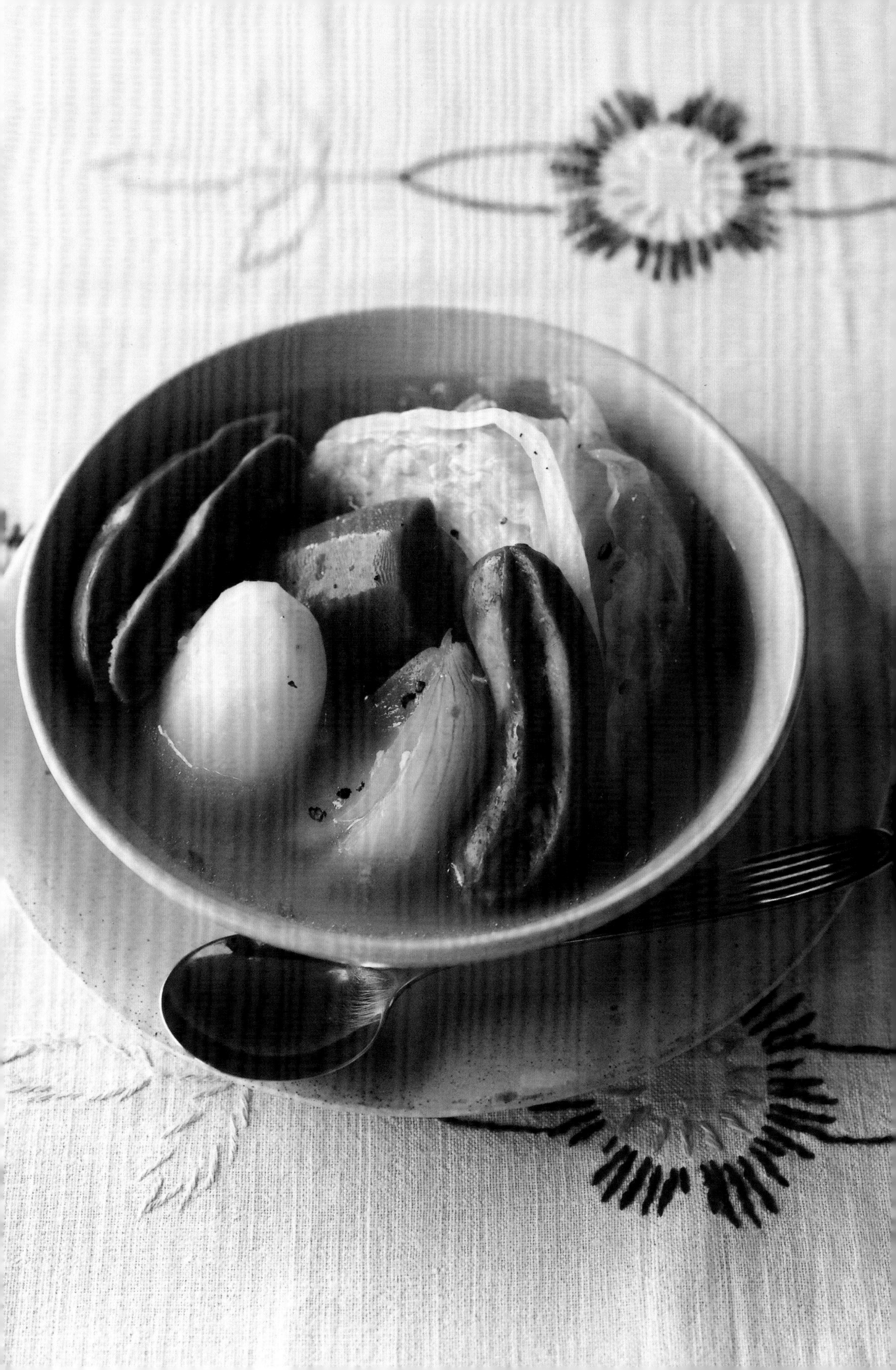

Seafoo
Dishes, Good for Beginners

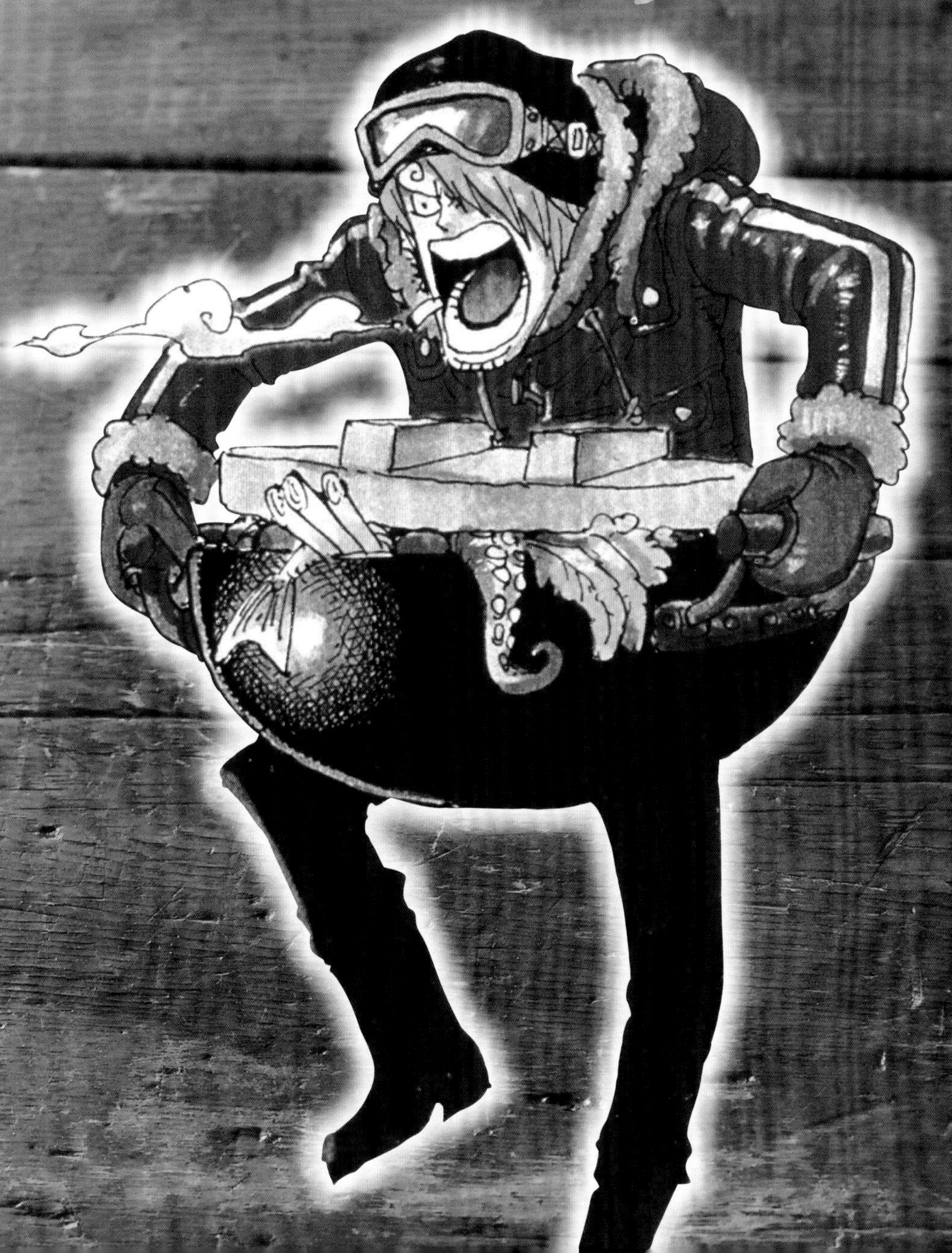

"Cooking fish is hard?" Nope. It's actually real easy, at least once you know the trick.
I've got a selection of knockout recipes to satisfy salty dogs and sultry dames,
so take this opportunity to learn the ropes, from fundamentals to practical lessons!!

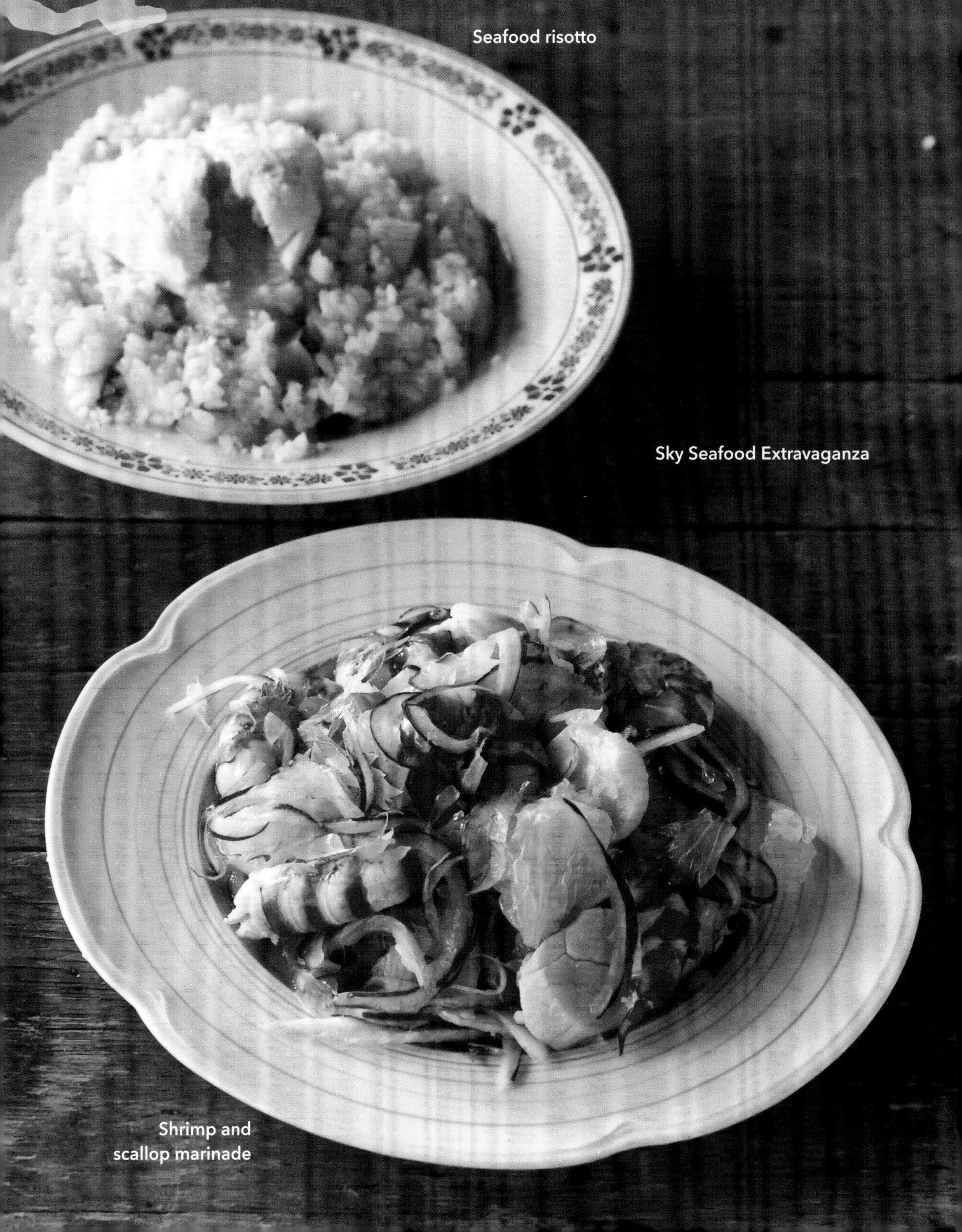

Seafood risotto

Sky Seafood Extravaganza

Shrimp and scallop marinade

Featuring the Products of Sky Island

Sky Seafood Extravaganza

Shrimp and scallop marinade

INGREDIENTS Serves 3-4

6 fresh scallops
10 shrimp (shell on)
1 grapefruit
1 celery stalk (with leaves)
½ red onion
1 knob of ginger root (⅓ oz./10 g)
1 lime's worth of juice
a little white pepper
½ tsp. salt
olive oil if desired

STEPS

① Place scallops in boiling water for 30 seconds, then remove and wash in cold water **(A)**. Cut in half to make coins. Remove the shrimp heads and back vein, setting shrimp heads aside for the next recipe, then boil with the shell on until they turn pink and pour into a strainer. When they are cool enough to touch, peel off the shell **(B)** and cut in half if too large. Remove peel and rind from grapefruit, then slice into wedges. Remove strings from celery, then slice diagonally. Slice red onion thinly and peel and cut ginger into julienne strips.

② Place shrimp and scallops into a bowl. Add lime juice, salt, and white pepper, and mix. Add red onion, celery, and ginger, and mix again. Add grapefruit pieces and chill in refrigerator.

③ After mixing again, transfer to serving dish and garnish with celery leaves. Add olive oil if desired.

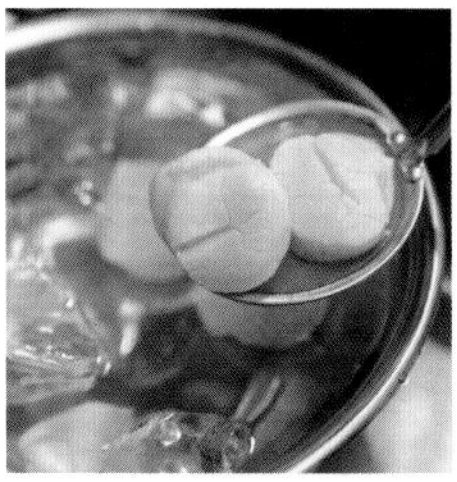

A

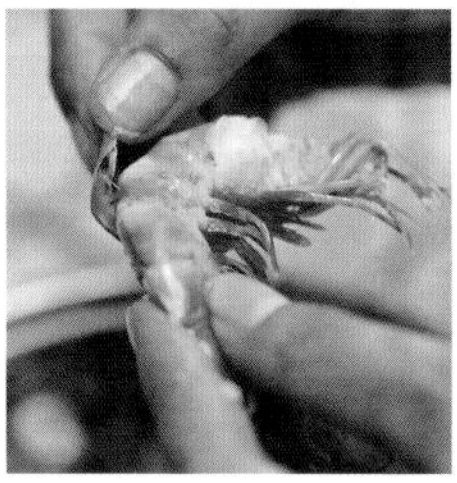

B

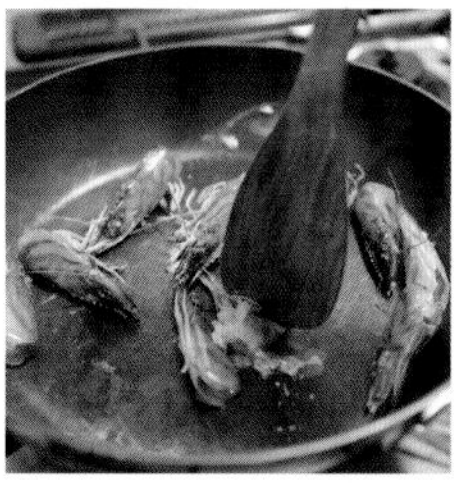

C

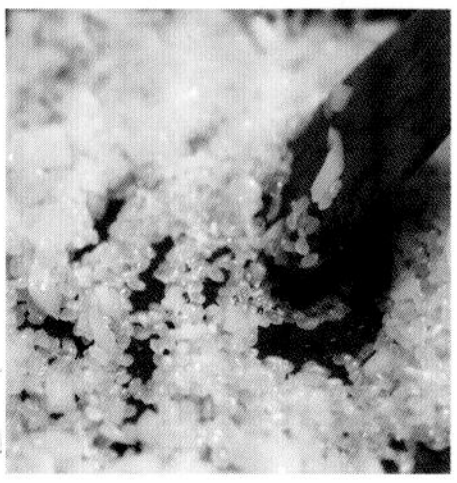

D

Seafood risotto

INGREDIENTS Serves 2

¾ cup (150 g) uncooked rice
10 shrimp heads
4 scallops, roughly ¼ lb.
¼ onion
¼ zucchini
1 ½ tbsp. butter
3 tbsp. white wine
½-⅔ tsp. salt
a little white pepper
about 3 cups (700 ml) chicken stock **(see p. 95)**
2 tbsp. parmesan cheese, grated
1 poached egg if desired

STEPS

① Place shrimp heads on frying pan and dry roast, flattening and crushing with a spatula **(C)**. Add chicken stock and boil for three minutes, then strain.

② Cut scallops into 0.6 inch (1.5 cm) pieces, mince onion, and cut zucchini to 0.4 inch (1 cm) pieces. Place butter in frying pan on medium heat and fry onion, adding rice once onion is translucent. Once rice is translucent **(D)**, add zucchini and white wine. Allow alcohol to cook off, then add some stock from ① and cook on high heat. Once boiling, maintain an even temperature by lowering if needed, with no more than 3-4 spots bubbling at any one time. Stir constantly and add more chicken stock as liquid evaporates, until it has boiled for 13-15 minutes (you may not need to use all of the stock).

③ When only the core of rice is still firm, add scallops and season with salt and white pepper.

④ Transfer to dishes and sprinkle with parmesan cheese. Add poached egg on top if desired.

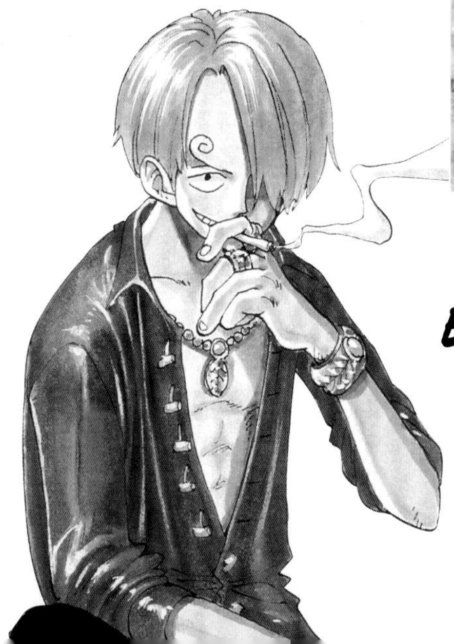

BOIL THOSE SUCKERS UP!!!

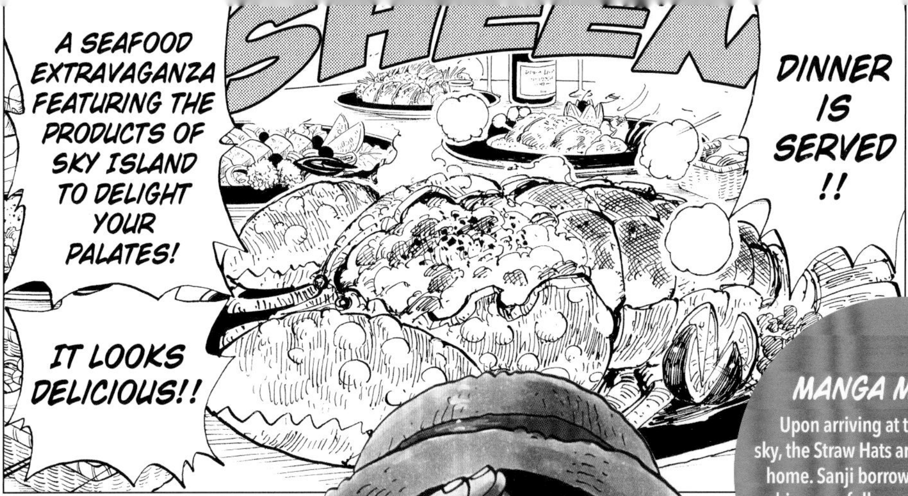
DINNER IS SERVED!!
SHEEN
A SEAFOOD EXTRAVAGANZA FEATURING THE PRODUCTS OF SKY ISLAND TO DELIGHT YOUR PALATES!
IT LOOKS DELICIOUS!!

MANGA MOMENT

Upon arriving at the island in the sky, the Straw Hats are invited to Conis's home. Sanji borrows the kitchen and whips up a full course meal with their sky ingredients. Everyone's satisfied with the indescribable sky island feast! **(FROM VOL. 26, CH. 240)**

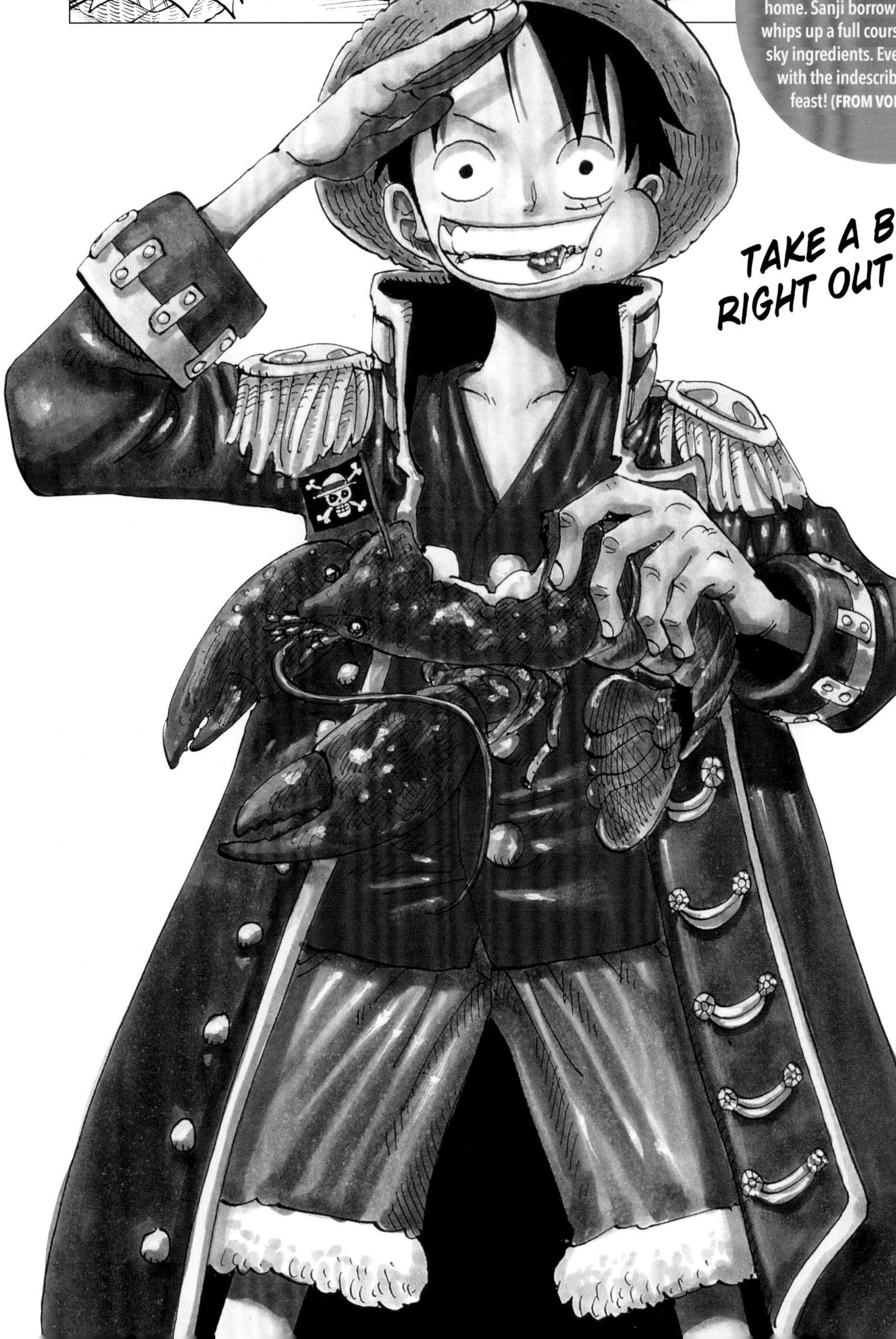
TAKE A BITE RIGHT OUT OF IT!!

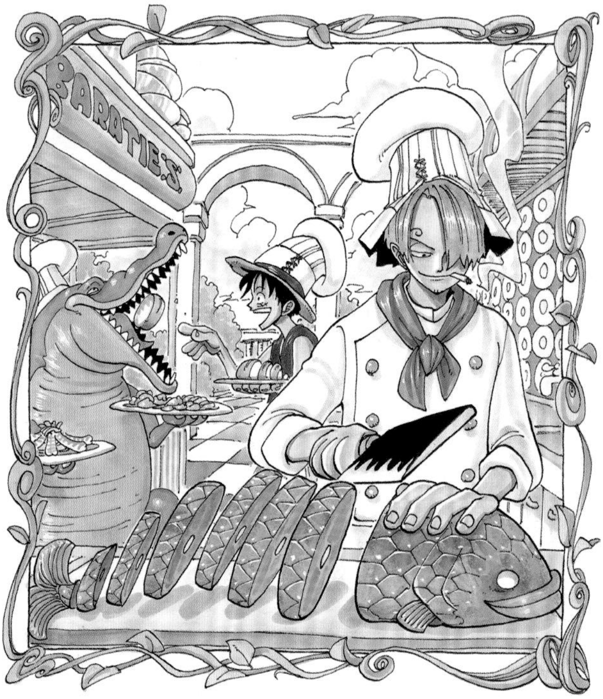

The Trunk Is Good

Elephant True Bluefin Sauté

Cooked blue marlin with a special sweet sauce

INGREDIENTS Serves 4

4 fillets of blue marlin (10-11 oz./300 g)
salt to taste
white pepper to taste
1 tbsp. olive oil

Sauce

- **½ onion**
- **2 tbsp. olive oil**
- **½-1 tsp. grated garlic**
- **2 tbsp. water**
- **2 tsp. honey**
- **⅔ tsp. salt**
- **1 tsp. soy sauce**
- **3 tbsp. hulled white sesame seeds**

STEPS

① Sprinkle salt and white pepper on marlin. Mince onion for sauce. Add olive oil to heated frying pan and cook marlin pieces on both sides. Remove once cooked through to 125°F, roughly 5–7 minutes per side for a 1 ½ inch thick steak **(A)**.

② Using the same frying pan, heat the olive oil for the sauce, then fry onions until translucent. Add garlic, water, honey, salt, soy sauce, and ground sesame **(B)**.

③ Serve marlin on a plate and drizzle sauce ② over it.

A

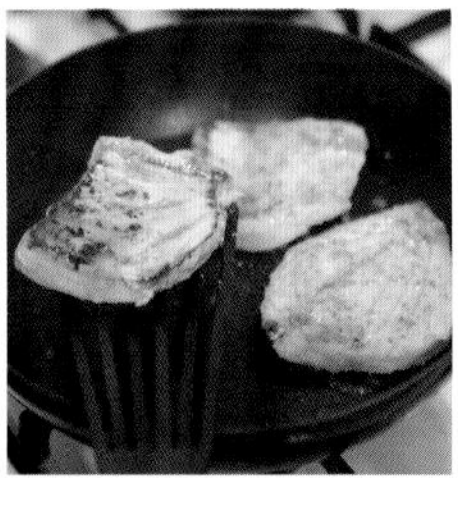

B

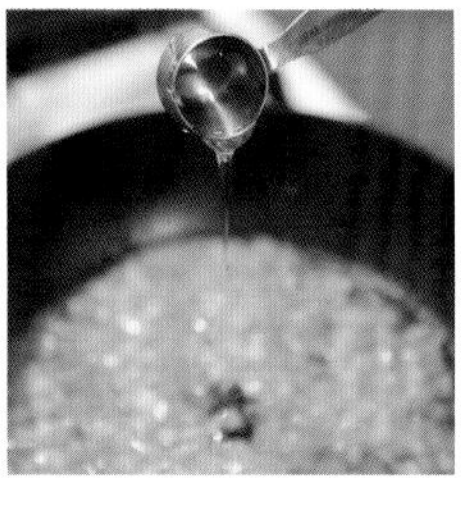

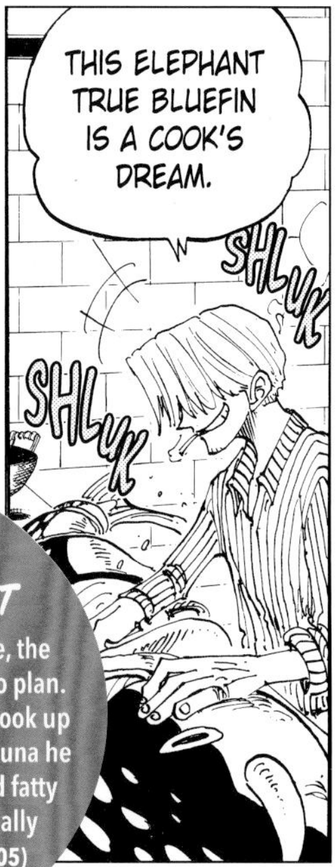
THIS ELEPHANT TRUE BLUEFIN IS A COOK'S DREAM.
SHLUK
SHLUK

MANGA MOMENT

After entering the Grand Line, the crew stops at the Twin Capes to plan. Sanji uses the opportunity to cook up the massive bluefin elephant tuna he bought in town. It's a rich and fatty fish, and the trunk is especially good. (FROM VOL. 12, CH. 105)

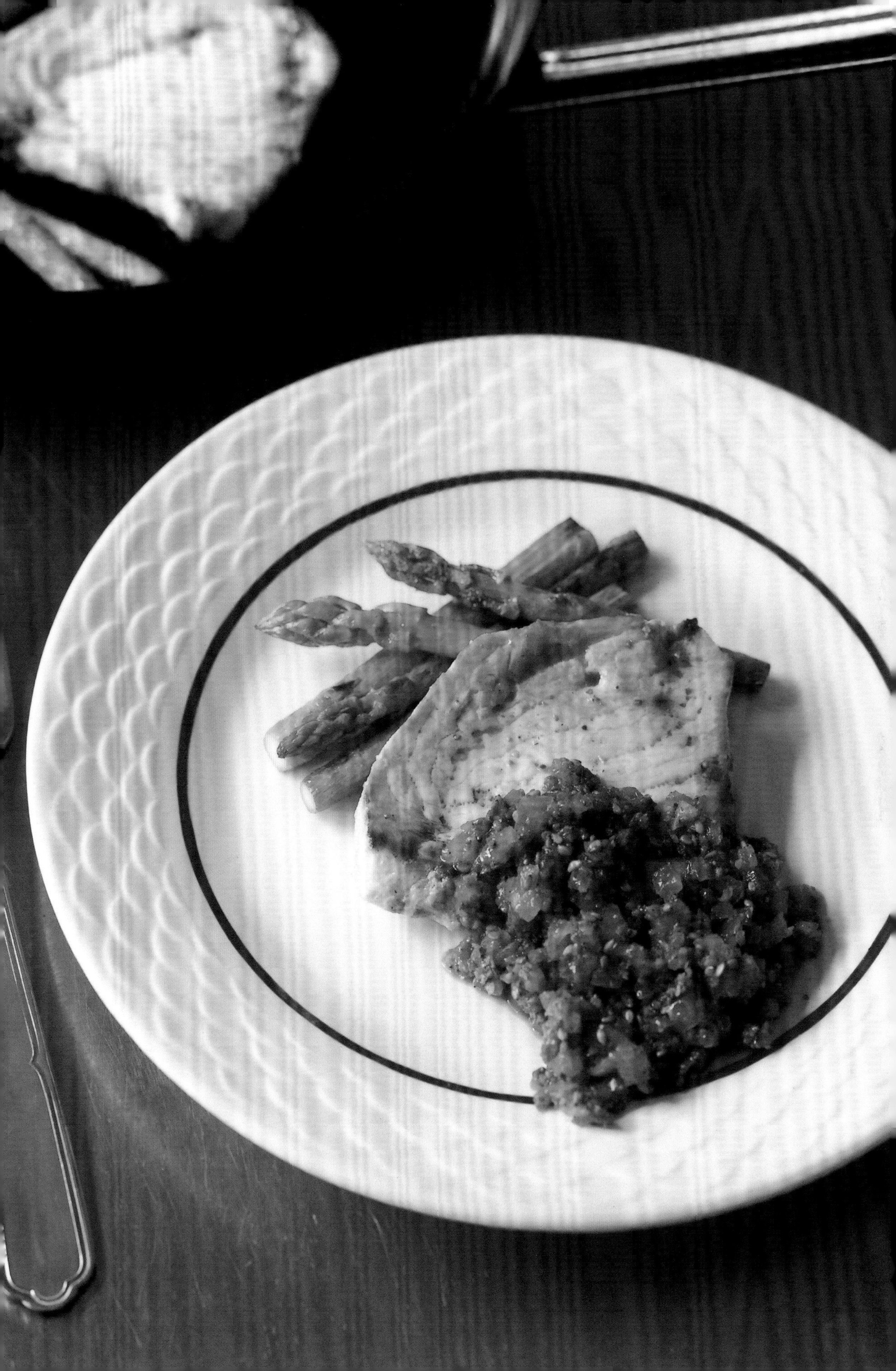

Fresh from the White Sea

Sky Fish Sauté

THIS MUST BE A SKY FISH.
NOLAND MENTIONED THEM IN HIS DIARY.
FWIP FWIP
IN ORDER TO SURVIVE IN THIS BOTTOMLESS SKY OCEAN...
...THEY'VE EVOLVED DIFFERENTLY FROM THEIR AQUATIC COUSINS.

MANGA MOMENT

The Straw Hat Crew heads for the island in the sky and lands on top of the clouds. The fish that dwell in the white sea above have evolved to match their unique environment. The crew is stunned at the strange specimen, but the flavor gets Luffy's stamp of approval.
(FROM VOL. 26, CH. 237)

MMULP!!
(MORE PLEASE!!)

Fried horse mackerel with melted cheese

INGREDIENTS Serves 4

- 4 whole horse mackerel (21 oz./600 g)
- 1 ball of mozzarella cheese (3 ½ oz./100 g)
- salt to taste
- white pepper to taste
- roughly 4 tsp. flour
- 1 egg
- 6 tbsp. panko
- vegetable oil

Sauce

- Mix (a.)
  - 1 tomato
  - ¼ onion
  - 6 tbsp. ketchup
  - 2 tsp. vinegar
  - 2 tsp. olive oil
  - hot sauce to taste
- red onion
- basil

STEPS

① Split the horse mackerel for frying, leaving a hinge. Cut the mozzarella into halves and then into ⅓ inch (8 mm) slices.

② Mince the tomato and onion for the sauce and mix with **(a.)**

③ Sprinkle salt and white pepper on mackerel, then place mozzarella slices in between the fillets **(A)**. Dip into flour, beaten egg, and panko in order.

④ Fill frying pan with about ⅓ inch (1 cm) of vegetable oil and heat to 320°F (160°C). Add breaded mackerel **(B)**. Fry about five minutes total, turning over once. Remove and place on a cooling rack over a paper towel-lined tray to drain oil.

⑤ Slice red onion thinly and garnish fish with sauce mixture and basil.

A

B

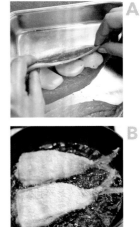

The inside looks like this!

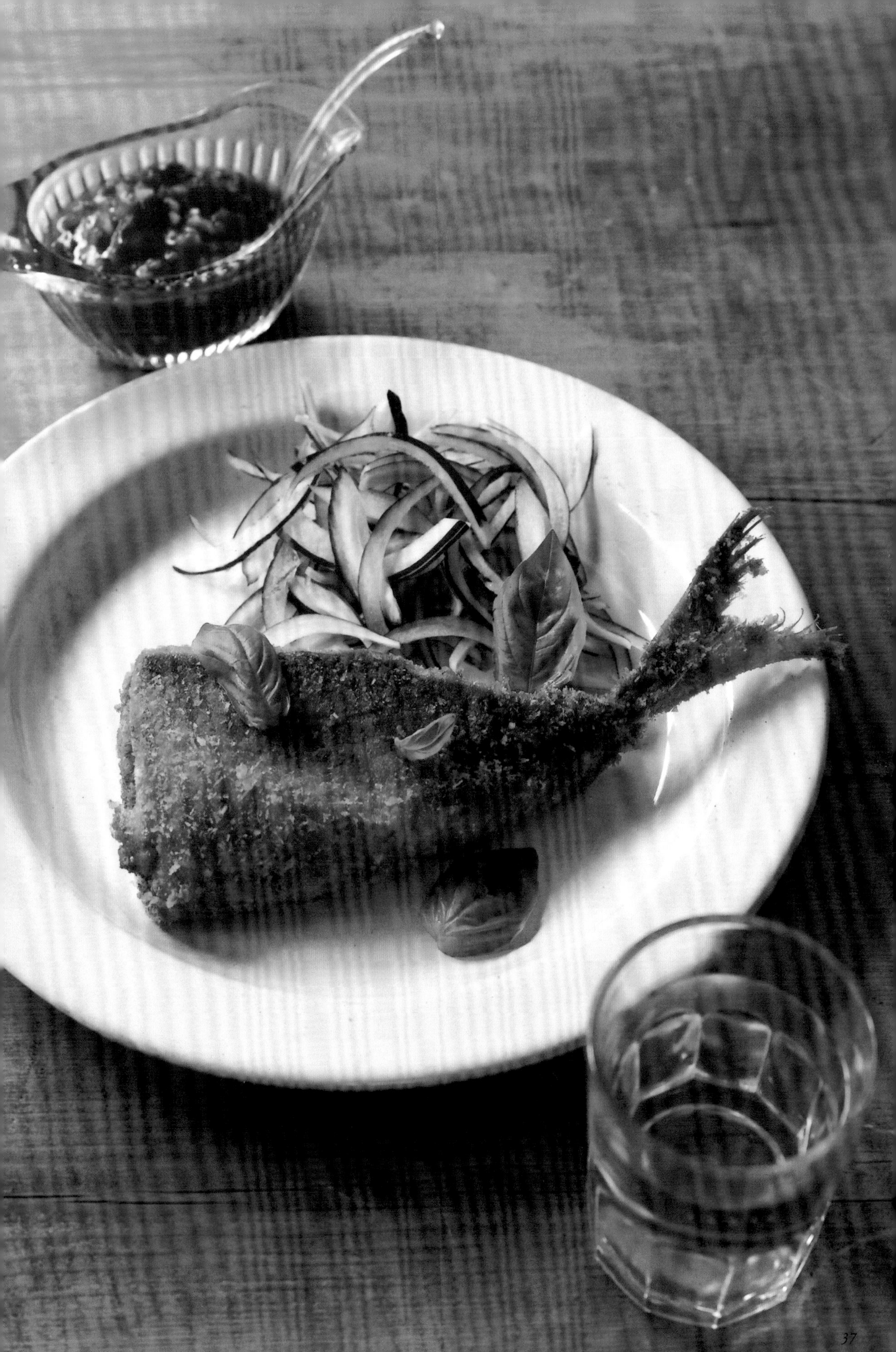

Monkey Mountain Allied Force's

Full-Course Mackerel Pike

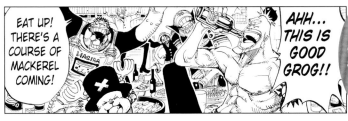

AHH... THIS IS GOOD GROG!!
EAT UP! THERE'S A COURSE OF MACKEREL COMING!
MASIRA

MANGA MOMENT

When the Monkey Mountain Allied Force learns the Straw Hats are heading for the island in the sky, they rejoice at finding a group of kindred souls chasing after their dreams. They feast on some mackerel pike Shoujou caught and speak of the dreams that drive them.
(FROM VOL. 25, CH. 229)

Honey mustard mackerel pike

INGREDIENTS Serves 3-4

2 mackerel pike (Pacific saury)
salt to taste

Mix (a.)
- 5 oz. (150 ml) vinegar
- 2 tbsp. sugar
- ½ tsp. salt

Mix (b.)
- 2 tbsp. yellow (or stone-ground) mustard
- ½ tbsp. honey
- ½ tsp. vinegar

dill if desired

STEPS

① Fillet pike, wash, and dry. Arrange on a deep tray, flesh side up, and sprinkle salt liberally **(A)**, then chill in refrigerator for 30 minutes. Mix together **(a.)** and **(b.)** during this time.

② Wash off the salt on the pike and dry again. Arrange on tray, skin side up, then pour mix **(a.)** over the top and chill again for 20 minutes.

③ Use fishbone pliers to remove fine bones. Pull off skin, starting from the head side **(B)**. Cut into bite-size pieces and dress with mix **(b.)**. Garnish with dill sprigs if desired.

Sesame-coated mackerel pike with a rich kabayaki sauce

INGREDIENTS Serves 2

2 mackerel pike (Pacific saury)
roughly 1 tsp. flour
white sesame seeds
1 lotus root (5 oz./140 g)
2 bell peppers

Mix (a.)
- 1 tbsp. soy sauce
- scant tbsp. sugar
- 2 tbsp. saké

vegetable oil

STEPS

① Fillet pike, dip skin side in flour, then coat flesh side with sesame seeds **(C)**. Peel lotus root and cut into ⅓ inch (1 cm) slices. Cut bell peppers into four equal slices, leaving the seeds and stem. Mix together **(a.)**.

② Add vegetable oil to a heated frying pan and cook lotus root and peppers on medium heat, covering both sides. Remove.

③ Add more vegetable oil to pan and cook skin side of pike for 3-4 minutes until browned, then flip over and cook flesh side. Blot with a paper towel to remove excess oil, then place on bed of sesame seeds. Transfer to plate, add lotus root and peppers ② and drizzle **(a.)** mixture over **(D)**.

THIS IS DARN GOOD PIKE!!!

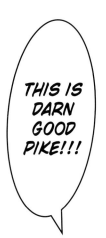

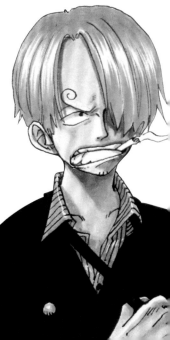

A

C

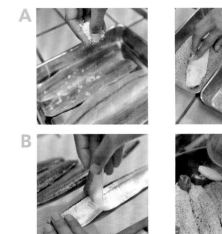

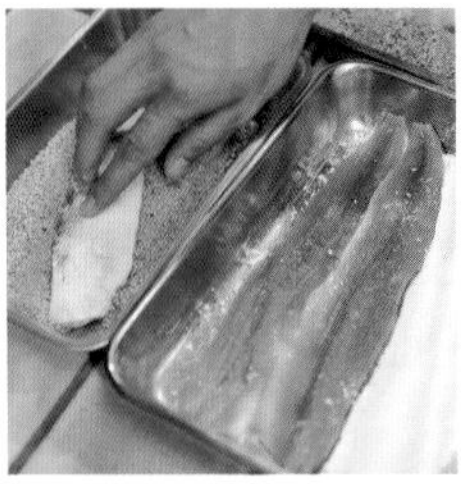

B

D

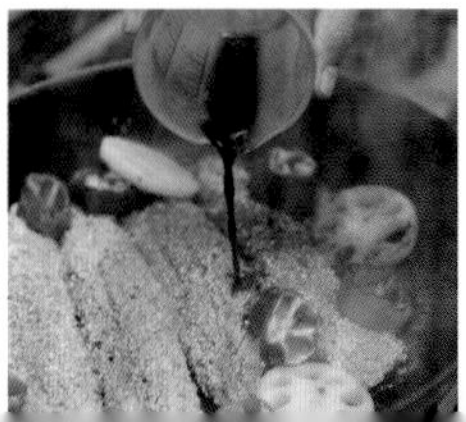

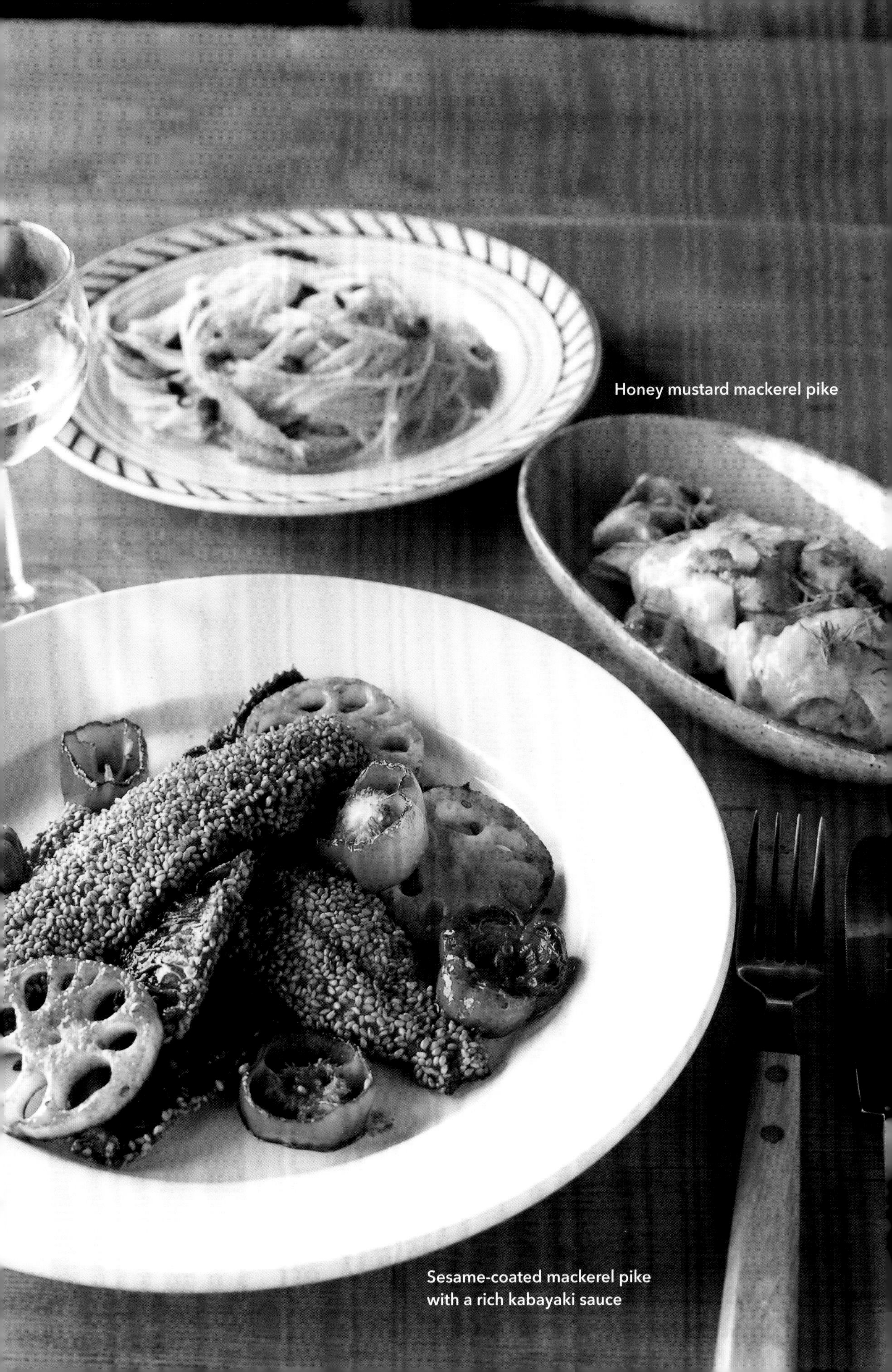

Honey mustard mackerel pike

Sesame-coated mackerel pike
with a rich kabayaki sauce

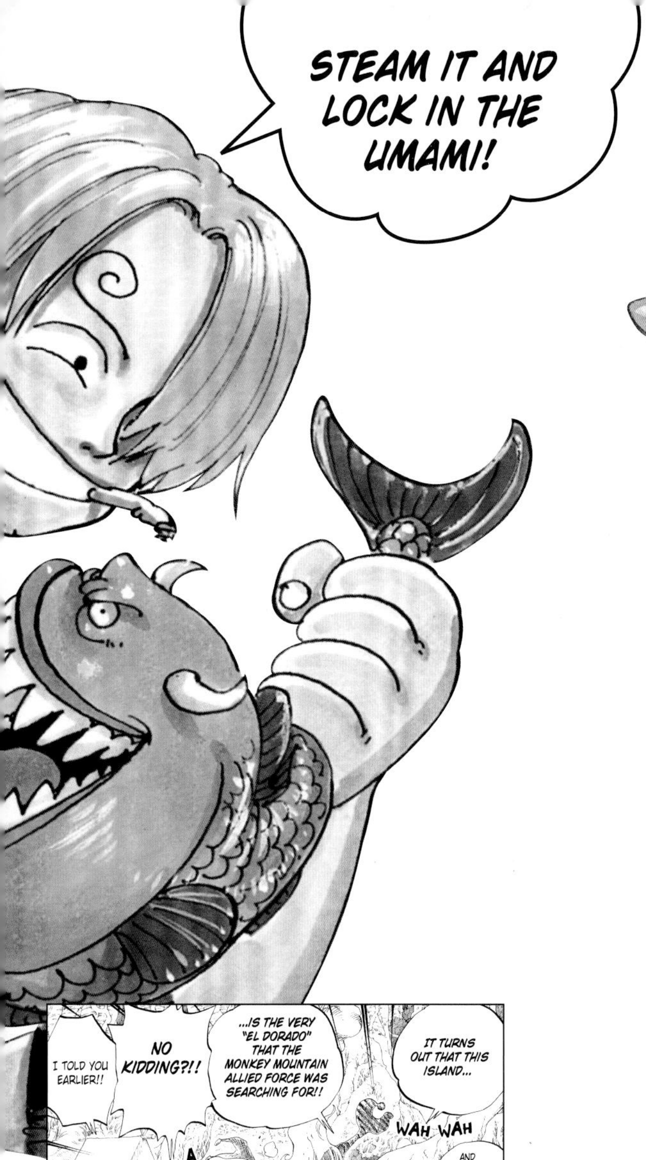
STEAM IT AND LOCK IN THE UMAMI!

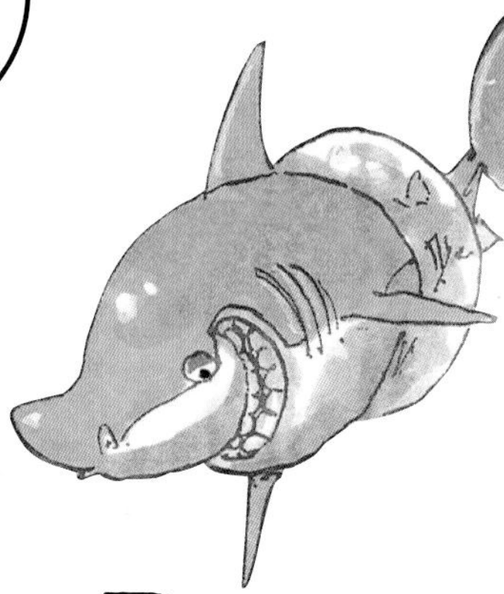

Roasted Sky Shark

From Sky Island

Sanji's take on steam-fried salmon!

INGREDIENTS Serves 4

3 fillets of salmon (12 ½ oz./360 g)
a little salt
a little white pepper
¼ head of cabbage
½ onion
½ carrot
a little vegetable oil
1 tbsp. saké
1 ½ tbsp. sugar
3 tbsp. miso
1 ½ tbsp. butter
½ tbsp. soy sauce

STEPS

① Lightly sprinkle salt and white pepper on salmon. Roughly cut the cabbage, slice onion into ⅓ inch (1 cm) pieces, and cut carrot into short strips.

② Pour oil onto a heated frying pan and cook salmon, skin side down, on medium heat for 2-3 minutes, until browned.

③ Turn over salmon, then add cabbage, onion, and carrot. Swirl in saké. Sprinkle sugar and miso here and there, and add dabs of butter on top of the miso clumps **(A)**. Carefully cover with aluminum foil and steam for 6-7 minutes **(B)**.

④ Remove foil, tear salmon into chunks, and mix contents. Add soy sauce and turn off heat.

A

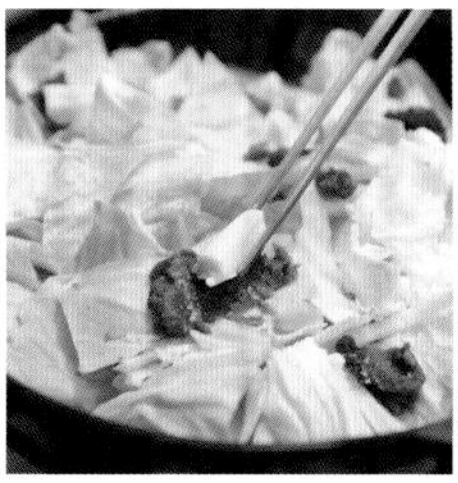

B

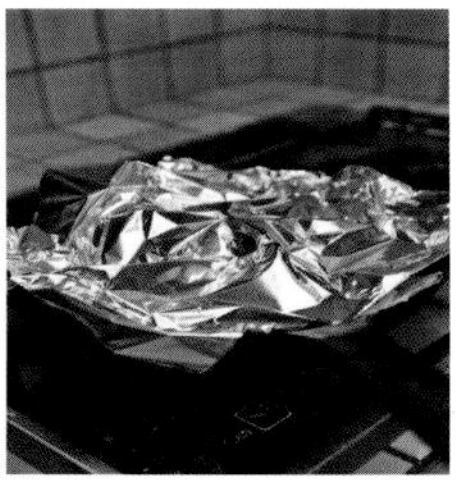

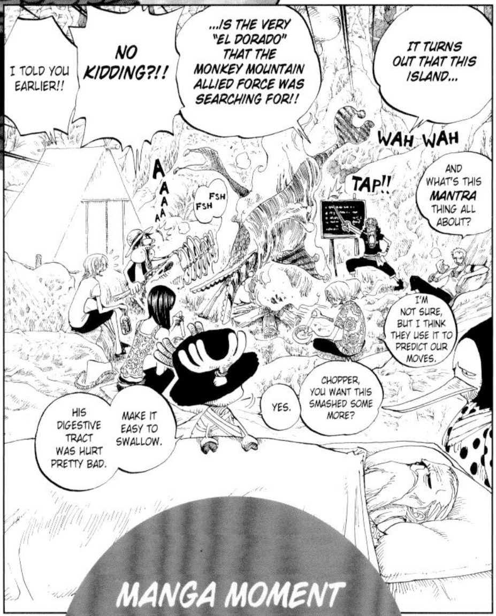
IT TURNS OUT THAT THIS ISLAND...
...IS THE VERY "EL DORADO" THAT THE MONKEY MOUNTAIN ALLIED FORCE WAS SEARCHING FOR!!
NO KIDDING?!!
I TOLD YOU EARLIER!!
WAH WAH
AND WHAT'S THIS MANTRA THING ALL ABOUT?
TAP!!
A A A A
FSH FSH
I'M NOT SURE, BUT I THINK THEY USE IT TO PREDICT OUR MOVES.
CHOPPER, YOU WANT THIS SMASHED SOME MORE?
YES.
MAKE IT EASY TO SWALLOW.
HIS DIGESTIVE TRACT WAS HURT PRETTY BAD.

MANGA MOMENT

After being split into two groups, the crew gets back together to share their findings. They camp at the lakeside this night because of damage to the *Merry Go*. An outdoor excursion calls for a rougher style of cooking.
(FROM VOL. 27, CH. 252)

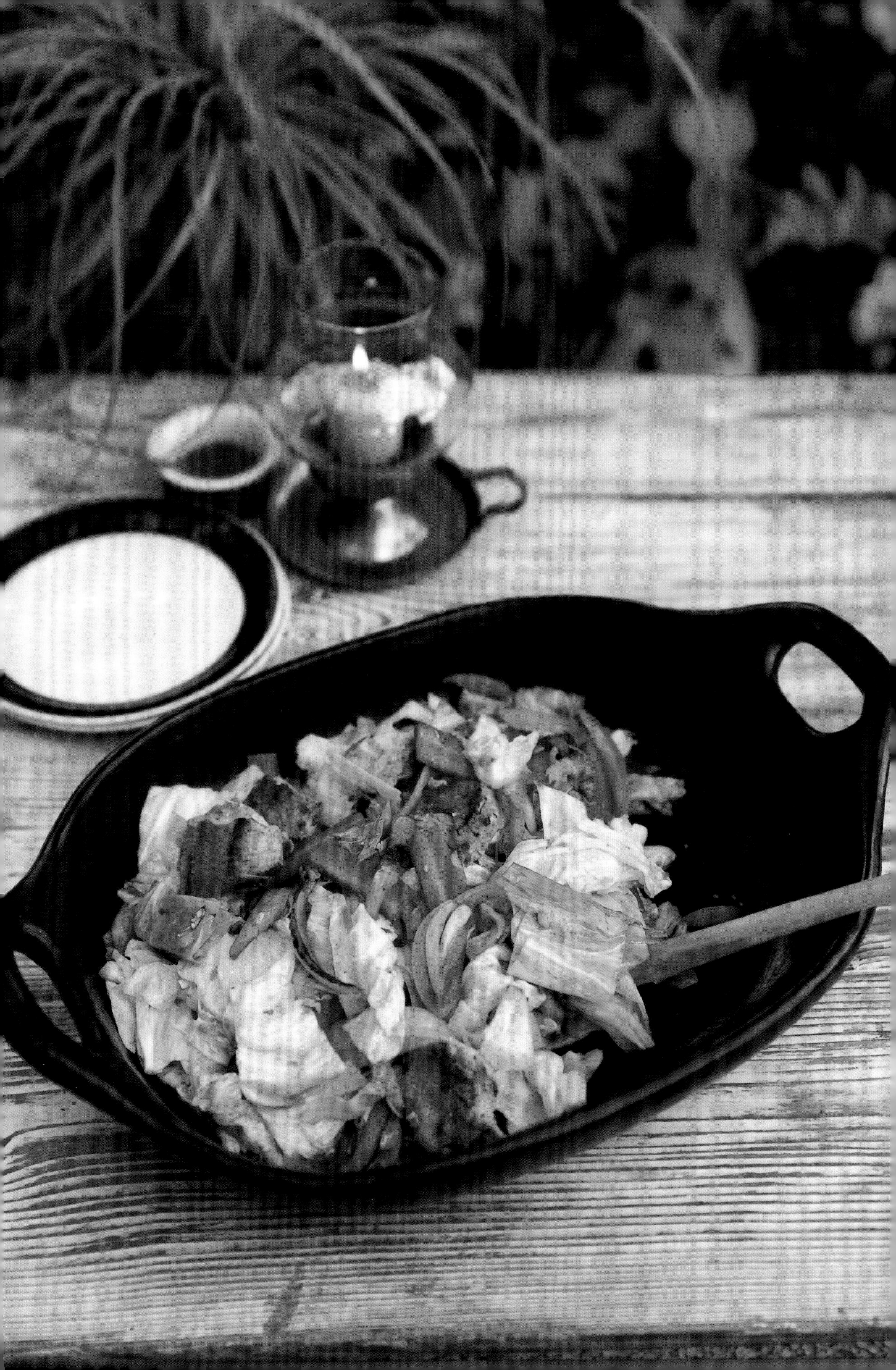

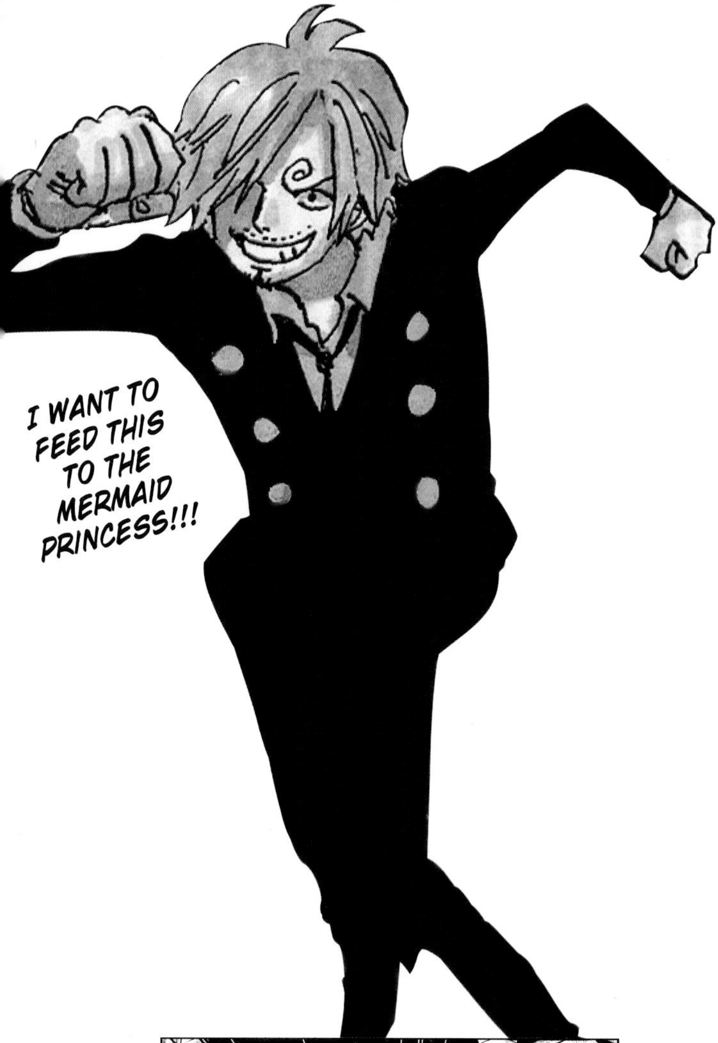
I WANT TO FEED THIS TO THE MERMAID PRINCESS!!!

The Mermaid Café's Kelp Brûlée

A rich steamed custard with a kelp-based sauce

INGREDIENTS Makes 4 cups
(¾ oz./100 ml each)
2 eggs
1 ¼ cups (300 ml) kombu and katsuobushi *dashi* broth (see p. 94)
½ tsp. salt
1 tsp. mirin
⅓ tsp. soy sauce
2 raw unbreaded chicken tenders (3 oz./80 g)
½ tsp. soy sauce
Kelp mixture
2 oz. (50 g) wakame kelp
⅔ cup (150 ml) kombu and katsuobushi *dashi* broth (see p. 94)
1 tsp. soy sauce
½ tbsp. potato starch

STEPS

① Crack eggs into a bowl. Add dashi broth, salt, mirin, and soy sauce, and mix. Cut chicken tenderloins in thin diagonal slices and season with soy sauce.

② Measure out chicken and egg base into four equal heatproof containers and scoop any air bubbles on surface **(A)**.

③ Cover containers with aluminum foil and let steam for 15–20 minutes in a steam cooker **(B)**.

④ Create kelp mixture. Add dashi broth, mild soy sauce and potato starch to a pot and mix well over low heat. When it has thickened, add strip-cut kelp on top, turn off heat and serve on top of steamed portion ③.

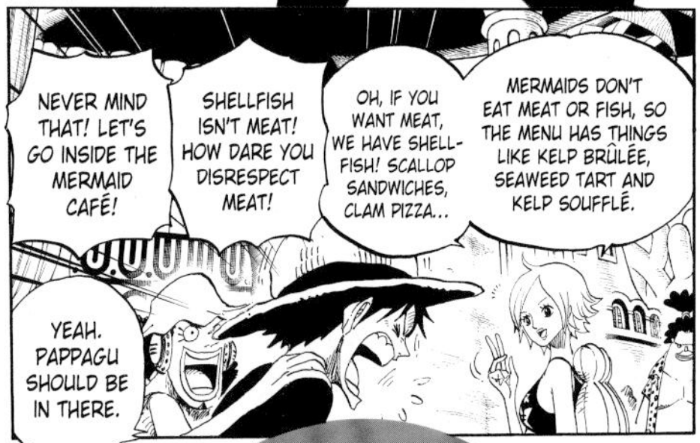
MERMAIDS DON'T EAT MEAT OR FISH, SO THE MENU HAS THINGS LIKE KELP BRÛLÉE, SEAWEED TART AND KELP SOUFFLÉ.
OH, IF YOU WANT MEAT, WE HAVE SHELL-FISH! SCALLOP SANDWICHES, CLAM PIZZA...
SHELLFISH ISN'T MEAT! HOW DARE YOU DISRESPECT MEAT!
NEVER MIND THAT! LET'S GO INSIDE THE MERMAID CAFÉ!
YEAH. PAPPAGU SHOULD BE IN THERE.

MANGA MOMENT

When the crew arrives at Fish-Man Island, the mermaid Camie takes them to the café where she works. But there's no meat on the menu there! Luffy has trouble accepting the truth.
(FROM VOL. 62, CH. 610)

A

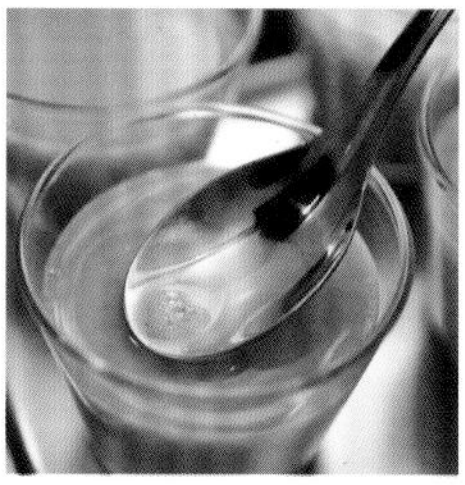

B

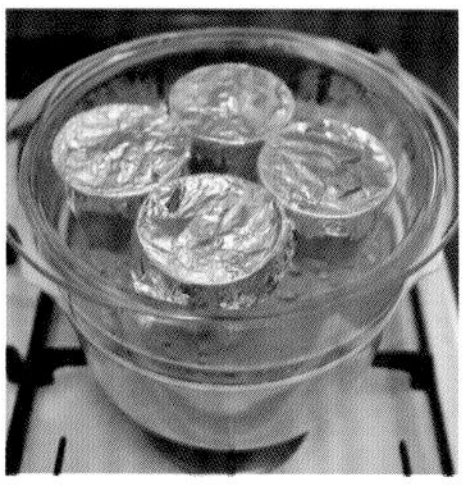

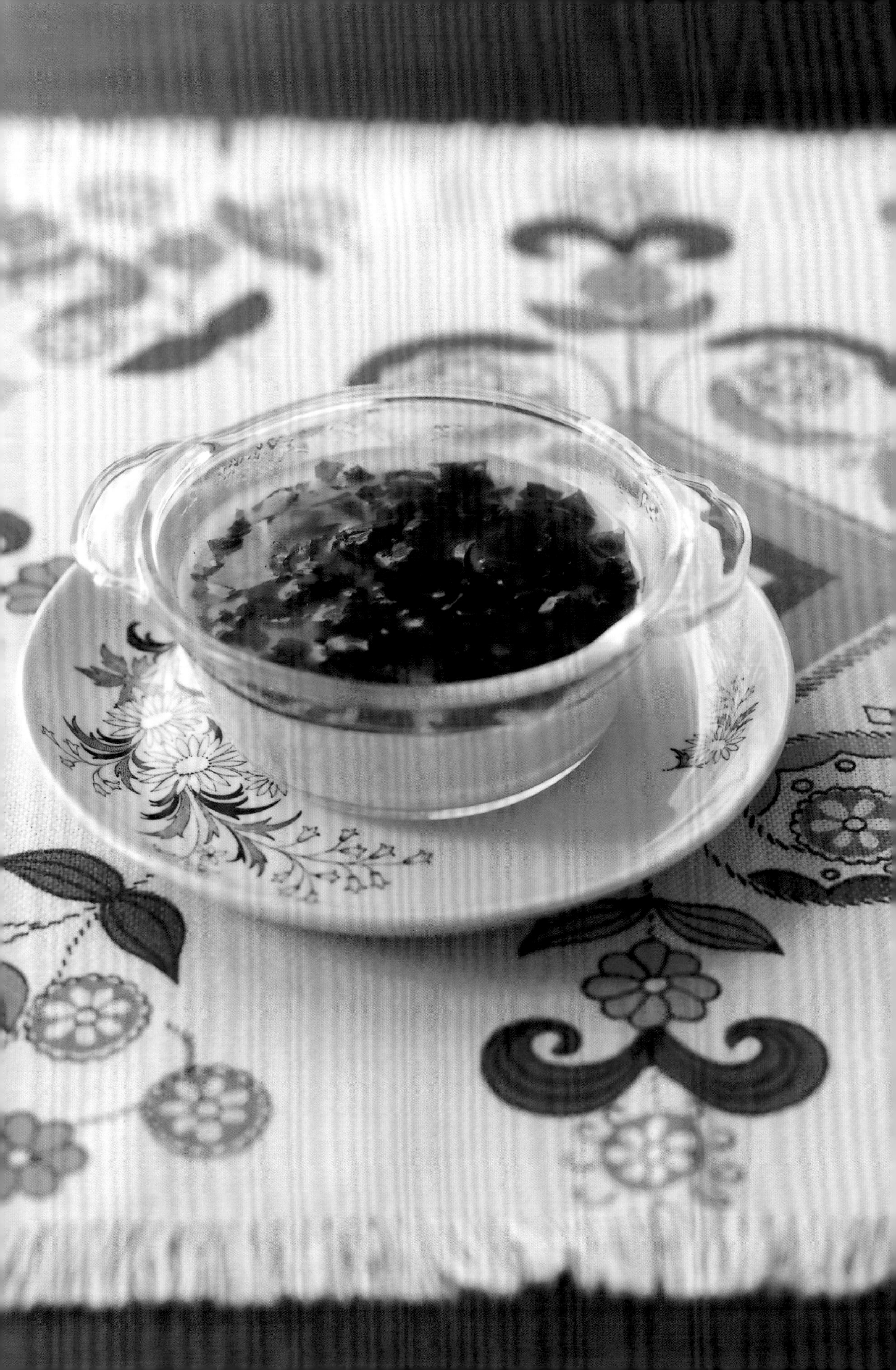

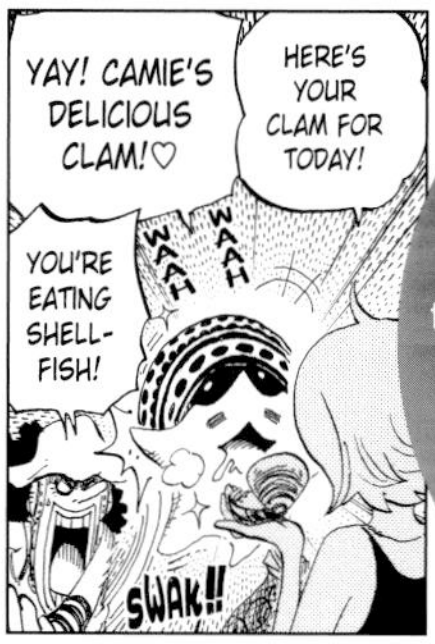
HERE'S YOUR CLAM FOR TODAY!
YAY! CAMIE'S DELICIOUS CLAM!♡
WAAH
WAAH
YOU'RE EATING SHELL-FISH!
SWAK!!

MANGA MOMENT

Camie's friend Pappagu brags to Luffy that he lives off of savage sea beast meat. But his secret favorite is the clams Camie harvests around her home. He looks forward to her delivery every day.

(FROM VOL. 62, CH. 610)

A

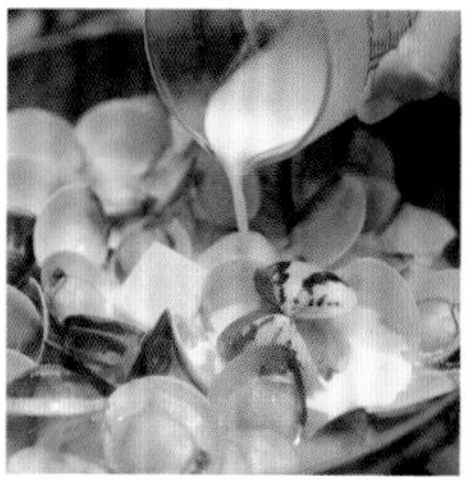

B

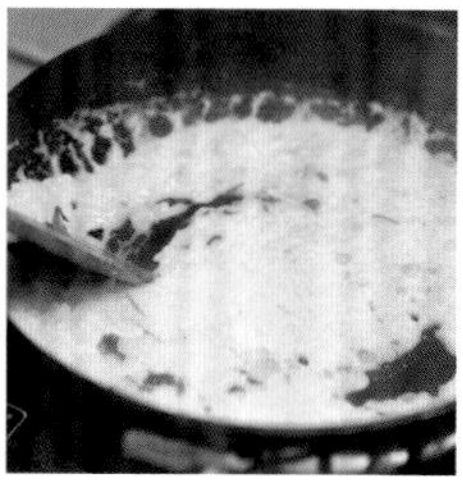

C

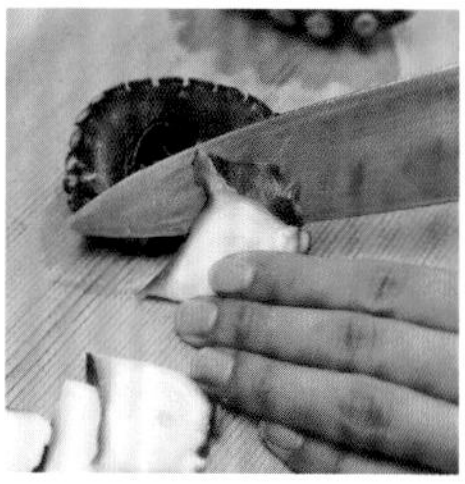

Camie's

Delicious Clams

Creamy and steamed in wine

INGREDIENTS Serves 4

17-18 oz. (500 g) clams in shell
¼ onion
1 clove garlic
3 ½ oz. (100 ml) white wine
a little white pepper
1 tbsp. butter
1 ¾ oz. (50 ml) heavy cream
flat-leaf parsley
rice if desired

STEPS

① Place clams in bowl of salted water at roughly seawater salinity. Cover with aluminum foil and put in a dark place for 2-3 hours until they have purged grit.

② Mince onions. Cut garlic in half vertically, remove stem, and crush with the flat of the knife. Chop parsley roughly.

③ Place clams, onions, garlic, and white wine in a frying pan, turn on heat, and cover. Once the clams open, sprinkle white pepper, add butter, and pour heavy cream **(A)**. Transfer to dish and sprinkle parsley. Cook leftover liquid **(B)** and pour over rice for a risotto if desired.

Perfect Finger Food!

Sliced Octopus

Nice savory octopus snacks

INGREDIENTS Serves 4

5 ½ oz. (150 g) fresh sushi-grade octopus
¼ onion
½ tbsp. vinegar
2 pinches of salt
1 tbsp. olive oil
a little paprika

STEPS

① Mince onion and soak in water. Slice octopus diagonally **(C)** and arrange on plate.

② Mix salt into vinegar, then mix in olive oil.

③ Pour ② on octopus. Dry out onions and scatter over octopus. Sprinkle paprika.

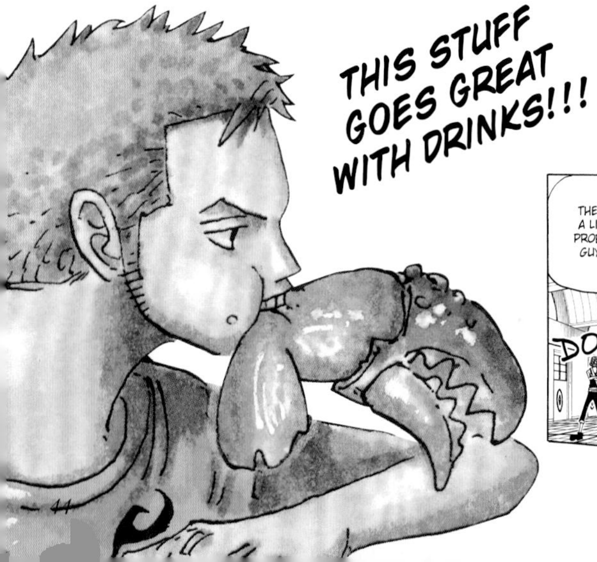
THIS STUFF GOES GREAT WITH DRINKS!!!

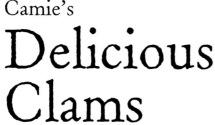

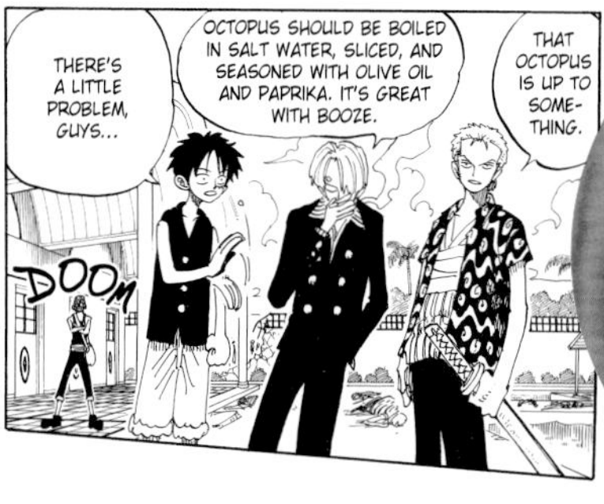
THAT OCTOPUS IS UP TO SOME-THING.
OCTOPUS SHOULD BE BOILED IN SALT WATER, SLICED, AND SEASONED WITH OLIVE OIL AND PAPRIKA. IT'S GREAT WITH BOOZE.
THERE'S A LITTLE PROBLEM, GUYS...
DOOM

MANGA MOMENT

The Straw Hats challenge Arlong's crew for how they've tormented Nami and abused her for her navigational skills. Once the battle starts, Sanji describes to Hachi an ideal recipe for eating octopus.

(FROM VOL. 10, CH. 83)

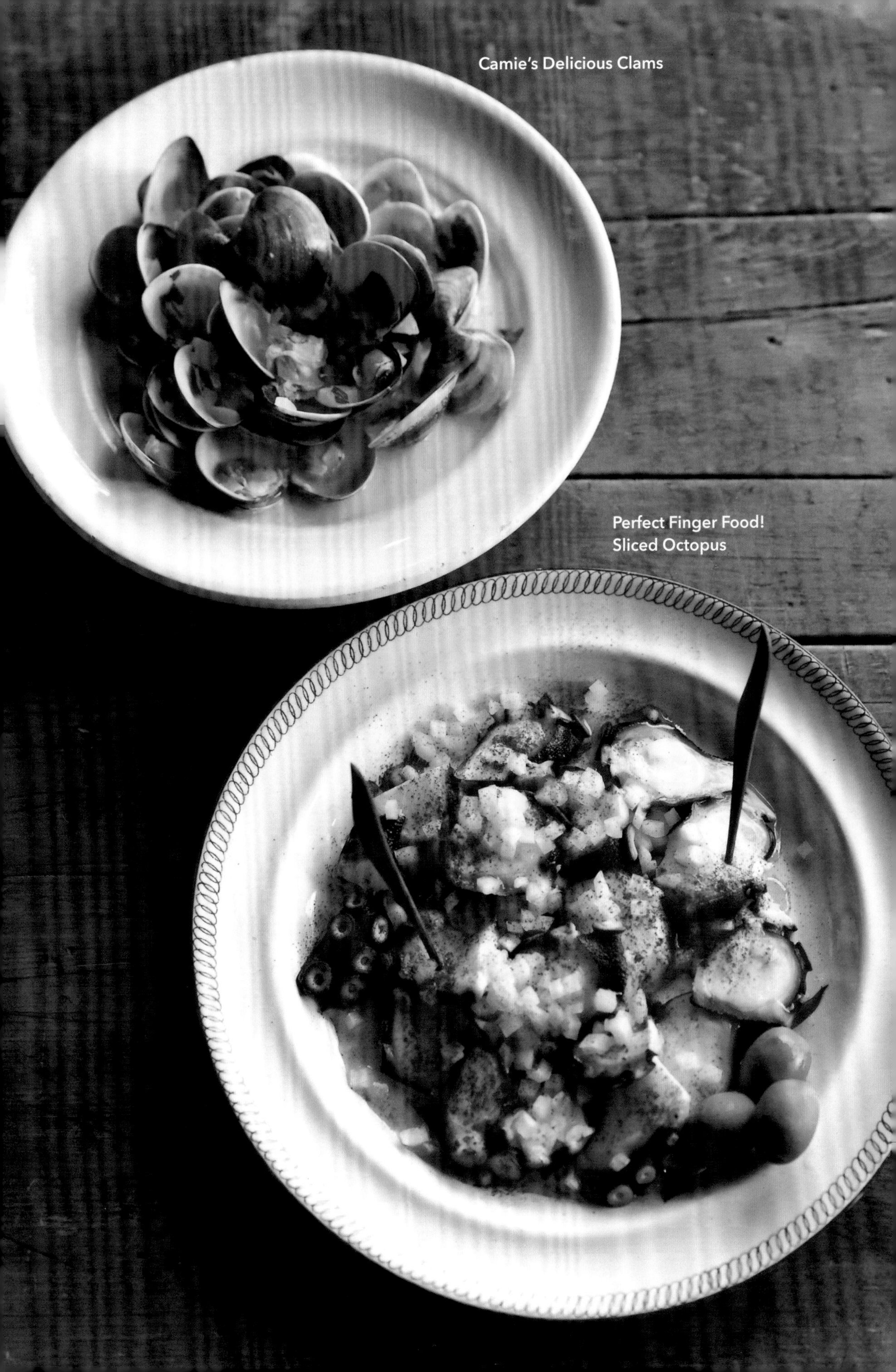
Camie's Delicious Clams
Perfect Finger Food!
Sliced Octopus

Healthy Veget

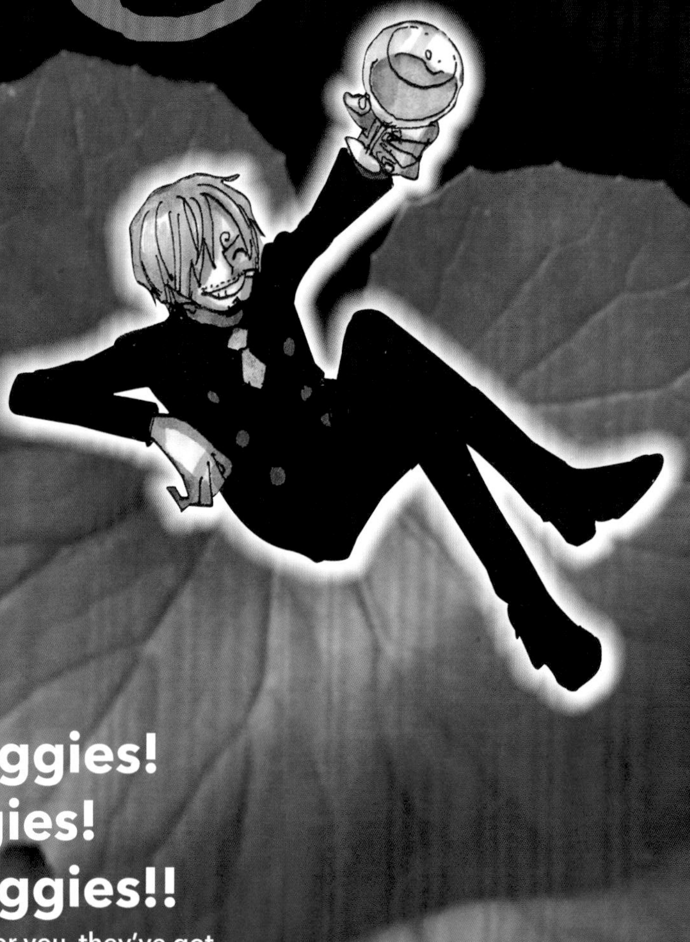

First come veggies! Second, veggies! Third, also veggies!!

Vegetables aren't just good for you, they've got a kind of elixir inside of them that cleanses your heart too. So, in the name of romance, I've put together some recipes that are low-calorie, but satisfying and delicious. They've all easy and quick to make. Eat them every day!

ble Recipes

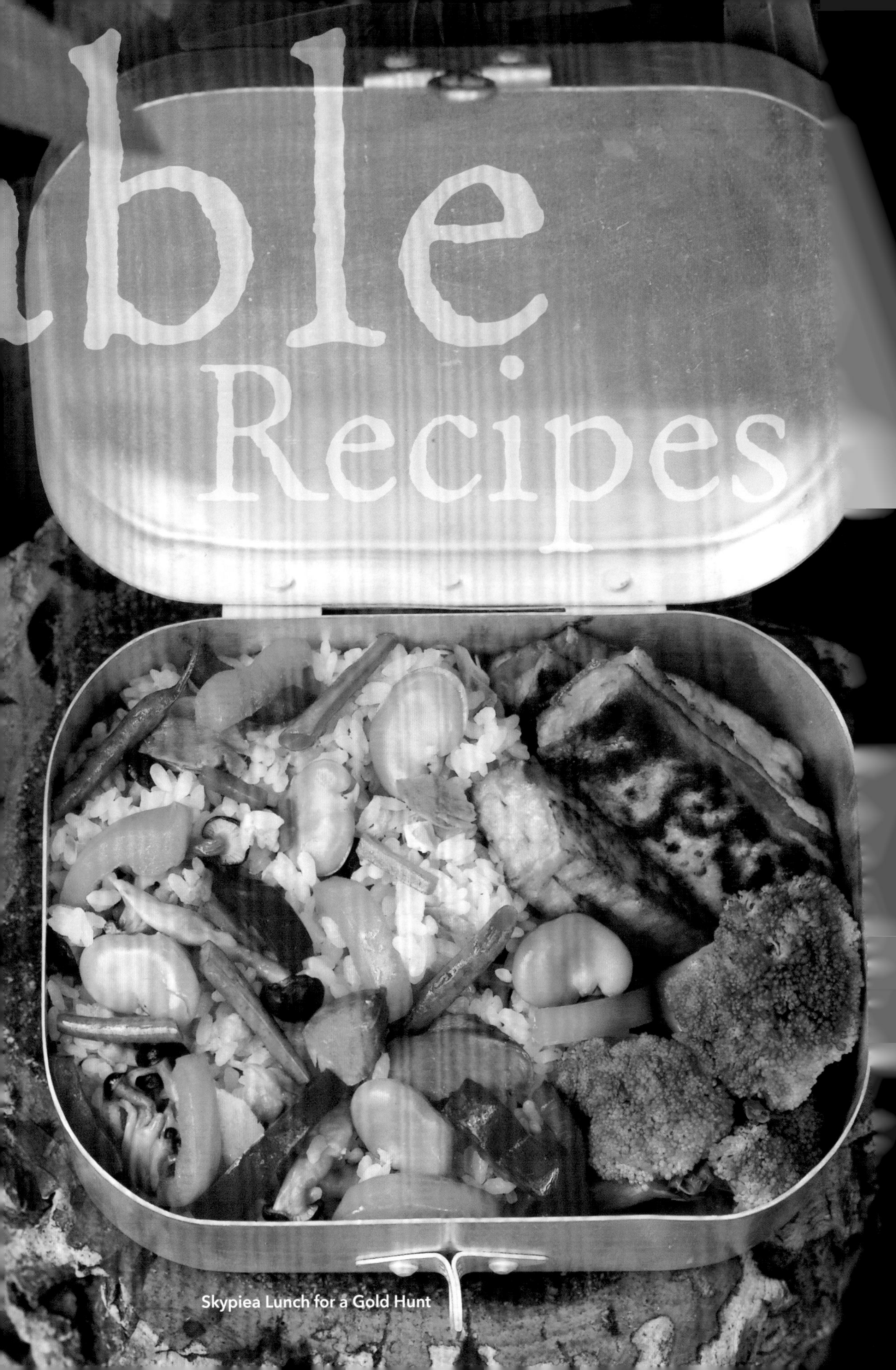

Skypiea Lunch for a Gold Hunt

Skypiea Lunch

for a Gold Hunt

A satisfying lunch packed with veggies

INGREDIENTS Serves 3–4

Colorful Salmon Rice

Rice

1 ½ cups (300 g) uncooked rice
1 fillet (4 oz./100-120 g) salted salmon
⅓ large carrot
1 slice (⅕ oz./40 g) of *abura-age* fried tofu
½ pack (3 oz./80 g) shimeji, shiitake, or enoki mushrooms
½ tbsp. mild soy sauce
½ tsp. salt
1 sheet kombu (4x4 in./10x10 cm)

Veggies

½ each of red and yellow bell peppers
10 green bean pods
3 oz. (80 g) fava beans
1 tsp. vegetable oil
2 pinches of salt
½ tsp. sugar
2 tbsp. water
½–1 tsp. soy sauce

Fried Tofu Ham Sandwiches Serves 2

1 block *atsu-age* thick fried tofu
2 slices ham
up to 2 tbsp. all-purpose flour
vegetable oil
½–1 tsp. soy sauce

salt-boiled broccoli

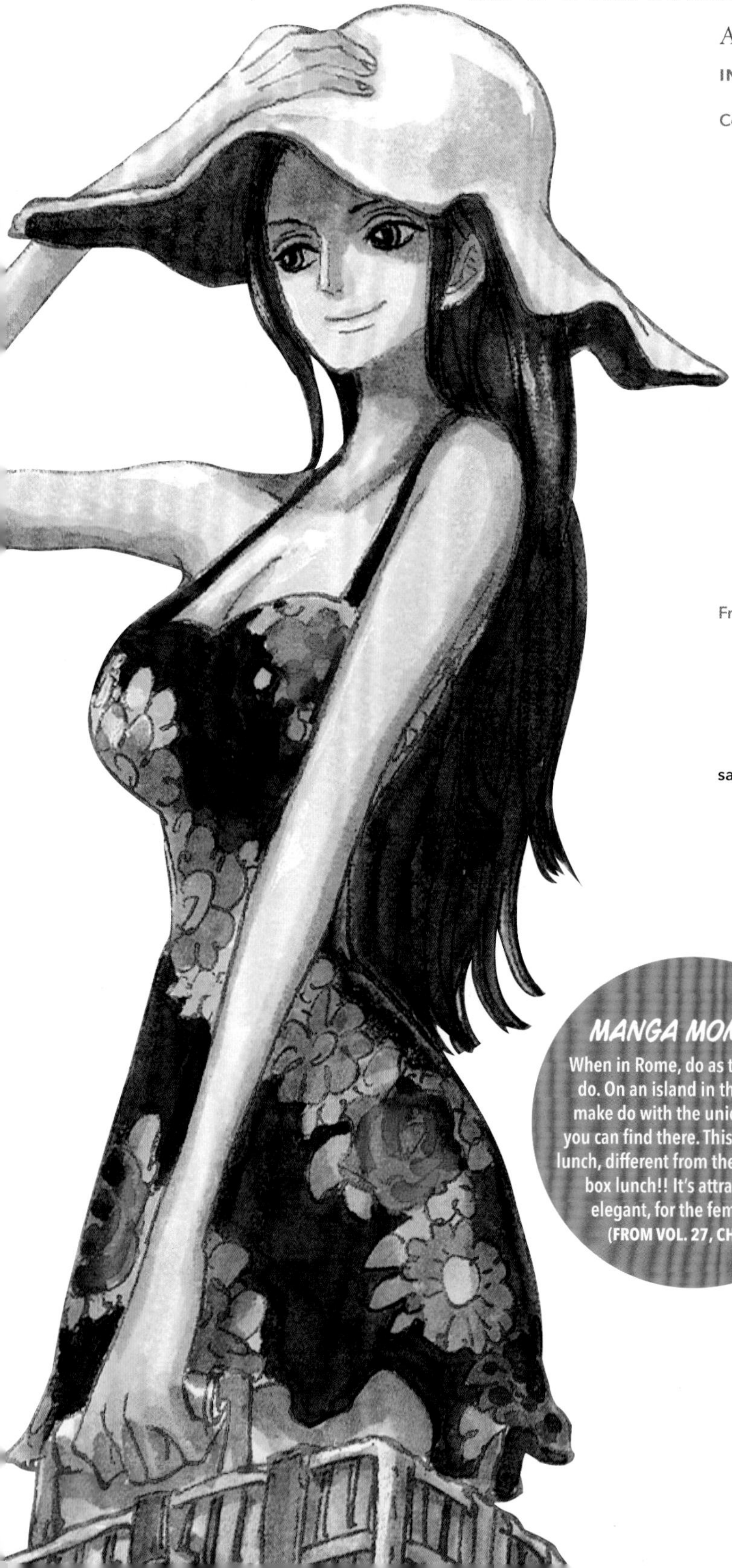

MANGA MOMENT

When in Rome, do as the Romans do. On an island in the sky, you make do with the unique flavors you can find there. This is a healthy lunch, different from the usual pirate box lunch!! It's attractive and elegant, for the female eye.
(FROM VOL. 27, CH. 253)

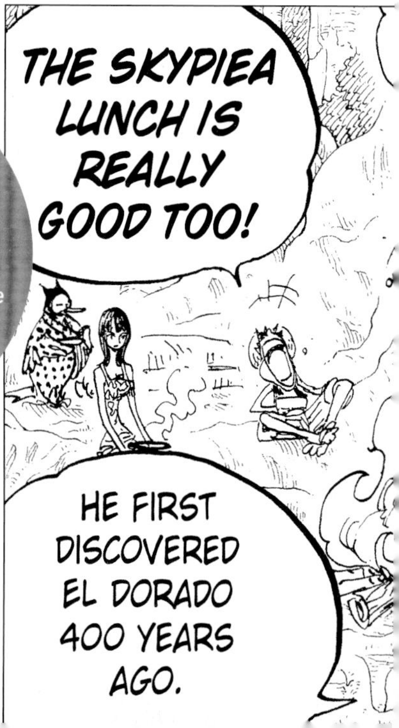
THE SKYPIEA LUNCH IS REALLY GOOD TOO!
HE FIRST DISCOVERED EL DORADO 400 YEARS AGO.

STEPS

Rice

① Wash rice and leave sitting in cold water. Cut carrot into sticks ¾ inch (2 cm) long. Use a paper towel to press out excess oil from abura-age, then mince it. Remove base from shimeji block and separate into small bunches. Cook both sides of salmon on a grill pan.

② Add rice and soy sauce to rice cooker and add water to 1 ½ cup line. Add salt, kombu, carrot ①, abura-age, mushrooms, and salmon. Turn on cooker **(A)**.

③ When rice is cooked, remove kombu and salmon. Remove bones from salmon, then return to rice cooker and stir, breaking up the salmon.

Veggies

① Remove stem and seeds from bell peppers and cut to bite size. Cut green beans into 1 inch (3 cm) pieces. Boil fava beans and peel skin **(B)**.

② Heat up vegetable oil in a pan and fry bell peppers and green beans until they are soft **(C)**. Add salt, sugar and water. Cook until liquid evaporates, then add soy sauce and turn off heat. Pack rice mixture into bento lunch box, then add bell peppers, green beans, and fava beans on top.

Fried Tofu Ham Sandwiches

① Cut atsu-age fried tofu into ⅔ inch (1.5 cm) pieces. Cut lengthwise down the middle two-thirds of the way through. Cut ham slices to match size of incision and fit inside, then coat with flour **(D)**.

② Place tofu sandwiches in frying pan with vegetable oil and cook both sides on medium heat. Drizzle with soy sauce and turn off heat.

A

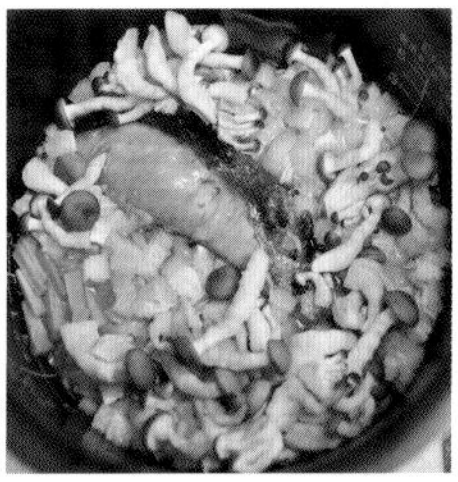

B

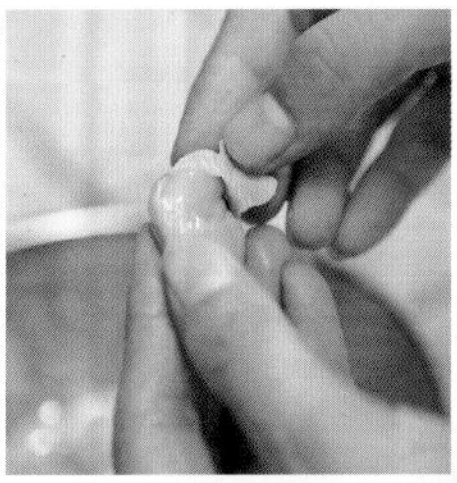

C

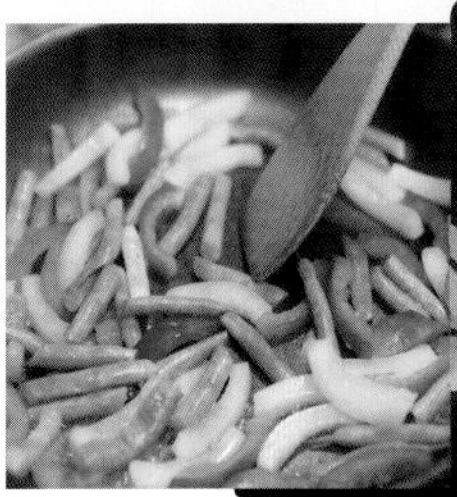

D

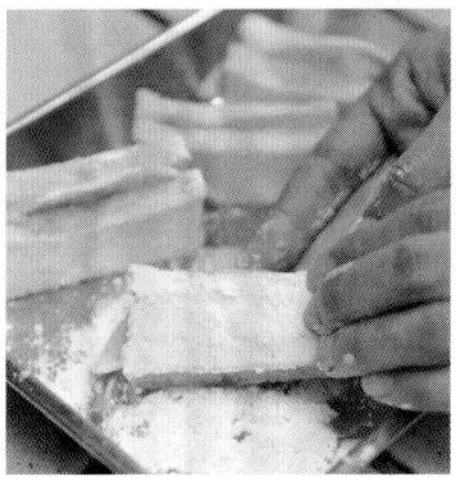

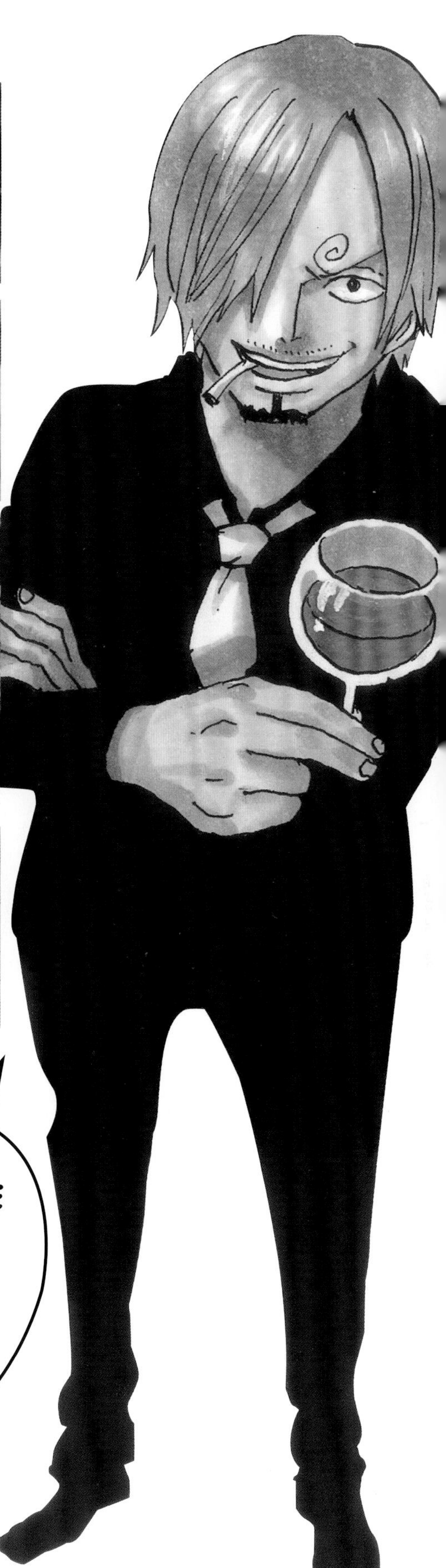
MANAGEABLE CALORIES FOR THE LADIES!!!

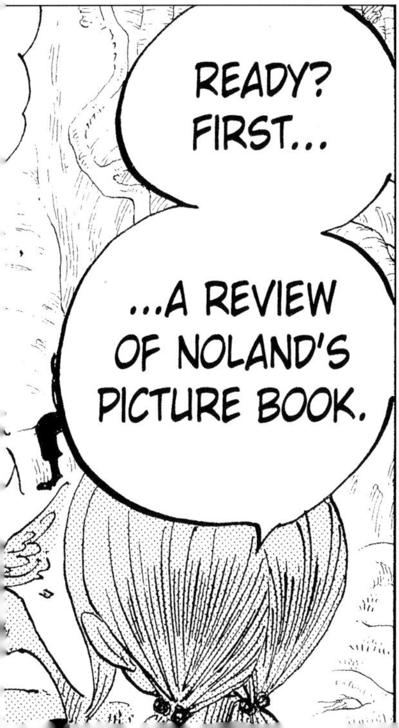
READY? FIRST...
...A REVIEW OF NOLAND'S PICTURE BOOK.

Water Seven's

Water-Water Cabbage

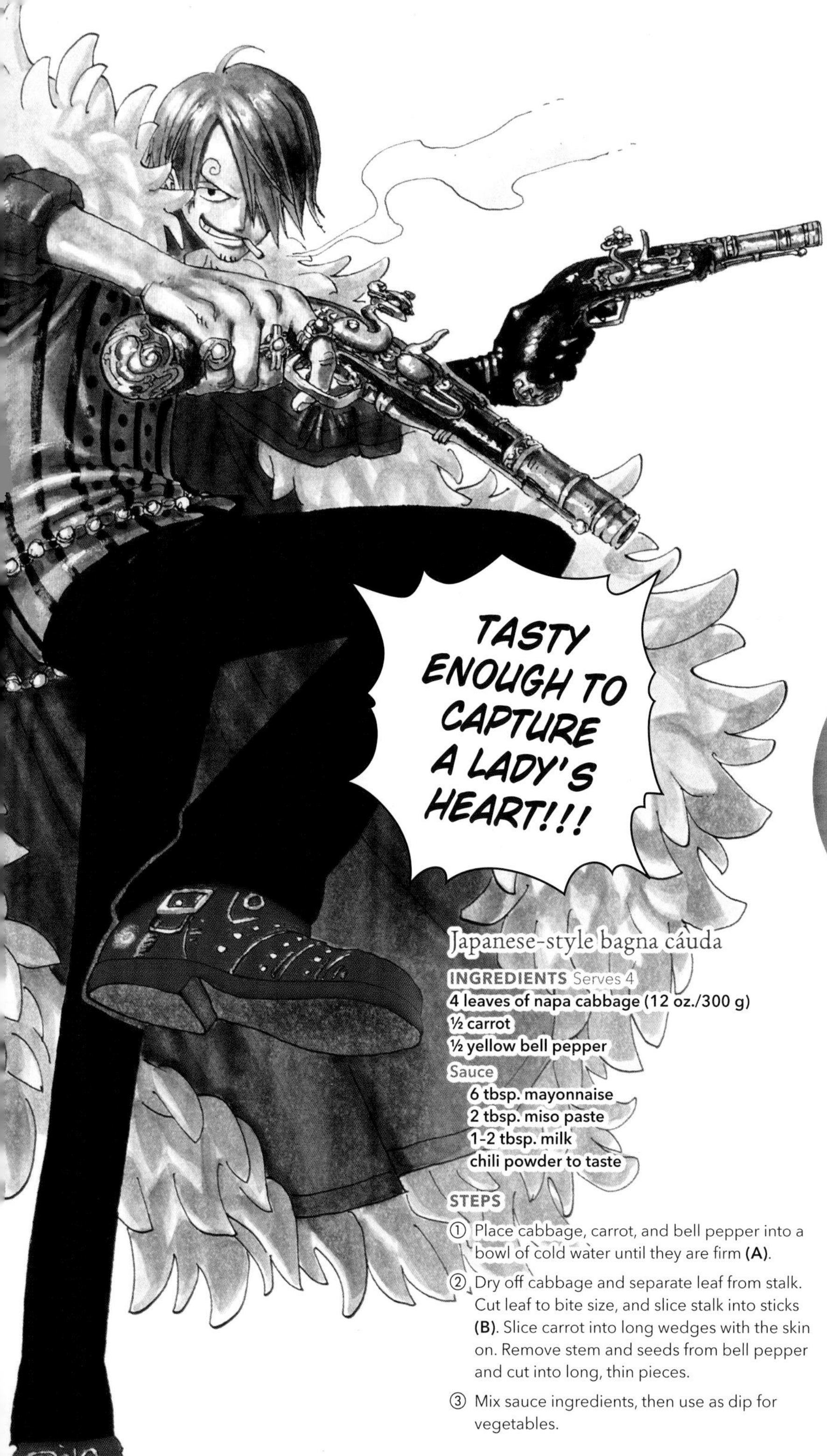
TASTY ENOUGH TO CAPTURE A LADY'S HEART!!!

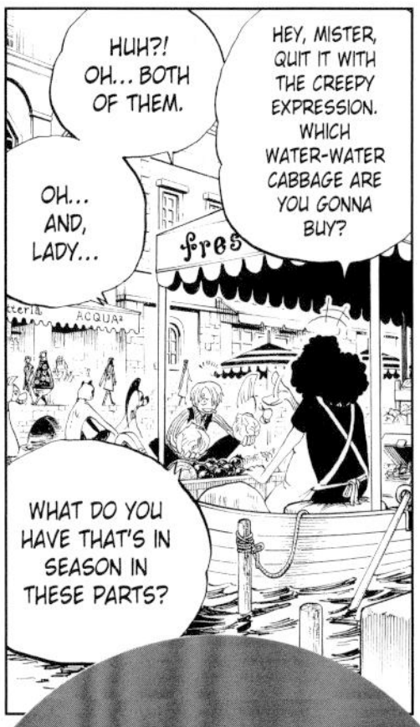
HEY, MISTER, QUIT IT WITH THE CREEPY EXPRESSION. WHICH WATER-WATER CABBAGE ARE YOU GONNA BUY?
HUH?! OH... BOTH OF THEM.
OH... AND, LADY...
WHAT DO YOU HAVE THAT'S IN SEASON IN THESE PARTS?

MANGA MOMENT

Part of a cook's job is procuring groceries! Sanji went shopping in Water Seven and found some Water-Water Cabbage soaked in crisp, clear water. Like with the Water-Water Meat, the juiciness brings out the subtle sweetness of the cabbage.

(FROM VOL. 34, CH. 326)

Japanese-style bagna câuda

INGREDIENTS Serves 4

4 leaves of napa cabbage (12 oz./300 g)
½ carrot
½ yellow bell pepper

Sauce

- **6 tbsp. mayonnaise**
- **2 tbsp. miso paste**
- **1-2 tbsp. milk**
- **chili powder to taste**

STEPS

① Place cabbage, carrot, and bell pepper into a bowl of cold water until they are firm **(A)**.

② Dry off cabbage and separate leaf from stalk. Cut leaf to bite size, and slice stalk into sticks **(B)**. Slice carrot into long wedges with the skin on. Remove stem and seeds from bell pepper and cut into long, thin pieces.

③ Mix sauce ingredients, then use as dip for vegetables.

A

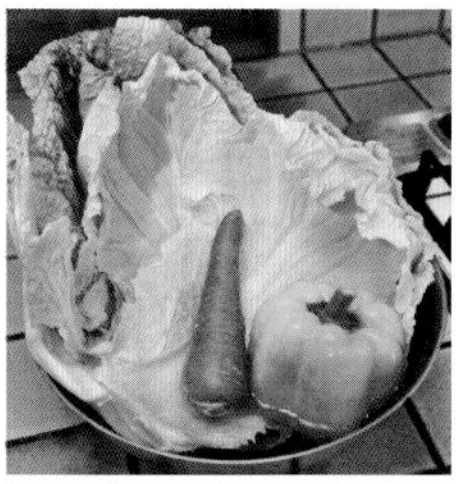

B

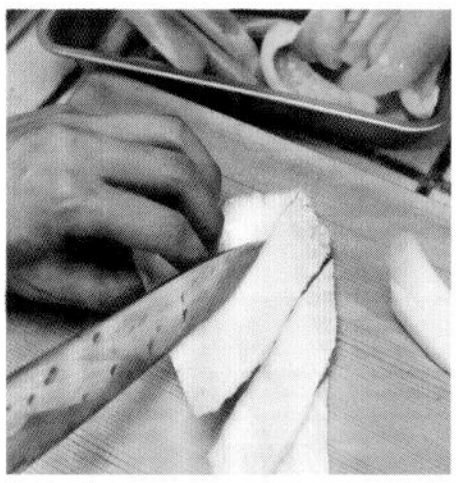

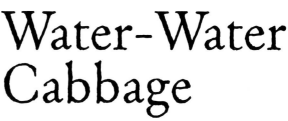

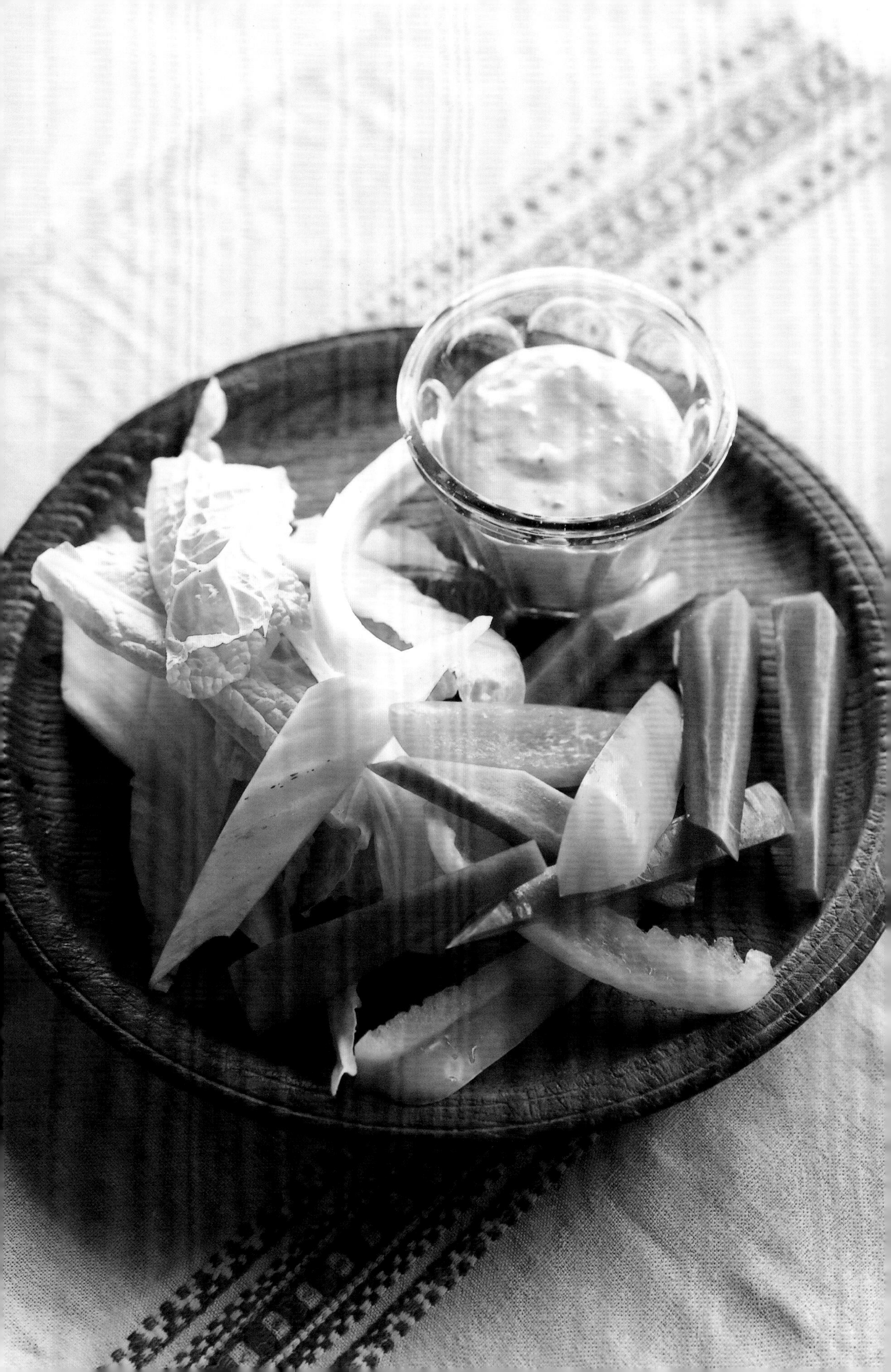

Island of Women's

Laughing Mushrooms

Packed with fragrant herbs

INGREDIENTS Serves 4

6 shiitake mushrooms
1 pack (6 oz./170 g) shimeji mushrooms
2 king oyster mushrooms
3 pieces of bacon
1 tbsp. vegetable oil
2 sprigs rosemary
½ tsp. salt
a little black pepper
a pat of butter

STEPS

① Remove the shiitake from their base and cut into ⅓ inch (1 cm) slices. Remove the shimeji from their base and separate into small bunches. Trim king oyster mushrooms to a length of 1 ½ inch (3 cm) and slice thinly. Cut bacon into ¼ inch (7 mm) slices.

② Put vegetable oil and rosemary into frying pan and heat on medium **(A)**. When oil is fragrant, fry bacon briefly, then add all mushrooms and mix. Cover and steam on low heat for 4 minutes.

③ Remove lid, add salt, and mix again. Cover again and continue steaming for 4–5 minutes, stirring occasionally, until liquid is gone and bacon is fried and no longer appears pink. If needed, add more salt and pepper for flavor, then add butter, mix, and turn off heat.

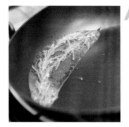

A

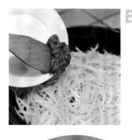

B

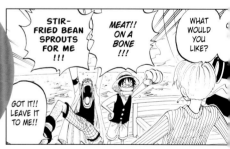

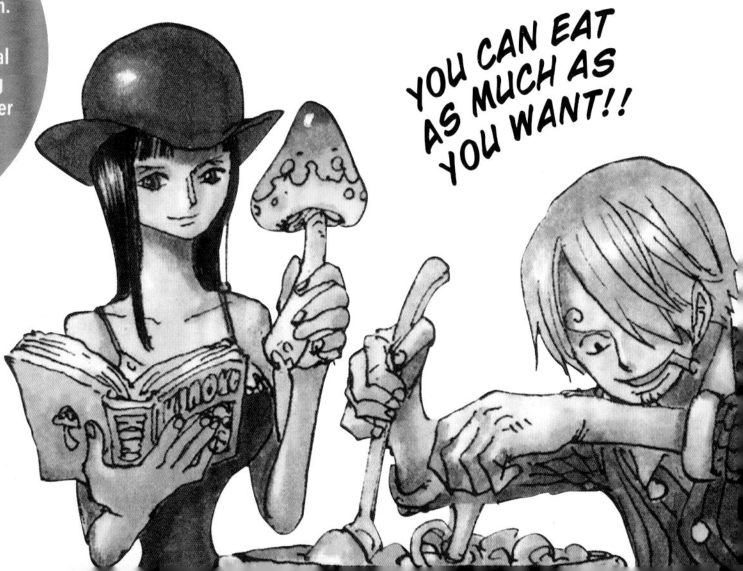

MANGA MOMENT

Amazon Lily, the island of women. Upon landing here alone, Luffy remembers his childhood survival lessons, and eats some laughing mushrooms. The bursts of laughter put him into a giddy mood!!
(FROM VOL. 54, CH. 514)

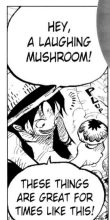

HEY, A LAUGHING MUSHROOM!
PLUP
THESE THINGS ARE GREAT FOR TIMES LIKE THIS!

Yosaku's Favorite

Stir-fried Bean Sprouts

A stir fry with anchovies and garlic

INGREDIENTS Serves 4

2 bags (roughly 1 lb./400 g) bean sprouts
2 cloves garlic, peeled
6 anchovies
olive oil
a little black pepper
a little salt

STEPS

① Mince garlic and chop anchovies finely.

② Put olive oil and garlic into a frying pan on medium heat. When garlic is golden, add bean sprouts and cook on high heat.

③ When bean sprouts are translucent, add anchovies and black pepper and mix **(B)**. Taste test and add more salt if needed.

MANGA MOMENT

It's off to Arlong Park in search of Nami!! Yosaku warns of Arlong's danger, but Luffy and Sanji are thinking more about food. When Sanji asks for requests, Yosaku demands stir-fried bean sprouts!!
(FROM VOL. 8, CH. 69)

WHAT WOULD YOU LIKE?
MEAT!! ON A BONE !!!
STIR-FRIED BEAN SPROUTS FOR ME !!!
GOT IT!! LEAVE IT TO ME!!

YOU CAN EAT AS MUCH AS YOU WANT!!

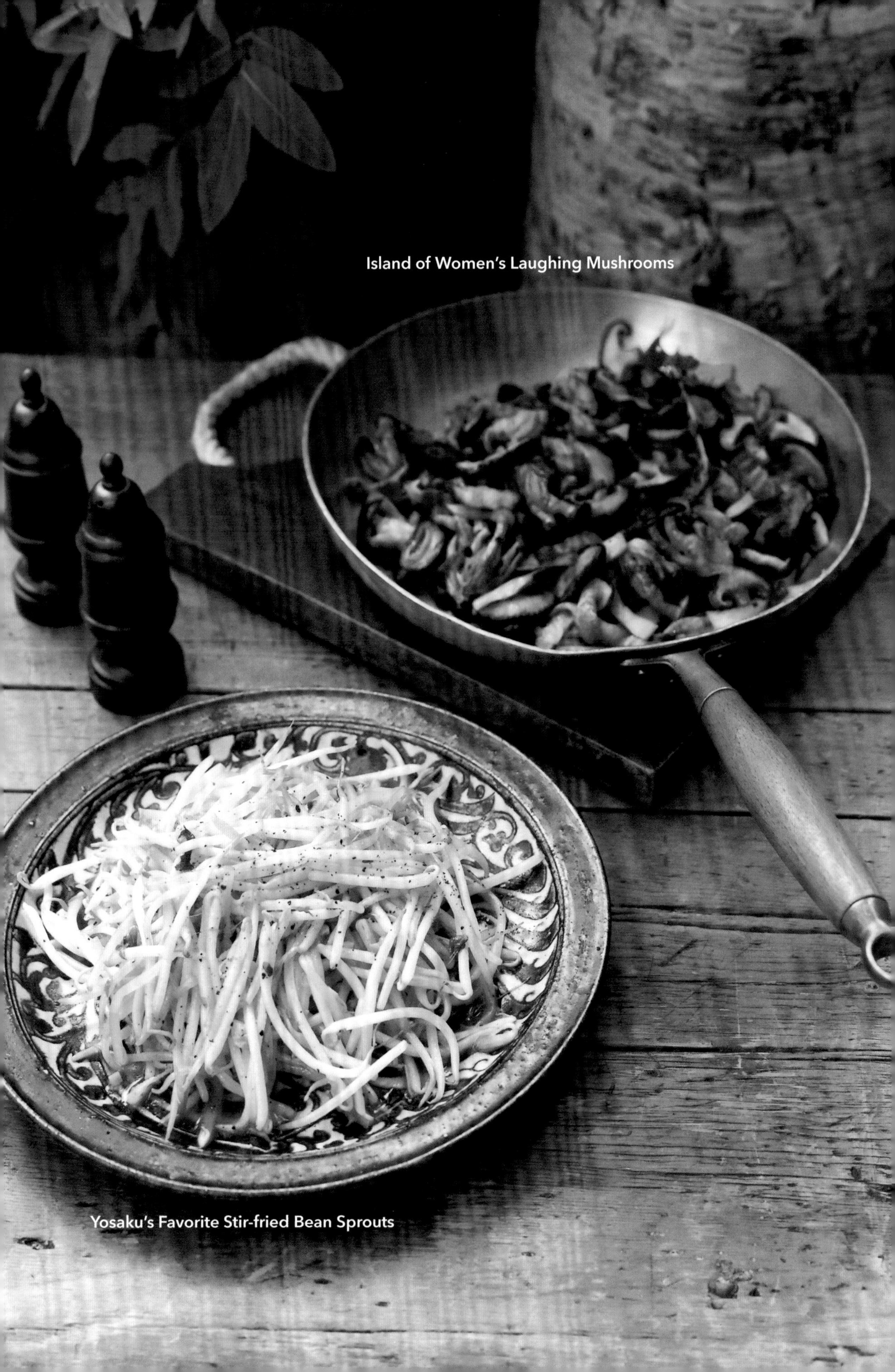
Island of Women's Laughing Mushrooms
Yosaku's Favorite Stir-fried Bean Sprouts

Early Summer

Pommes Paille

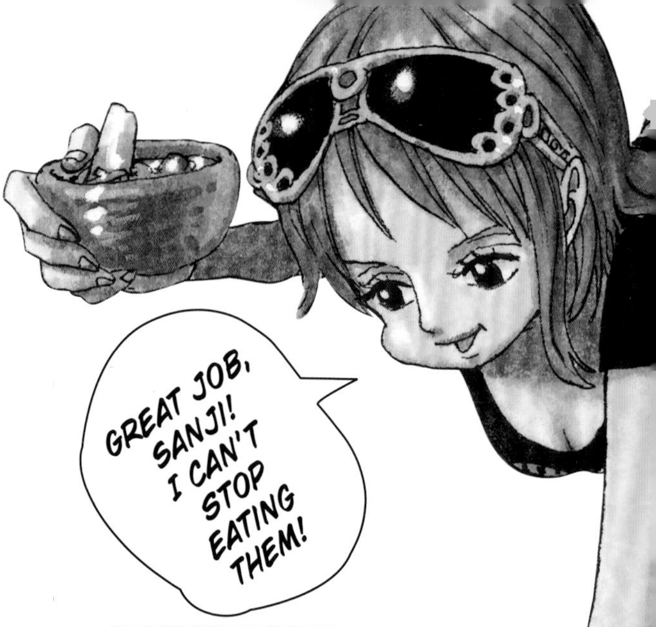
GREAT JOB, SANJI! I CAN'T STOP EATING THEM!

Crispy shoestring potatoes

INGREDIENTS Serves 4

3 potatoes, peeled
20 oz. (60 g) shredded cheese
vegetable oil
salt

STEPS

① Place finely cut shoestring potatoes in a using a mandoline at ⅛ inch setting if available, and mix with cheese **(A)**.

② Pour a generous amount (around ¼ cup) of oil on a frying pan. Pack ¼ of ① tightly and fry on low heat for 7–8 minutes. Turn over and fry another 7–8 minutes, until both sides are crispy **(B)**. Be careful not to prod too much while frying, as it will come apart. Once cooked, dab dry with paper towels, then sprinkle with salt.

③ Repeat for the other three portions.

A

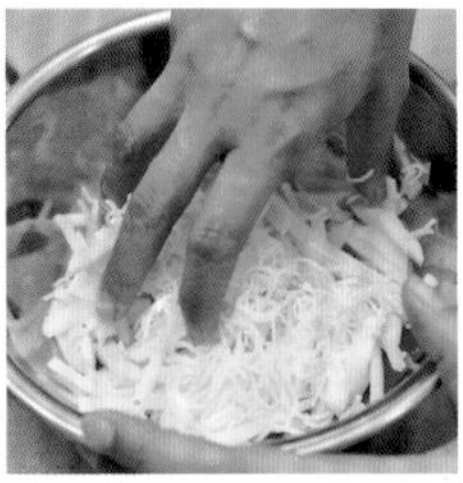

B

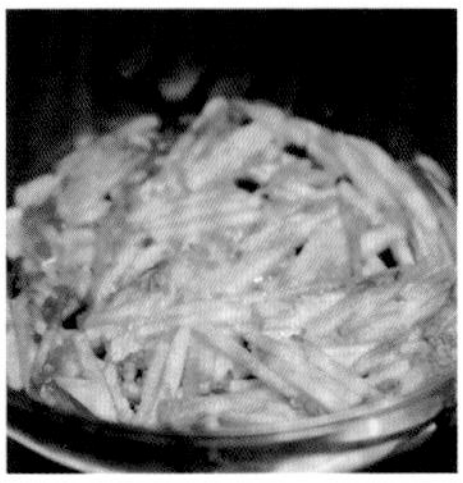

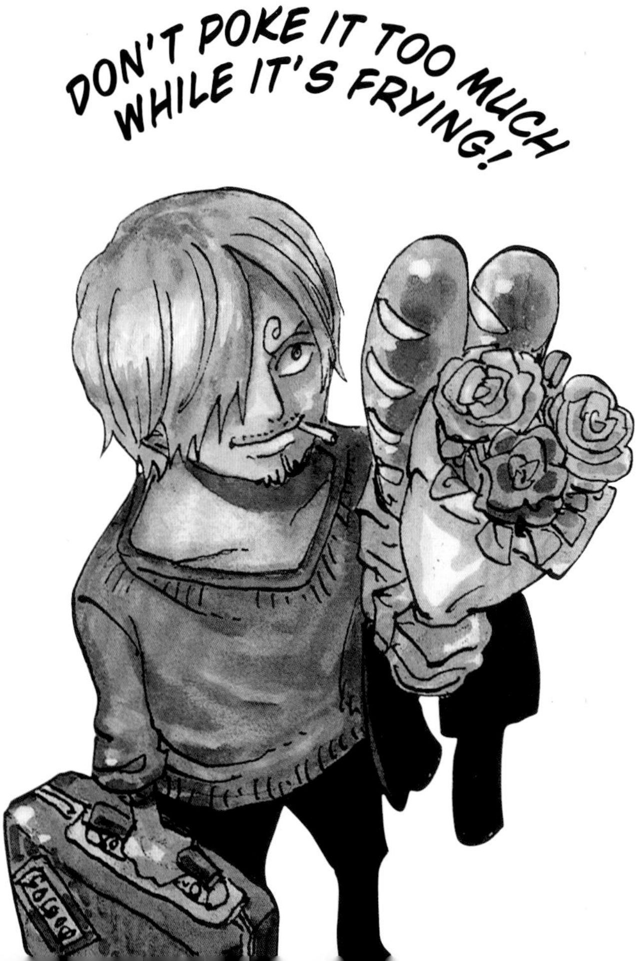
DON'T POKE IT TOO MUCH WHILE IT'S FRYING!

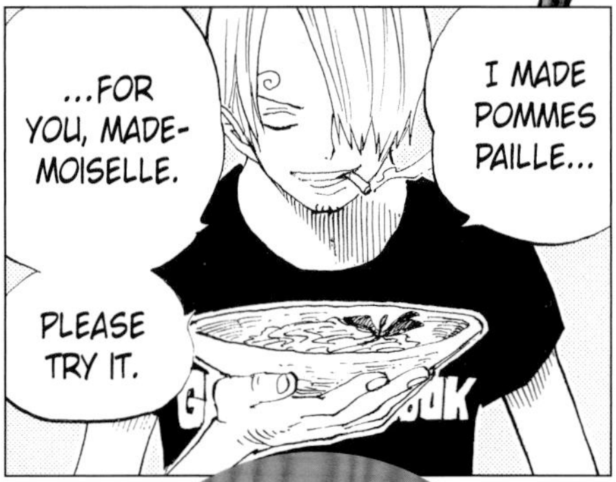
I MADE POMMES PAILLE...
...FOR YOU, MADE-MOISELLE.
PLEASE TRY IT.

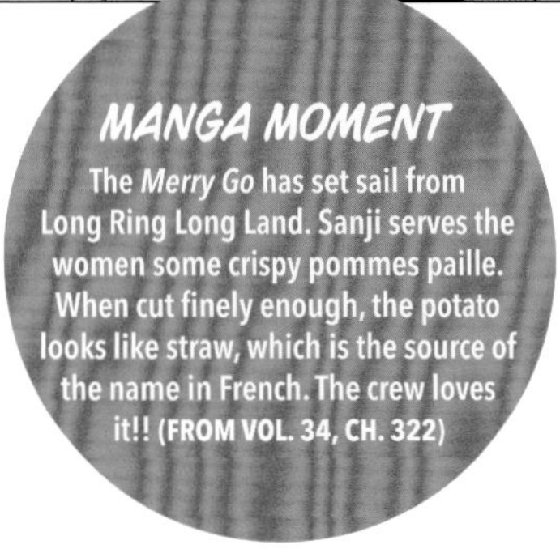

MANGA MOMENT

The *Merry Go* has set sail from Long Ring Long Land. Sanji serves the women some crispy pommes paille. When cut finely enough, the potato looks like straw, which is the source of the name in French. The crew loves it!! (FROM VOL. 34, CH. 322)

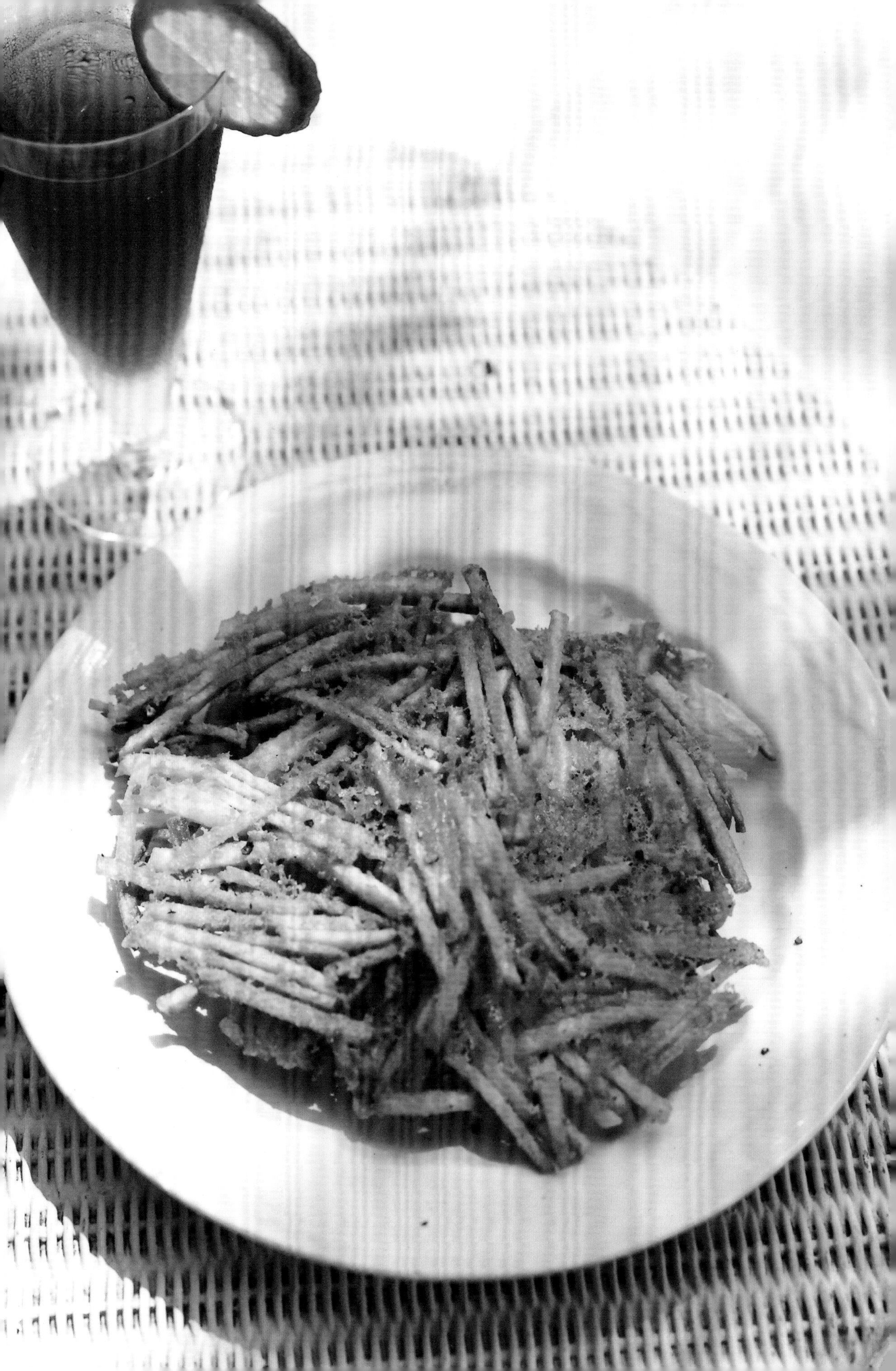

Former-Pirate Shakky's

Simmered Beans

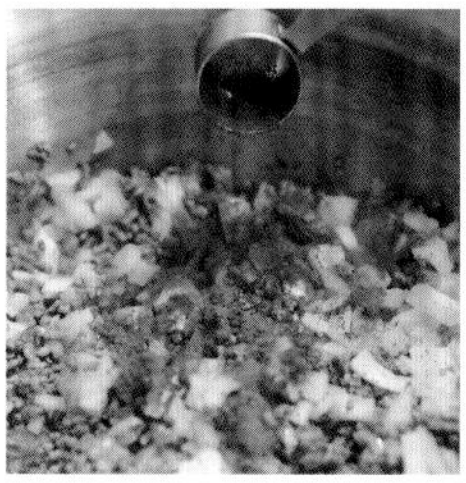

A

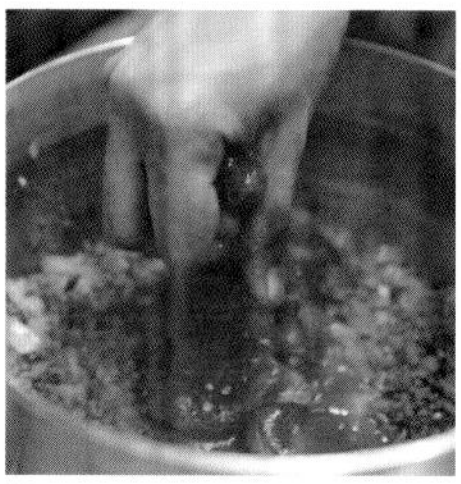

B

Spicy chili con carne

INGREDIENTS Serves 4

8 oz. (roughly 200 g) ground beef
1 can (14 oz./400 g) whole tomatoes
1 can (15 oz./432 g) red kidney beans
1 small onion
1 clove garlic, peeled
1 tbsp. olive oil
heaping ½ tsp. salt
1 ½ tsp. chili powder

STEPS

① Mince onion and garlic.

② Heat olive oil and garlic in a pot on medium heat. When garlic is browned after 30 seconds to a minute, add ground beef and stir-fry. When it changes color after about 3–4 minutes, add onion, salt, and chili powder **(A)** and stir-fry for 2–3 minutes.

③ Add tomatoes to pot, crushing first **(B)**. When mixture boils, skim the top. Drain red kidney beans and add to pot, then simmer for 10 minutes. Add salt to taste.

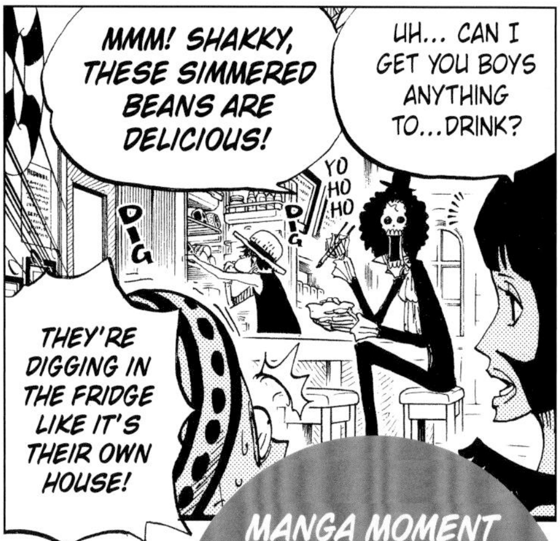
MMM! SHAKKY, THESE SIMMERED BEANS ARE DELICIOUS!
UH... CAN I GET YOU BOYS ANYTHING TO...DRINK?
YO HO HO
DIG
DIG
THEY'RE DIGGING IN THE FRIDGE LIKE IT'S THEIR OWN HOUSE!

MANGA MOMENT

Shakky's Rip-off Bar can be found in the Sabaody Archipelago. The two rudest members of the Straw Hat Crew plunder the fridge, where Brook finds some simmered beans. Shakky's homemade recipe has a rustic charm. Once you start eating, you can't stop!!
(FROM VOL. 51, CH. 498)

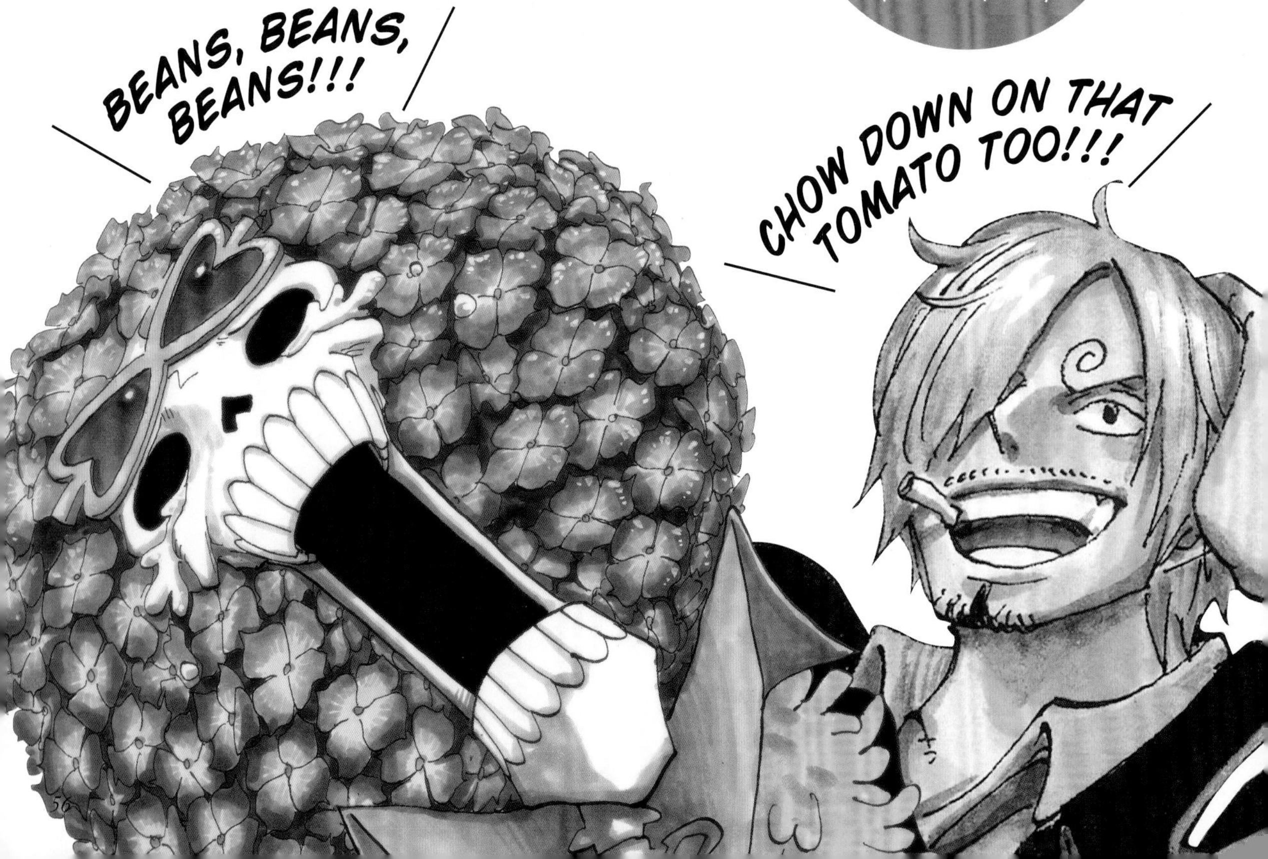
BEANS, BEANS, BEANS!!!
CHOW DOWN ON THAT TOMATO TOO!!!

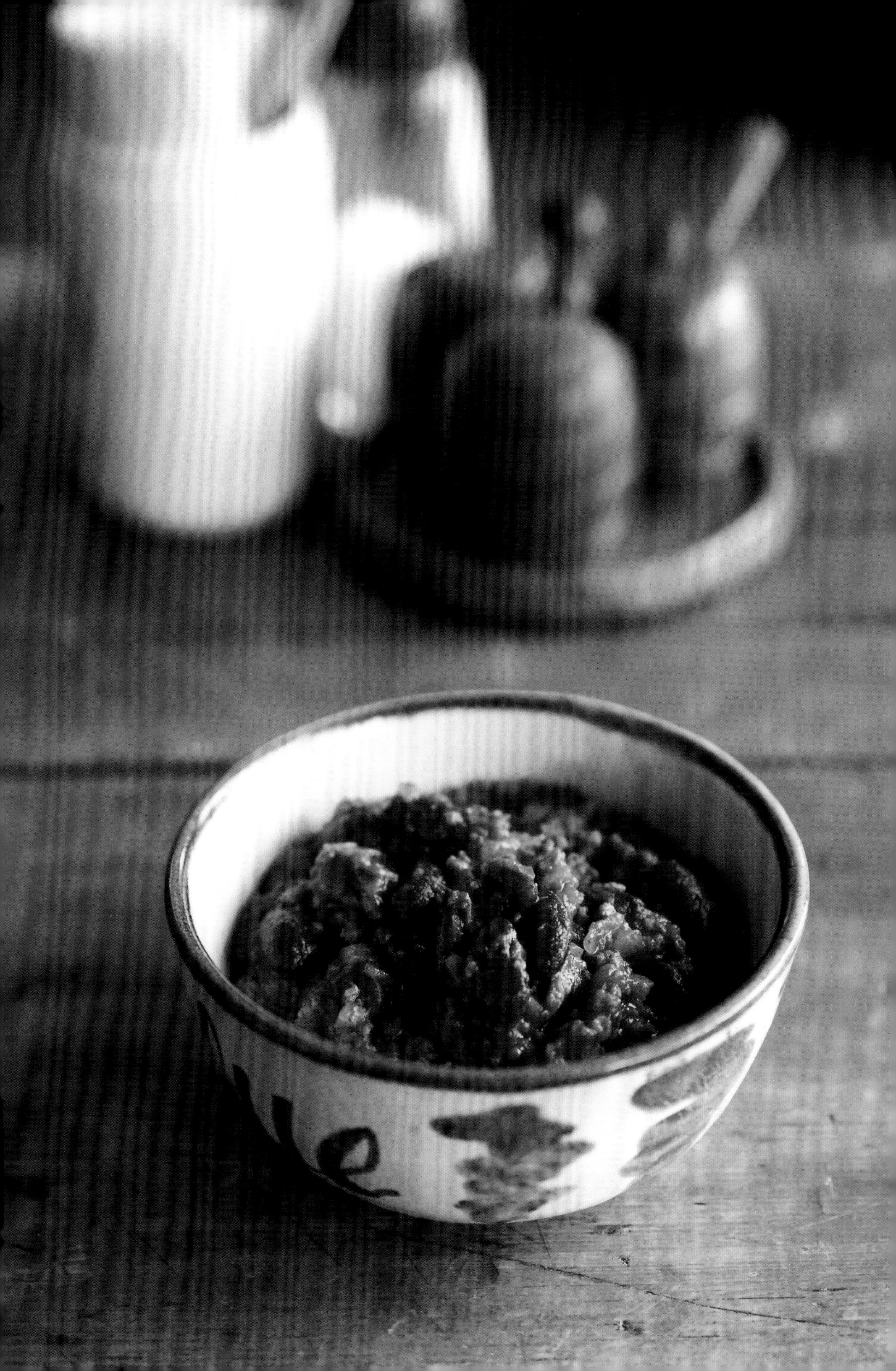

Satisfying Sa Meals

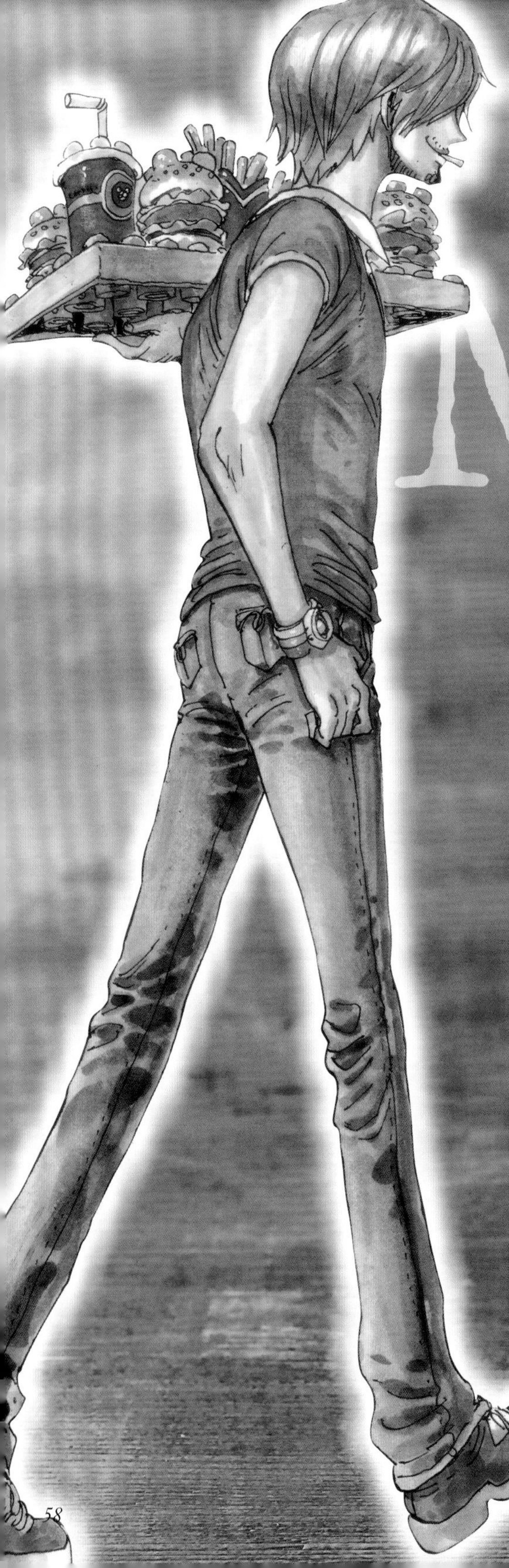

I'm glad you're all fine! C'mon, let's eat!

Hamburgers, curry, yakisoba... You can feed even the hungriest bunch with these bold, bountiful dishes. These recipes are packed with secrets that will leave your crew salivating.

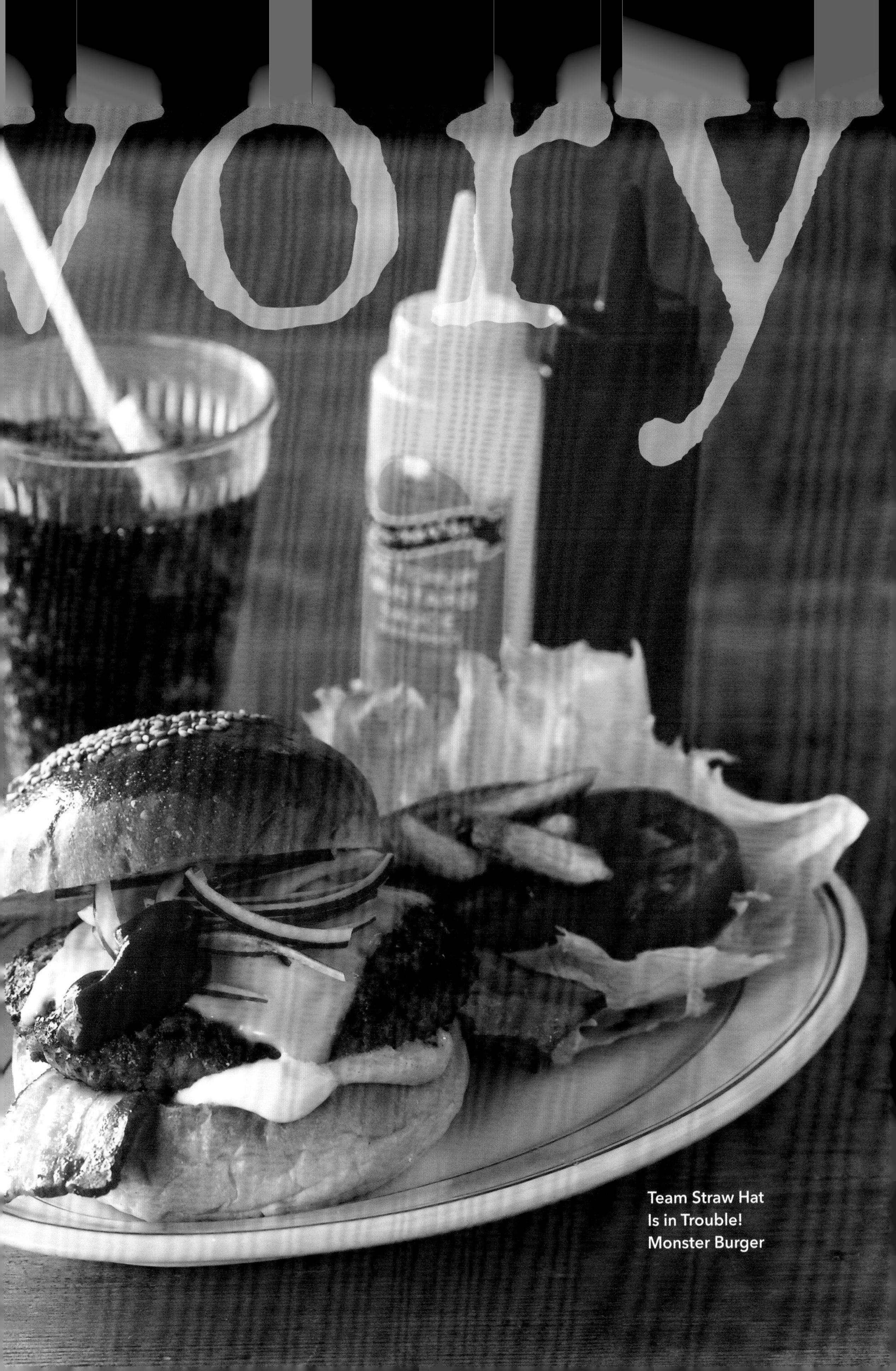
vory

Team Straw Hat
Is in Trouble!
Monster Burger

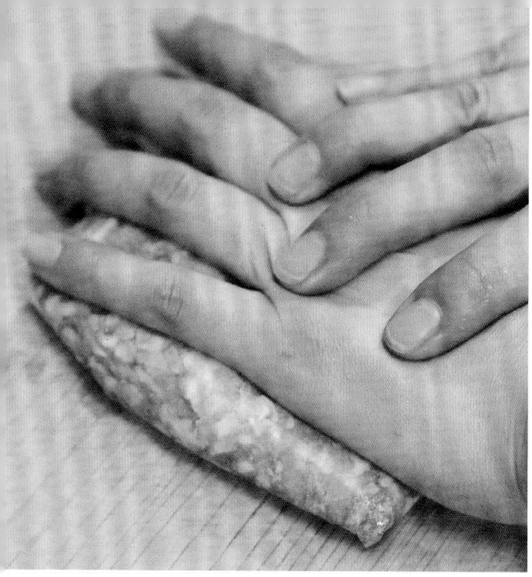

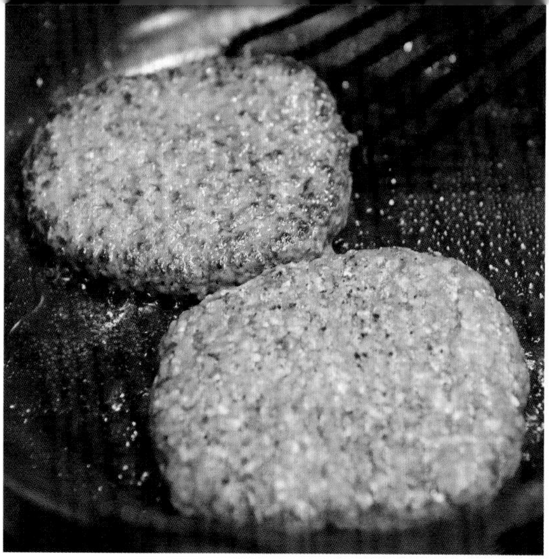

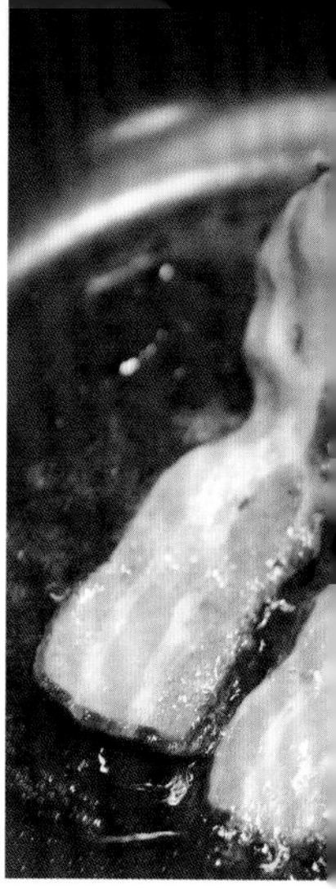

A

B

Team Straw Hat Is in Trouble!

Monster Burger

Supreme volume, supreme burger

INGREDIENTS Serves 4

4 sets of hamburger buns
21 oz. (600 g) ground beef
1 tomato
¼ red onion
whole pickles
vegetable oil
a little salt
a little black pepper
4 slices cheddar cheese
4 pieces bacon
4 pieces lettuce
mayonnaise
mustard
ketchup

STEPS

① Cut tomato into ⅓ inch (1 cm) slices. Slice red onion and pickles.

② Split ground beef into four equal parts. Wrap them individually in plastic wrap and press hard **(A)**. Mold into rounded patties ⅓ inch (1 cm) thick.

③ Heat up vegetable oil in a frying pan, then lay out the meat and season with salt and pepper. Cook for about 1 ½ minutes on medium, or until interior reaches 160°F. Flip over, season with salt and pepper, and cook for one and a half minutes again **(B)**. Set heat on low and place cheese slice on top, then cover and cook for 1 minute. Remove from pan. Place bacon in the same pan on medium heat and turn over to ensure both sides are cooked evenly **(C)**.

④ Separate buns and use a toaster to toast lightly. Spread on mayonnaise and mustard **(D)**, then add bacon, patty, onion, lettuce, tomato, and pickles in that order **(E)**. Lastly, add ketchup and place the top bun.

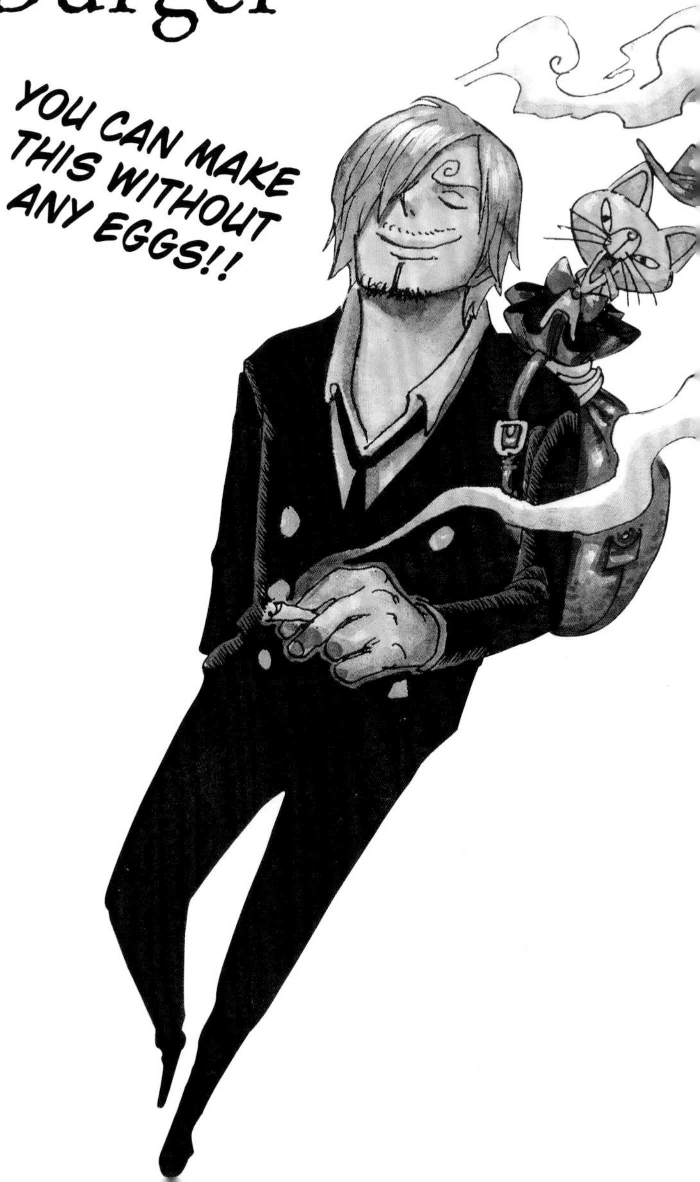
YOU CAN MAKE THIS WITHOUT ANY EGGS!!

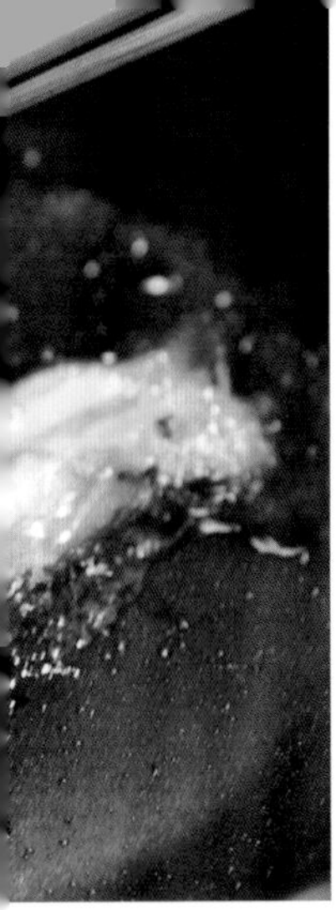

C

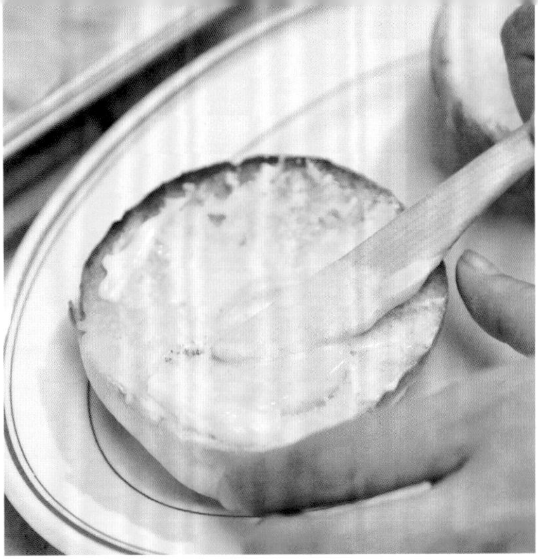

D

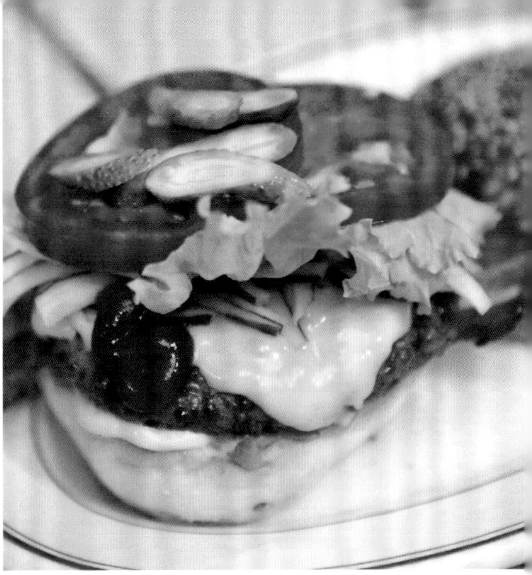

E

MANGA MOMENT

The Straw Hats attempt the Davy Back Fight, a competition that wagers your own crewmates. Zolo and Sanji have to face the Groggy Monsters, who use a three-part weapons combination in an attempt to turn the pair into mincemeat!

(FROM VOL. 33, CH. 312)

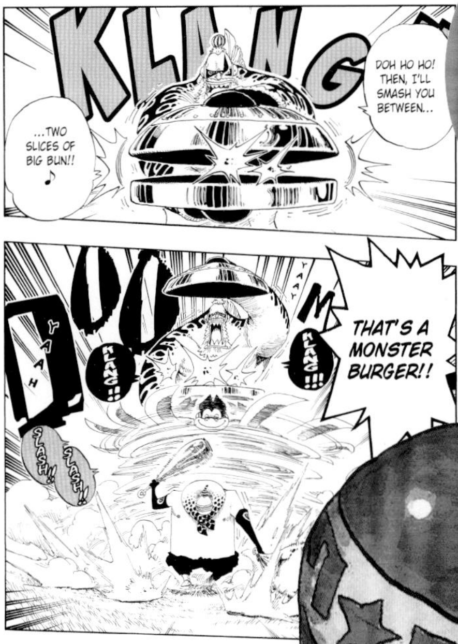
KLANG
DOH HO HO! THEN, I'LL SMASH YOU BETWEEN...
...TWO SLICES OF BIG BUN!! ♪
THAT'S A MONSTER BURGER!!
KLANG!!
KLANG!!
SLASH!!
SLASH!!

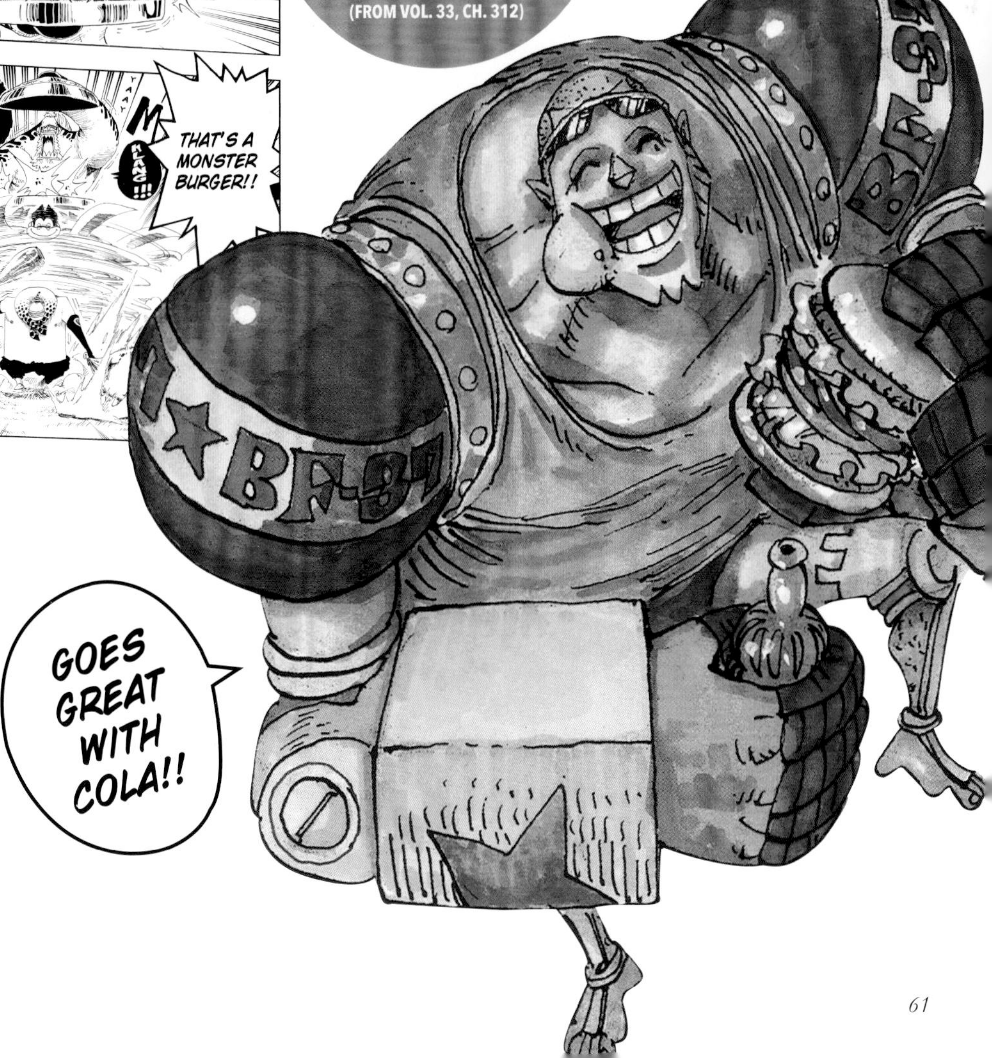
GOES GREAT WITH COLA!!
BF-37
BF-37

Tom's Workers

Kokoro's Curry Rice

Packed with spices!
A proper Indian-style curry

INGREDIENTS Serves 4

Filling
- 2 chicken breasts (18 oz./500 g)
- 1 tsp. salt
- a little black pepper
- 2 potatoes
- 1 carrot
- ¾ oz. (20 g) butter
- 4 servings of cooked rice

Sauce
- 2 cloves garlic, peeled
- 1 knob ginger, peeled
- 1 onion, peeled
- 1 celery stalk
- 2 tomatoes
- 3 tbsp. vegetable oil
- ½ tbsp. honey
- 3 tbsp. flour
- 3 tbsp. curry powder
- about 3 cups (700 ml) chicken stock (see p. 95)
- 2 bay leaves
- 1 ½ tsp. salt
- ½ tbsp. garam masala
- Chinese onion or soy-pickled vegetable relish, if desired

I COULD EAT PLATE AFTER PLATE OF THIS!

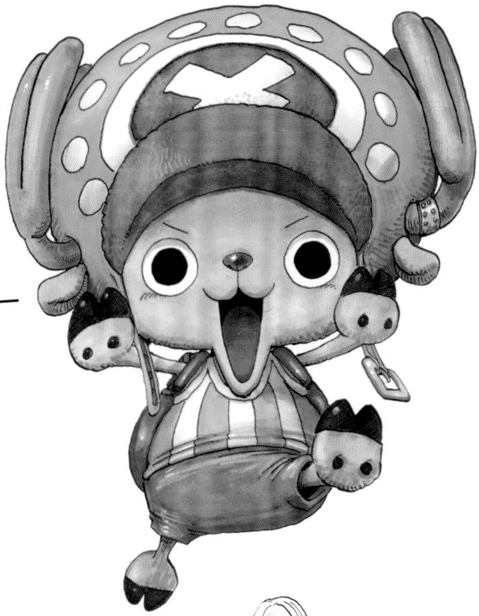

STEPS

① Cut chicken into bite-sized pieces and season with pepper and 1 tsp. salt. Peel potatoes and carrot and chop roughly. Mince garlic, ginger, onion, and celery. Cut tomatoes into large pieces.

② Pour 1 tbsp. vegetable oil into a pan and stir-fry garlic and ginger on medium heat. When fragrant, add onions and celery, cooking until they soften. Add honey and continue stir-frying briefly until the mixture begins to brown. **(A)**.

③ Add 2 tbsp. vegetable oil to ② on low heat, add flour and curry powder, and stir-fry for about 5 minutes. Add tomatoes **(B)** and fry another 2–3 minutes, stirring occasionally.

④ Once the tomatoes have shed their fluid, add chicken stock in 2–3 parts and mix thoroughly each time. If it boils, skim the top, then add bay leaves and 1 tsp. salt, and simmer on low heat.

⑤ Heat half of butter on a frying pan and add chicken ①. Cook on medium heat until browned and add to pot ④.

⑥ Heat the other half of the butter in the same frying pan and fry potatoes and carrots. When potato surface becomes translucent, add to pot ④ and simmer on low heat for 30–40 minutes, stirring occasionally, until mixture thickens. Season with remaining salt, add garam masala powder, mix, and turn off heat.

⑦ Serve rice on plate and pour curry on top. Add Chinese onion and vegetable relish if desired.

A

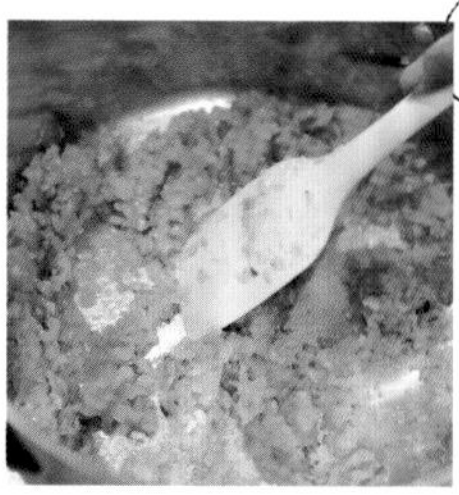

B

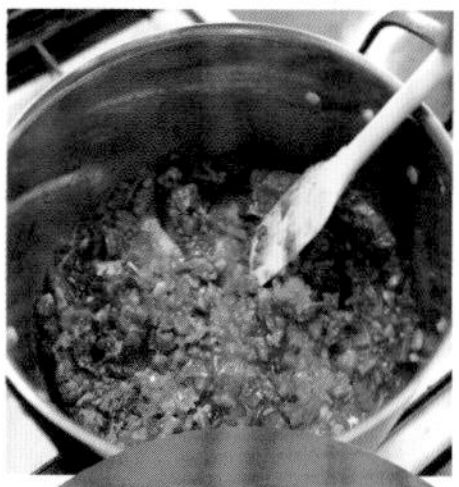

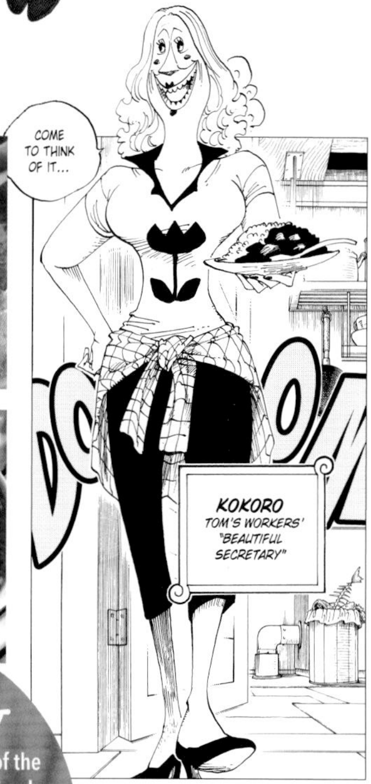
COME TO THINK OF IT...
KOKORO
TOM'S WORKERS' "BEAUTIFUL SECRETARY"

MANGA MOMENT

Tom's Workers was the name of the shipbuilding company where Franky once worked. Kokoro the secretary was in charge of taking care of the live-in employees. At mealtime, she served home-cooked meals they ate around the table, like a family.
(FROM VOL. 37, CH. 353)

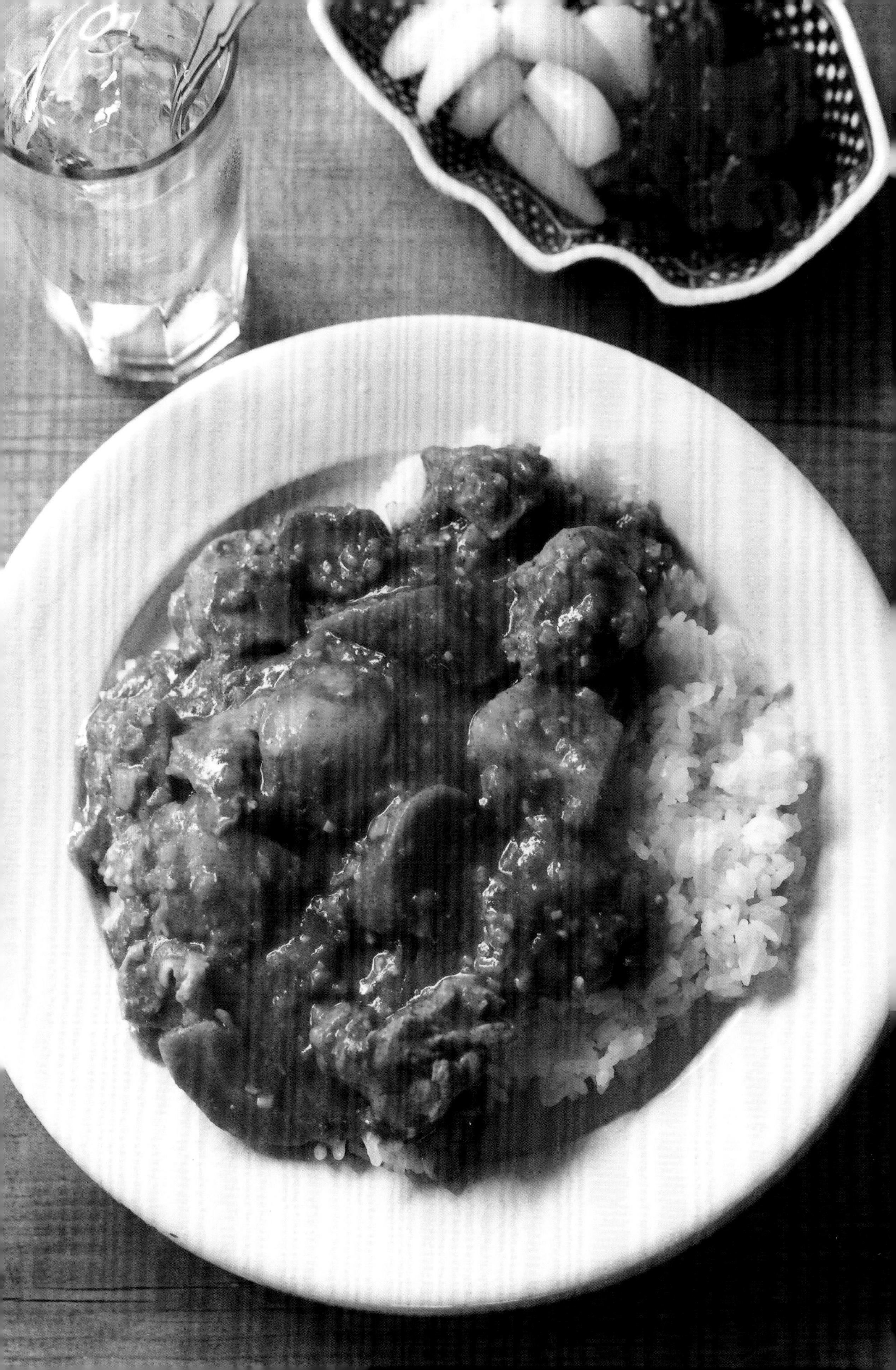

A

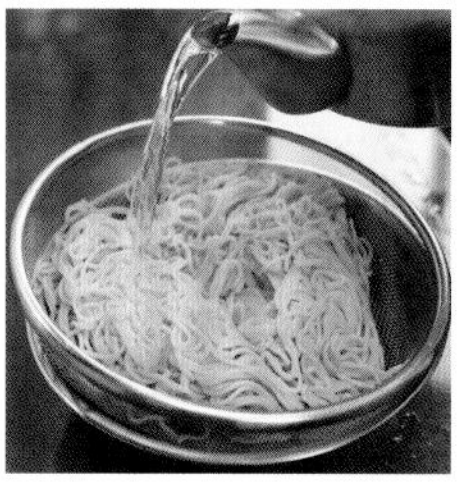

B

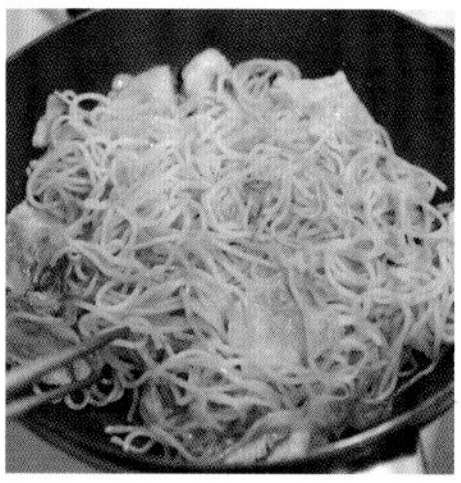

MANGA MOMENT

The Davy Back Fight has a festival atmosphere, with food carts lining the grounds. Even Tonjit, whose beloved horse was hurt by the Foxy Pirates, is enjoying the event. Luffy's chowing down on those noodles!

(FROM VOL. 33, CH. 306)

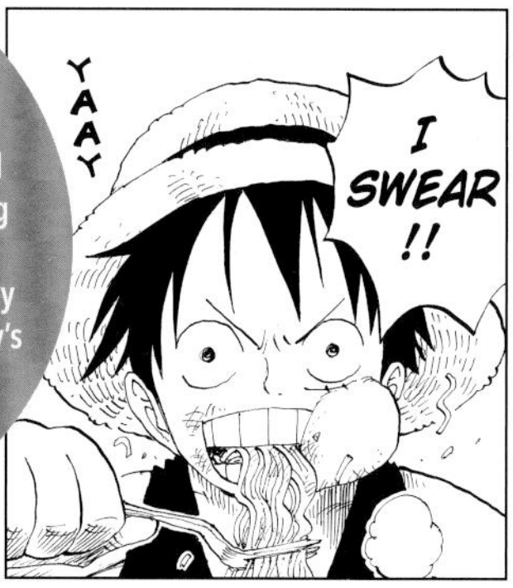
I SWEAR !!
YAAY

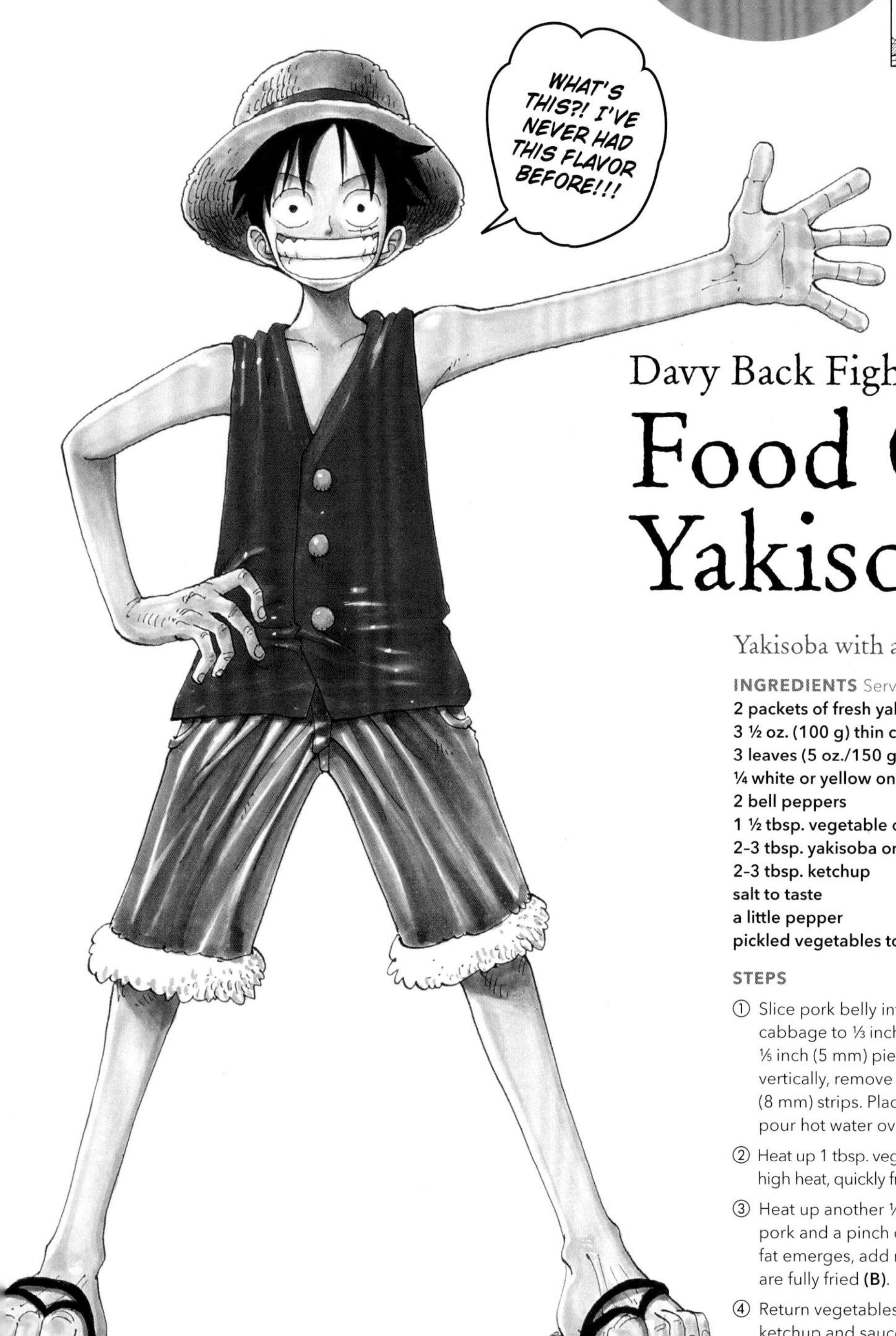
WHAT'S THIS?! I'VE NEVER HAD THIS FLAVOR BEFORE!!!

Davy Back Fight

Food Cart Yakisoba

Yakisoba with a pasta-style twist

INGREDIENTS Serves 2

2 packets of fresh yakisoba noodles
3 ½ oz. (100 g) thin cut pork belly
3 leaves (5 oz./150 g) cabbage
¼ white or yellow onion
2 bell peppers
1 ½ tbsp. vegetable oil
2–3 tbsp. yakisoba or Worcestershire sauce
2–3 tbsp. ketchup
salt to taste
a little pepper
pickled vegetables to taste

STEPS

① Slice pork belly into 1 inch (3 cm) pieces, cabbage to ⅓ inch (1 cm) pieces, and onion to ⅕ inch (5 mm) pieces. Slice bell peppers in half vertically, remove seeds, and cut into ¼ inch (8 mm) strips. Place noodles in a sieve and pour hot water over **(A)**.

② Heat up 1 tbsp. vegetable oil in a pan on medium-high heat, quickly fry vegetables, and remove.

③ Heat up another ½ tbsp. oil in the pan, add pork and a pinch of salt, and stir-fry. When the fat emerges, add noodles and cook until they are fully fried **(B)**.

④ Return vegetables ② to the pan. Combine ketchup and sauce and mix into pan. Add salt and pepper to taste. Transfer to serving plates and garnish with pickled vegetables.

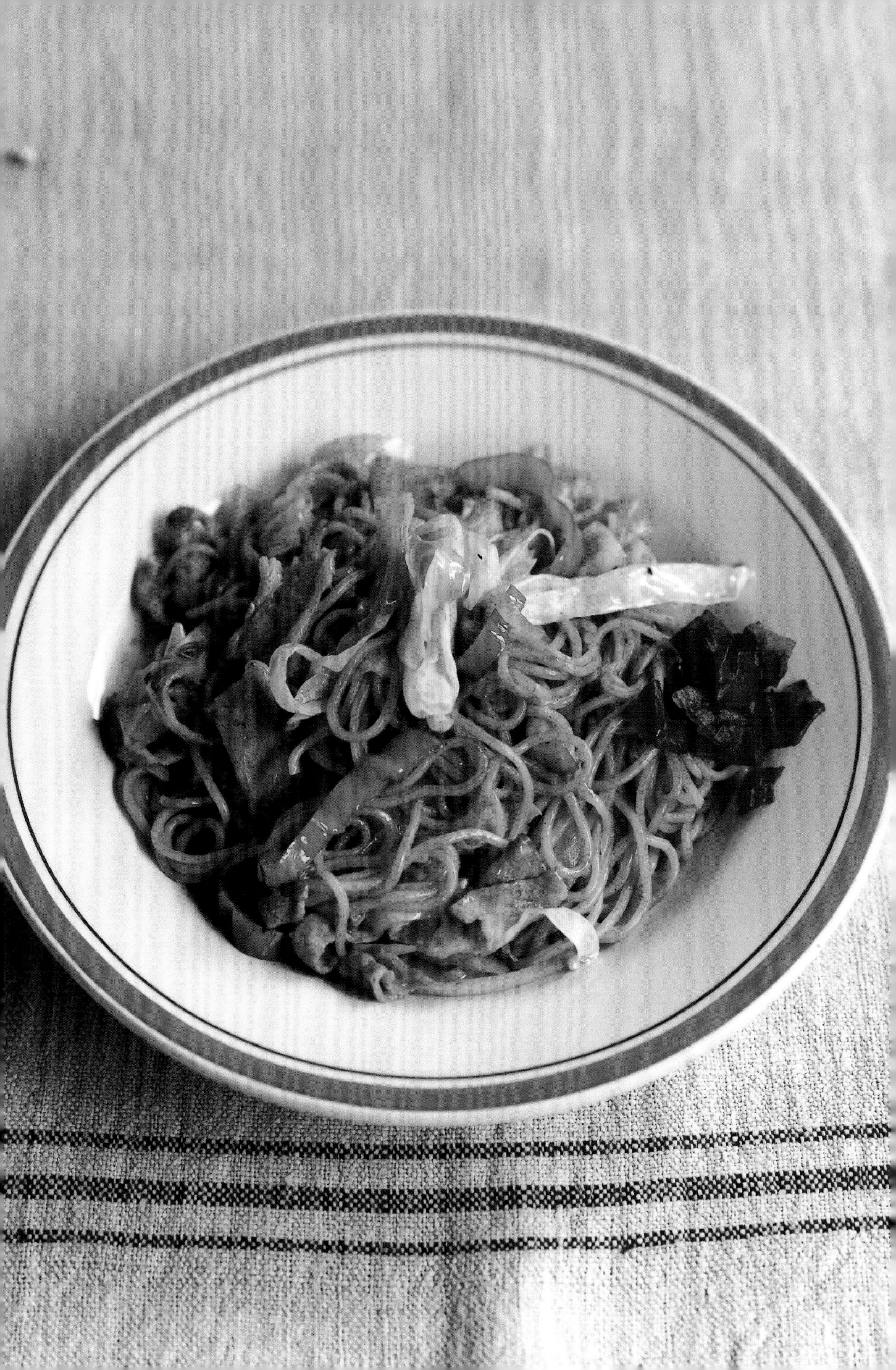

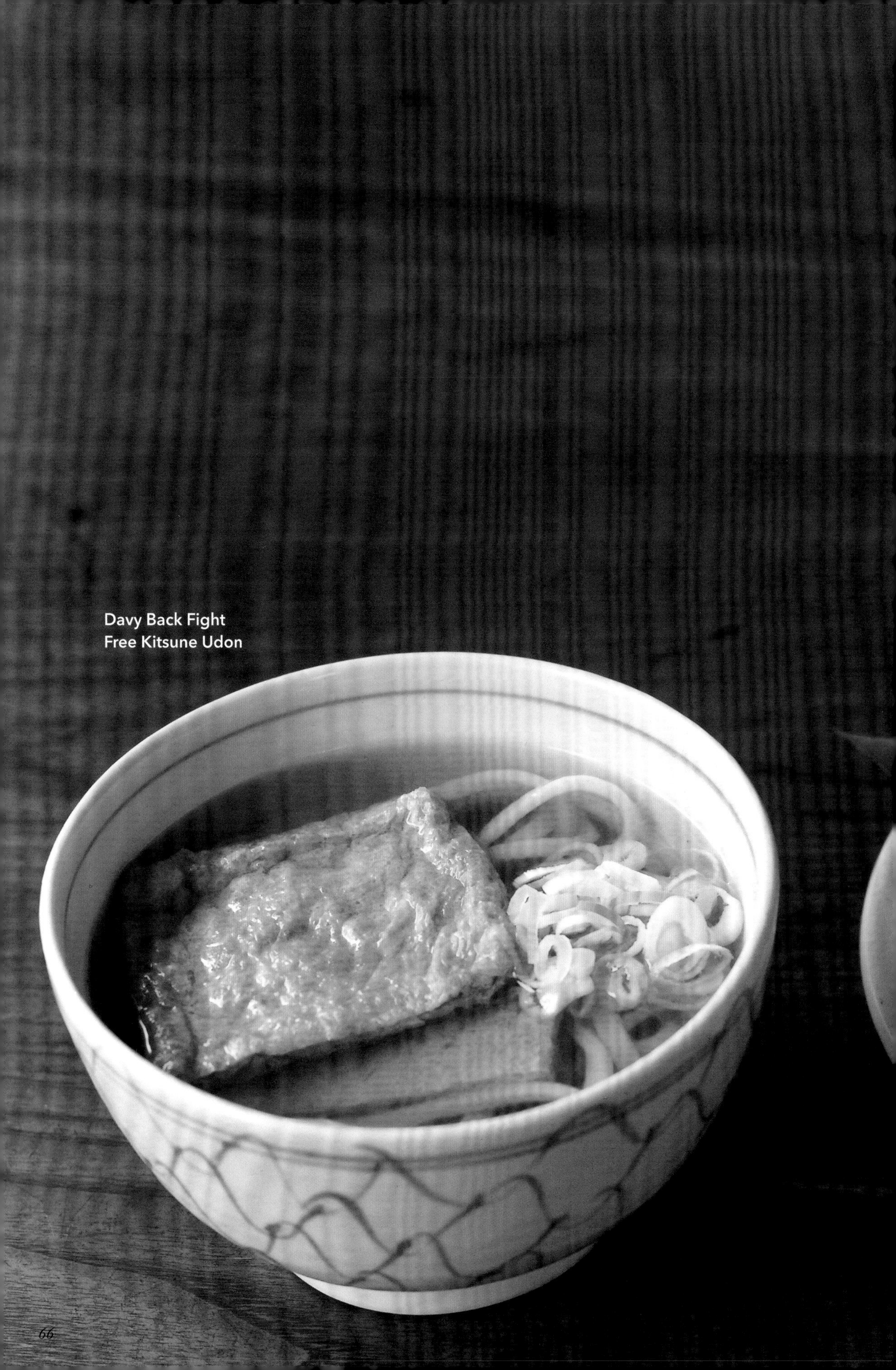

Davy Back Fight
Free Kitsune Udon

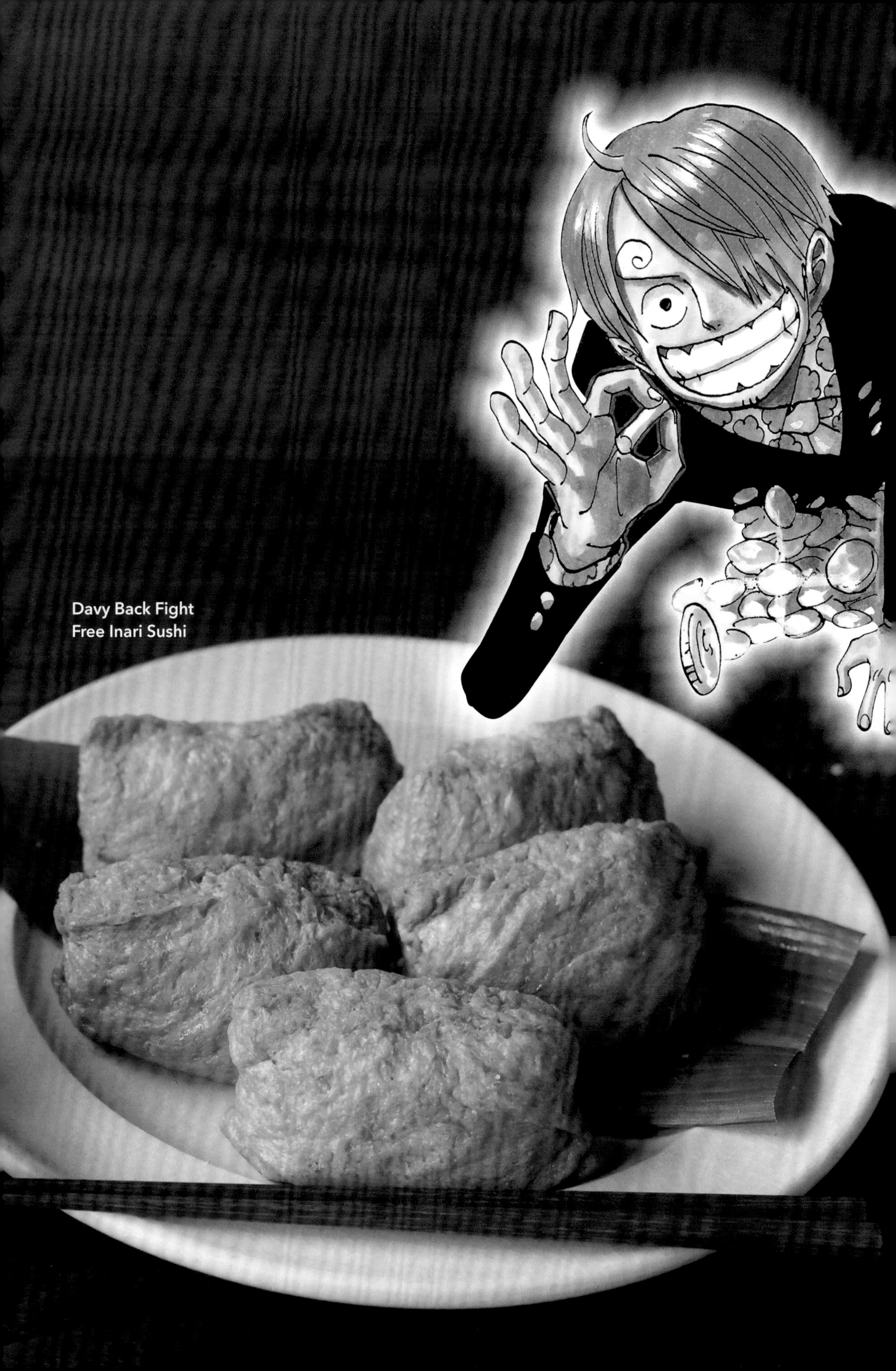

Davy Back Fight
Free Inari Sushi

Davy Back Fight

Free Inari Sushi

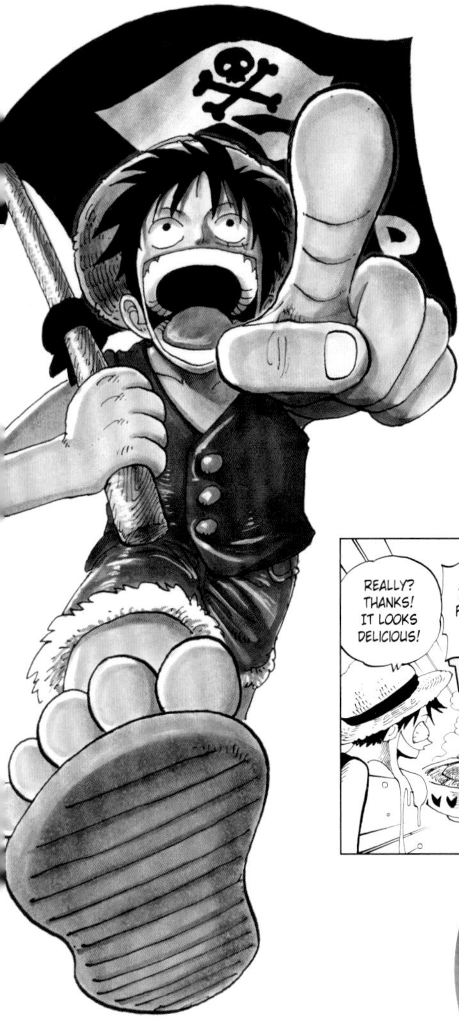

Sweet fried tofu pouches packed with rice

INGREDIENTS Makes 20

10 *abura-age* fried tofu pouches

Rice

- **2 ⅓ cups (450 g) uncooked rice**
- **1 sheet kombu (4x4 in./10x10 cm)**
- **1 tbsp. white sesame seeds**
- **yuzu citrus peel, if desired**

Vinegar mixture

- **4 tbsp. plus 1 ½ tsp. rice vinegar**
- **1 tbsp. sugar**
- **1 tsp. salt**

Fried tofu broth

- **2 cups water**
- **¼ cup saké**
- **¼ cup sugar**
- **¼ cup soy sauce**

Diluted vinegar

- **1 cup of water with a splash of vinegar**

HERE, SUSHI AND RAMEN!
IT'S FREE !!
REALLY? THANKS! IT LOOKS DELICIOUS!

MANGA MOMENT

In the midst of the Donut Race, the first round of the Davy Back Fight, Foxy sees his chance to interfere! His henchmen lure Luffy away with some inari sushi, golden brown and tempting. The sweet scent of the tofu keeps him distracted.
(FROM VOL. 33, CH. 308)

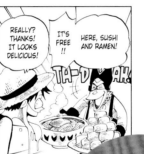

STEPS

Vinegared rice

① Combine ingredients for vinegar mixture.

② Wash rice, let it soak, and drain. Place rice, water (not for the diluted vinegar), and kombu in a rice cooker, and cook until slightly tough, with less water than normal. When rice is cooked, remove kombu and transfer rice to rice container while hot. Add vinegar mix ① to rice, soaking evenly, and mix briskly. Add sesame seeds and yuzu peel and mix thoroughly **(A)**. Air out with a fan, then cover with a wet kitchen towel and chill.

Fried tofu

③ Cut abura-age pieces in half crosswise to make two pockets and roll flat with cooking chopsticks or rolling pin **(B)**. Peel open interior to make pouches, then arrange on sieve and soak in hot water. Remove and place in chilled water, then rinse briefly and dry.

④ Combine and stir broth ingredients in a pot and heat on medium. When it is bubbling, arrange tofu pouches ③ inside and place a drop lid (aluminum foil will do) directly on top, then simmer on low heat for about 30 minutes. Stop the heat and allow flavors to mingle **(C)**.

Combine

⑤ Separate vinegared rice into 4 equal parts, then split those parts into 5, roughly ¼ cup (50 g) portions. Place your fingers into diluted vinegar and lightly form the rice with your hands.

⑥ Lightly press the tofu pouches dry, then pack with vinegared rice **(D)**.

A

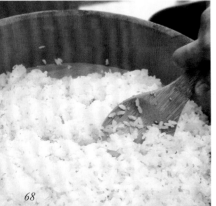

B

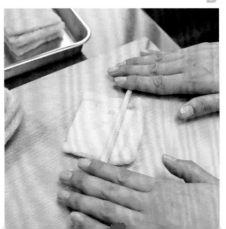

C

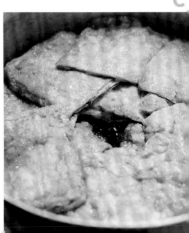

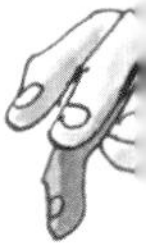

Davy Back Fight

Free Kitsune Udon

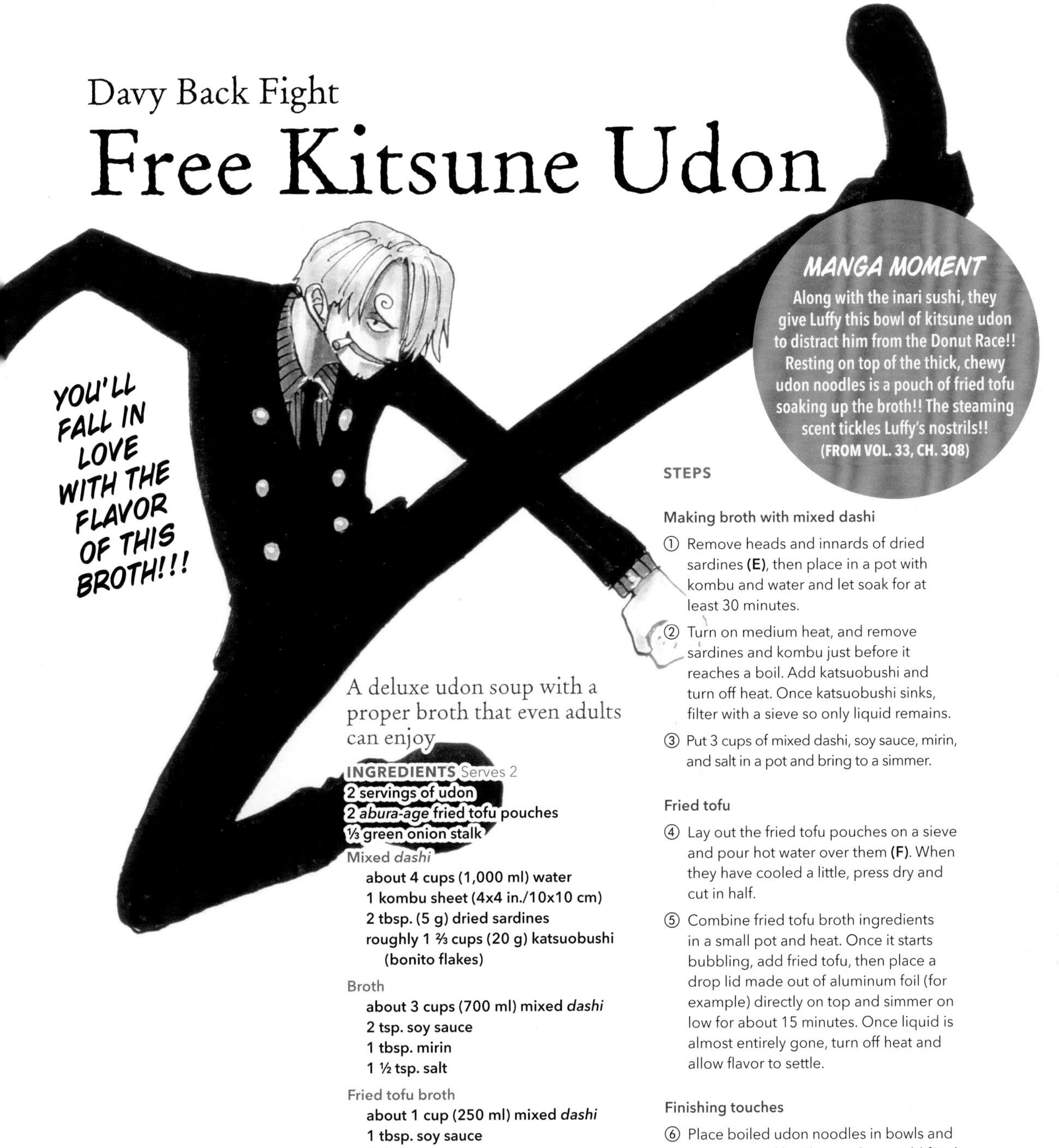
YOU'LL FALL IN LOVE WITH THE FLAVOR OF THIS BROTH!!!

MANGA MOMENT

Along with the inari sushi, they give Luffy this bowl of kitsune udon to distract him from the Donut Race!! Resting on top of the thick, chewy udon noodles is a pouch of fried tofu soaking up the broth!! The steaming scent tickles Luffy's nostrils!!
(FROM VOL. 33, CH. 308)

A deluxe udon soup with a proper broth that even adults can enjoy

INGREDIENTS Serves 2

2 servings of udon
2 *abura-age* fried tofu pouches
⅓ green onion stalk

Mixed *dashi*
- **about 4 cups (1,000 ml) water**
- **1 kombu sheet (4x4 in./10x10 cm)**
- **2 tbsp. (5 g) dried sardines**
- **roughly 1 ⅔ cups (20 g) katsuobushi (bonito flakes)**

Broth
- **about 3 cups (700 ml) mixed *dashi***
- **2 tsp. soy sauce**
- **1 tbsp. mirin**
- **1 ½ tsp. salt**

Fried tofu broth
- **about 1 cup (250 ml) mixed *dashi***
- **1 tbsp. soy sauce**
- **1 tbsp. sugar**
- **1 pinch of salt**

STEPS

Making broth with mixed dashi

① Remove heads and innards of dried sardines **(E)**, then place in a pot with kombu and water and let soak for at least 30 minutes.

② Turn on medium heat, and remove sardines and kombu just before it reaches a boil. Add katsuobushi and turn off heat. Once katsuobushi sinks, filter with a sieve so only liquid remains.

③ Put 3 cups of mixed dashi, soy sauce, mirin, and salt in a pot and bring to a simmer.

Fried tofu

④ Lay out the fried tofu pouches on a sieve and pour hot water over them **(F)**. When they have cooled a little, press dry and cut in half.

⑤ Combine fried tofu broth ingredients in a small pot and heat. Once it starts bubbling, add fried tofu, then place a drop lid made out of aluminum foil (for example) directly on top and simmer on low for about 15 minutes. Once liquid is almost entirely gone, turn off heat and allow flavor to settle.

Finishing touches

⑥ Place boiled udon noodles in bowls and pour warmed broth over them. Add fried tofu and sliced spring onions on top.

D

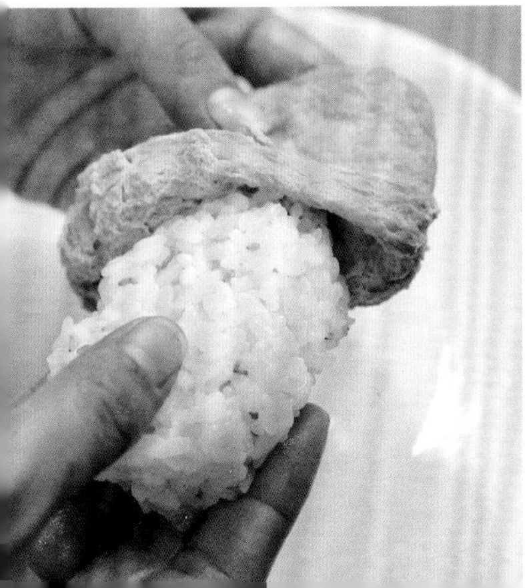

E

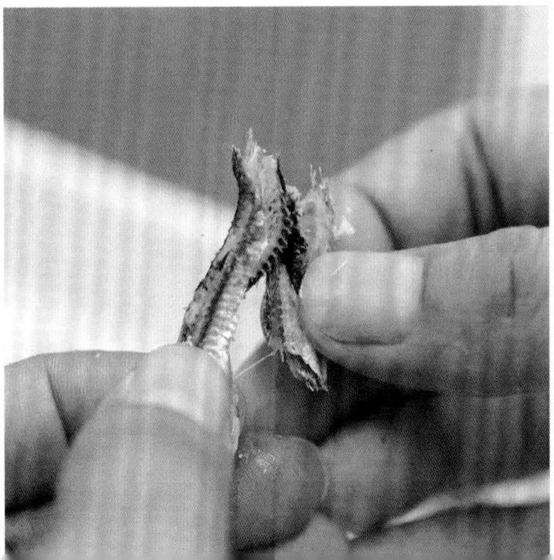

F

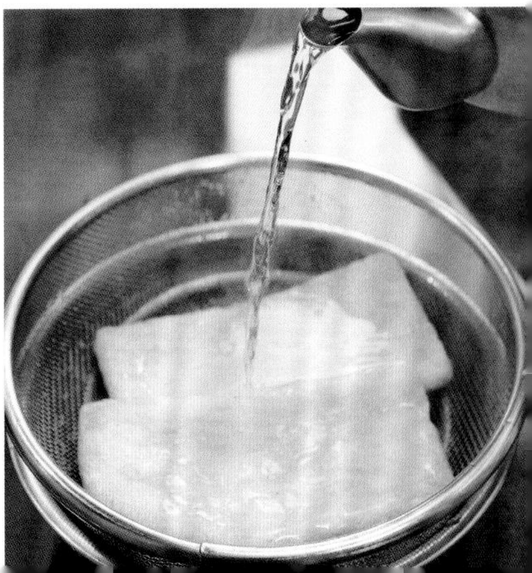

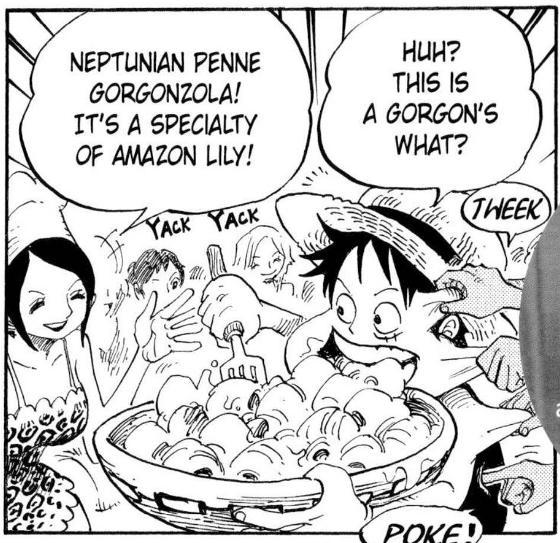
NEPTUNIAN PENNE GORGONZOLA! IT'S A SPECIALTY OF AMAZON LILY!
HUH? THIS IS A GORGON'S WHAT?
TWEEK
YACK YACK
POKE!

MANGA MOMENT

The night before he leaves Amazon Lily, the island of women, Luffy gets to chow down at a feast surrounded by women. Because the island is surrounded by a nest of enormous aquatic Neptunians, their meat is the centerpiece for many bold dishes.
(FROM VOL. 53, CH. 522)

A

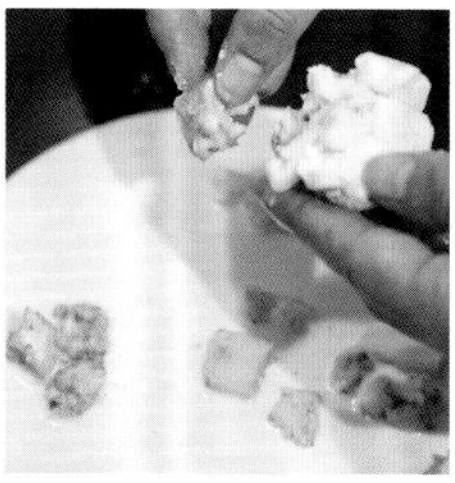

B

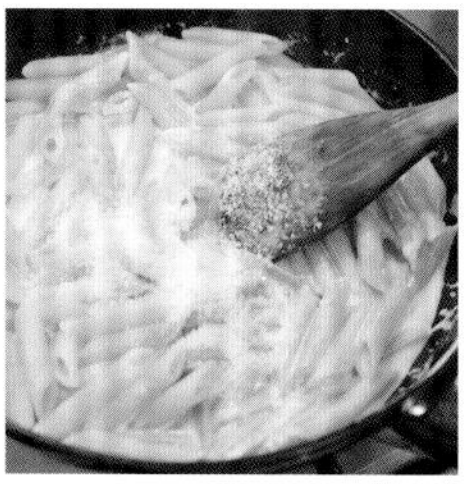

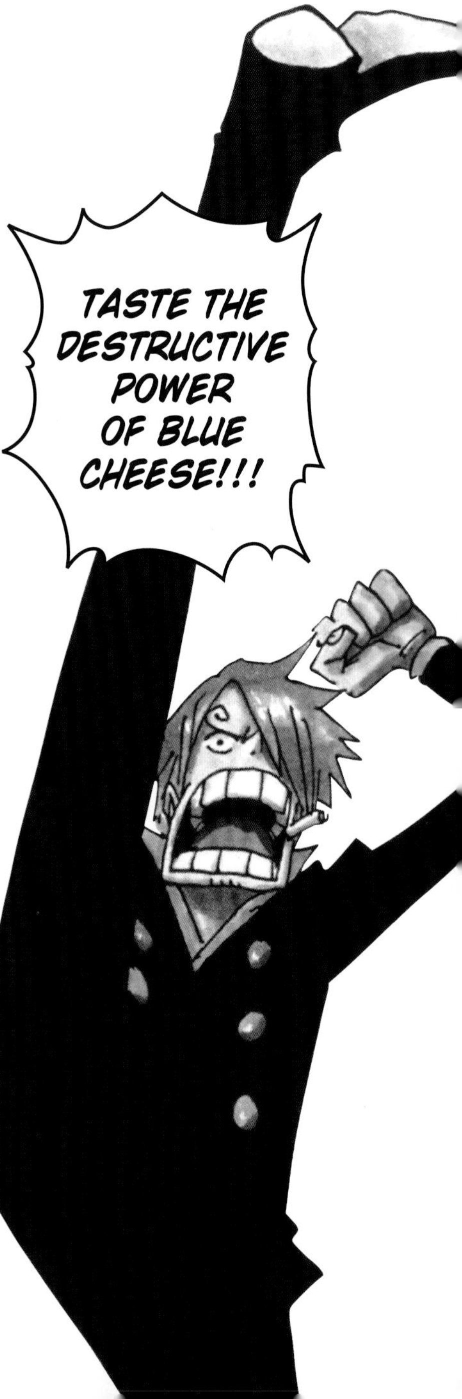
TASTE THE DESTRUCTIVE POWER OF BLUE CHEESE!!!

Neptunian Penne Gorgonzola

Rich pasta made with two kinds of cheese

INGREDIENTS Serves 2

6 ½ oz. (180 g) penne
2 slices ham
⅓-½ cup (100 ml) milk
a little under ½ cup (100 ml) heavy cream
⅓ cup (50 g) blue cheese
2-3 tbsp. grated parmesan cheese
a little black pepper
flat-leaf parsley
6-7 cups (1,500 ml) water
1 tbsp. salt

STEPS

① Boil about 6-7 cups (1,500 ml) of water, add 1 tbsp. (15 g) of salt, and boil penne for 1 minute less than indicated on the package. Slice ham into ¼ inch (5 mm) pieces.

② Starting with ⅓ cup milk and adding more as needed, heat milk and cream in a pan on medium heat about 2 minutes before penne is cooked. Mix in crumbled blue cheese **(A)**. When it is half melted, add penne and ham and simmer for 1 minute or until sauce has thickened. Add parmesan and mix.

③ Lastly, add pepper to taste, and sprinkle chopped parsley on top.

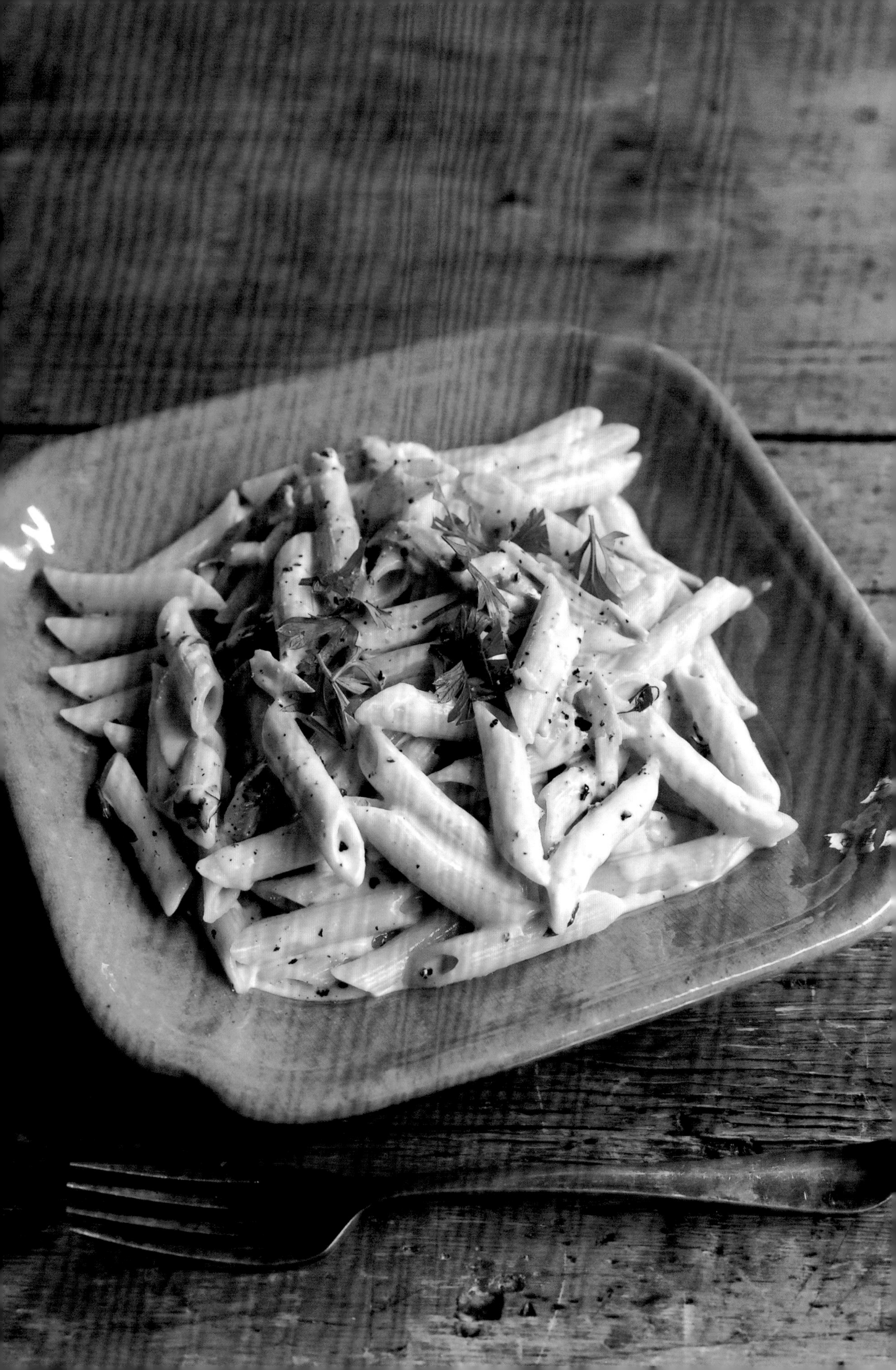

IT'S ALL IN HOW YOU USE THE PICKS.

For Ladies Only

Special Octopus Fritters

Healthy takoyaki made with fried tofu rather than egg!

AND SO...
ALL RIGHT, CREW, LET'S GO!!
TO JAYA, THE LAND OF MEAT!!
YEAH !!
IN YOUR DREAMS.
...THEY SAIL FOR THE MYSTERIOUS LAND OF JAYA.
NAMI, ROBIN...
I MADE SOME SPECIAL OCTOPUS FRITTERS--FOR LADIES ONLY. ♡

MANGA MOMENT

The crew searches a wrecked ship in search of clues to the sky island. An octopus pops out of the junk they haul up, so Sanji gets to work cooking it up. The guys get normal octopus in their food, but he puts extra special love into the ladies'.

(FROM VOL. 24, CH. 222)

INGREDIENTS Makes 20-30

- 3 ½ oz. (100 g) boiled octopus legs
- 1 cup (140 g) flour
- 1 tbsp. (10 g) potato starch
- ½ oz. (15 g) pickled red ginger
- 1 *abura-age* fried tofu pouch
- 2 green onions
- 2 cups (500 ml) water
- 1 egg
- 1 tsp. powdered bonito (*dashi* powder)
- 1 ½ tsp. salted kelp strips
- ½ tsp. salt
- vegetable oil
- Worcestershire sauce, ponzu, seaweed flakes, katsuobushi, extra green onions to taste

*If you have no salted kombu or powdered bonito, change 2 cups of water to 2 cups of kombu and katsuobushi *dashi* broth (see p. 94).

STEPS

A

B

① First, mix and sift flour and potato starch. Slice boiled octopus roughly into ⅓-½ inch (1 cm) pieces. Mince pickled red ginger. Press fried tofu between paper towels to remove excess oil, then mince. Slice green onions finely.

② Mix water and egg, then add salted kombu, powdered bonito, and salt and mix well. Add flour and potato starch and mix until there are no more clumps.

③ Rub vegetable oil onto a takoyaki grill on medium heat, then pour batter mix ② until brimming. Place one piece of octopus into each grill indentation, then sprinkle pickled ginger, tofu, and green onions liberally **(A)**.

④ When batter at the edge of grill firms up, use two long toothpicks or skewers to carefully turn each fritter 90 degrees at a time in the molds, repeating until they are thoroughly fried and browned all around **(B)**.

⑤ Remove from grill and place on a plate, then pour sauce, ponzu, seaweed flakes, katsuobushi, and spring onions on top as desired.

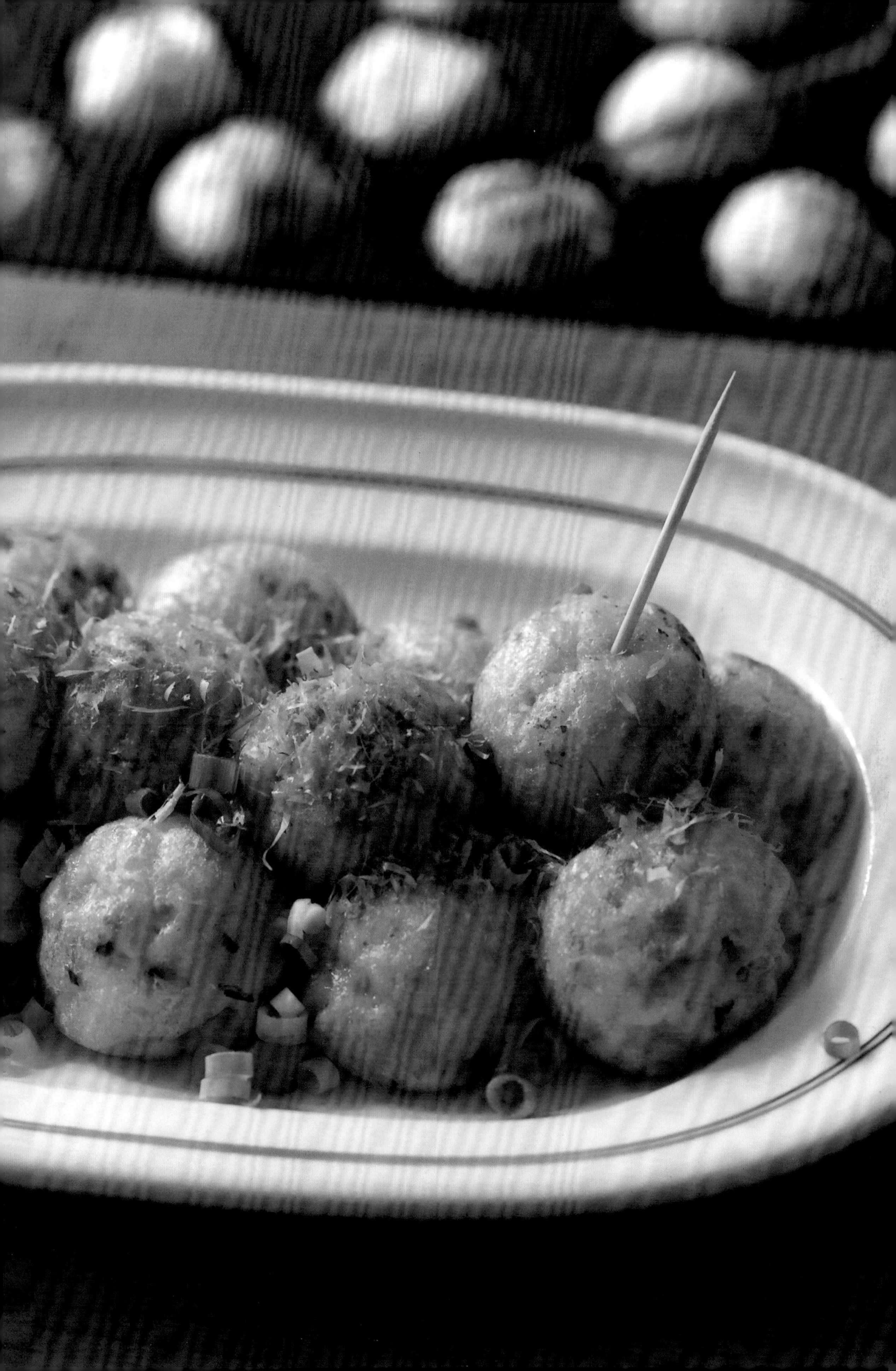

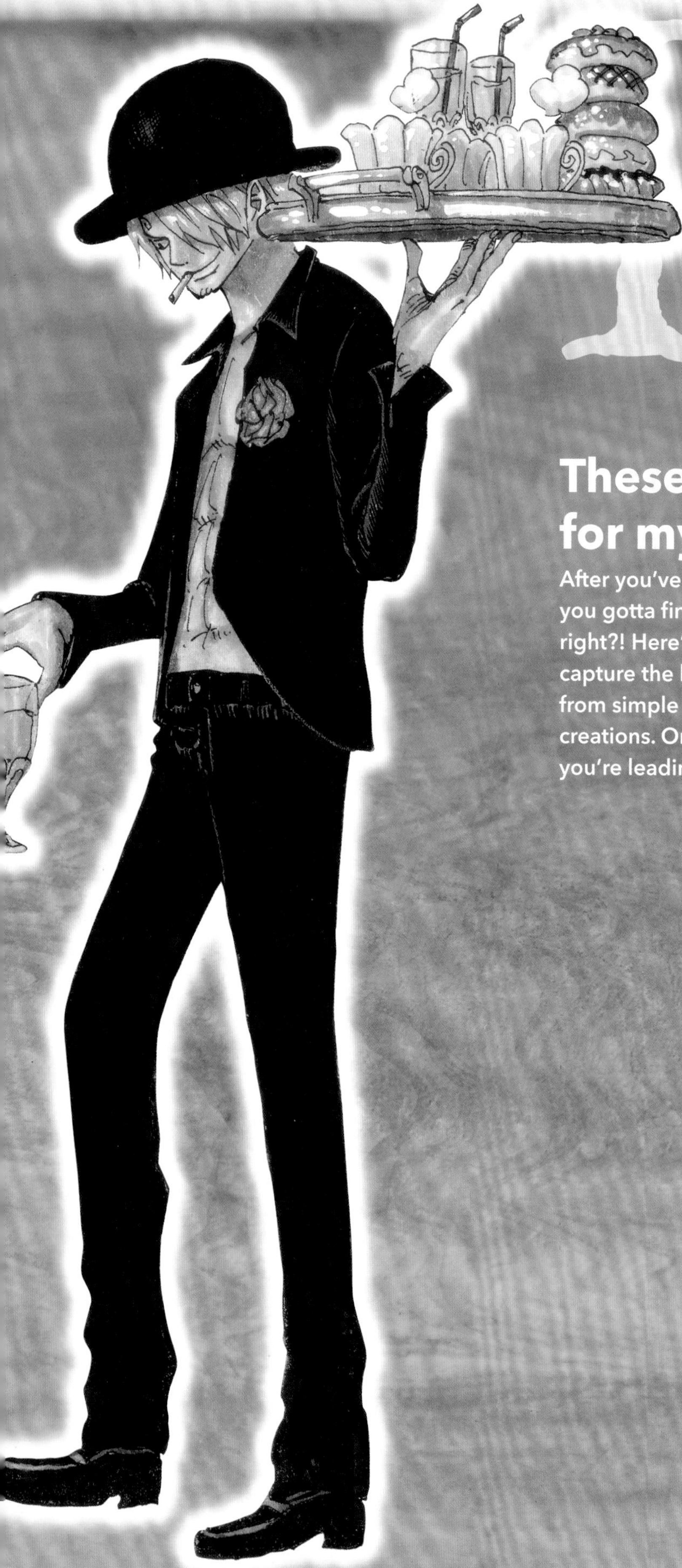

De

These are just for my loves!

After you've had a filling meal, you gotta finish up with a dessert, right?! Here's a lineup of sweets to capture the hearts of those you love, from simple examples to elaborate creations. Once you can make these, you're leading a charmed life!!

Refreshing
sserts

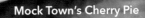
Mock Town's Cherry Pie

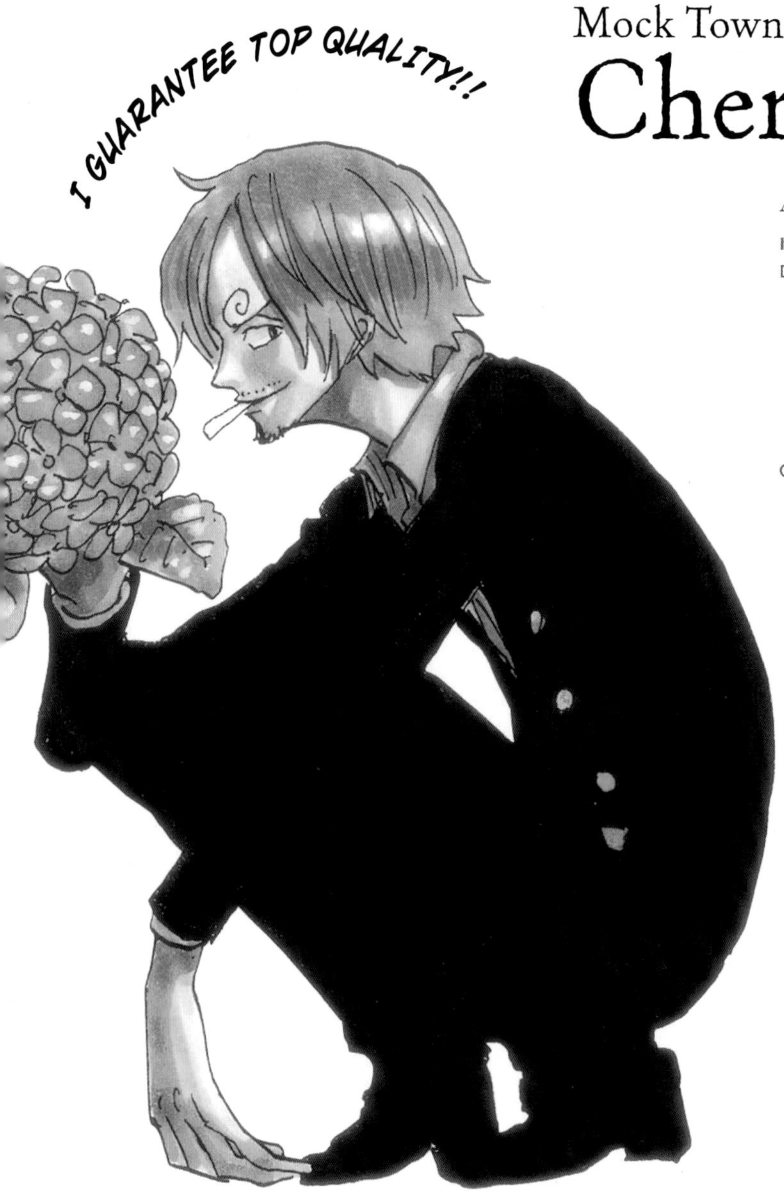
I GUARANTEE TOP QUALITY!!

Mock Town

Cherry Pie

A handmade tart with fruit on top

INGREDIENTS Makes a pie 8 ¼ in. (21 cm) across

Dough
- ½ cup (60 g) cake flour
- ½ cup (60 g) bread flour
- roughly 5 ¾ tbsp. (80 g) salted butter
- 2 tsp. (10 g) milk
- ½ egg
- 3 ¾ tsp. (15 g) granulated sugar
- dusting flour, as needed

Custard cream
- 2 egg yolks
- 4 tbsp. plus 2 tsp. (65 g) granulated sugar
- 2 tsp. (10 g) cornstarch
- 2 tsp. (10 g) cake flour
- 1 cup (230 ml) milk
- 2 tbsp. lemon juice
- roughly 1 ½ tbsp. (20 g) salted butter
- 18 Bing cherries

MANGA MOMENT

In the bar in Mock Town, where the crew stops to find information on the sky island, Luffy sits next to a man eating the same items off the menu. Yet they have the exact opposite reaction to each thing! Will this difference in taste lead to a rivalry?!
(FROM VOL. 24, CH. 223)

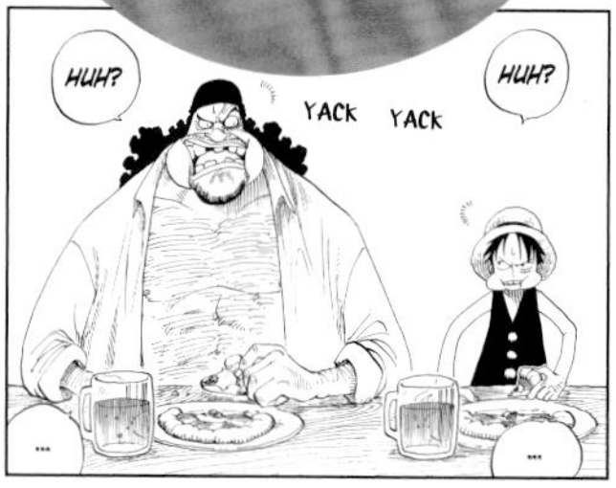
HUH?
YACK YACK
HUH?
...
...

A

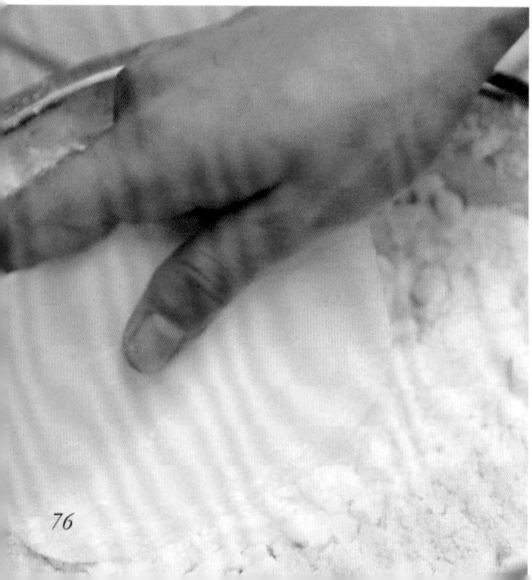

B

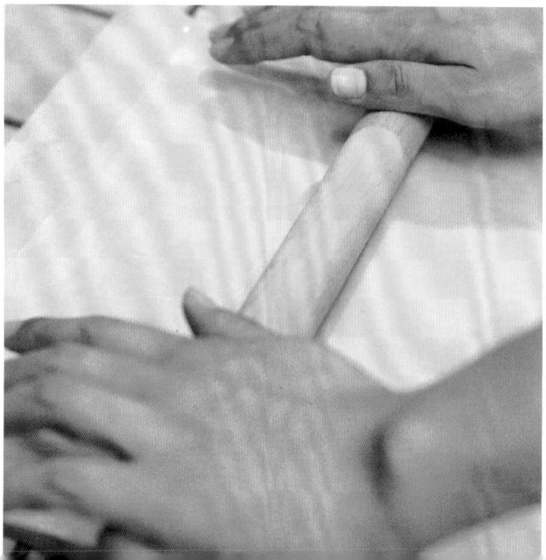

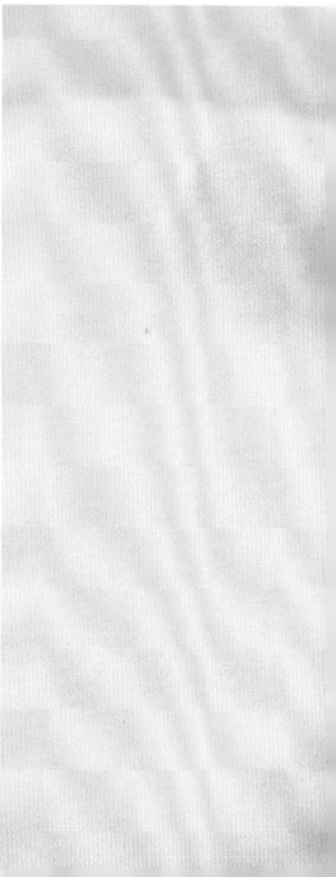

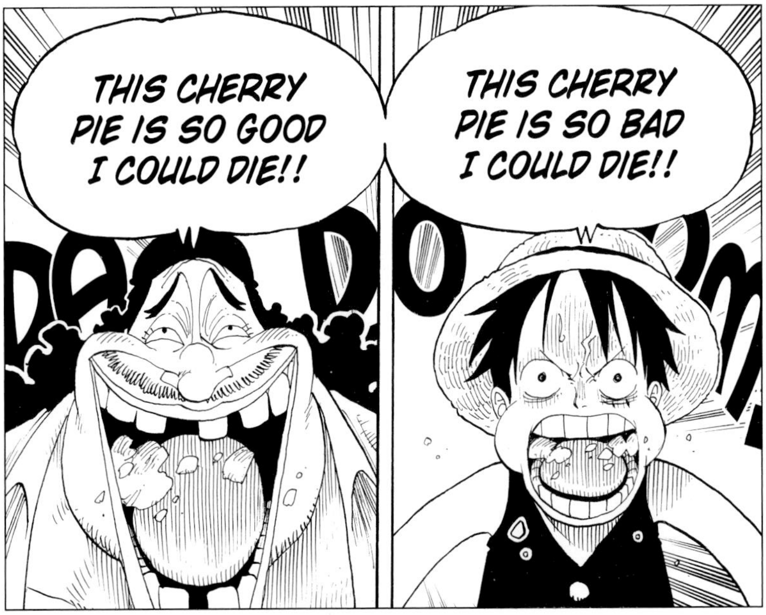
THIS CHERRY PIE IS SO BAD I COULD DIE!!
THIS CHERRY PIE IS SO GOOD I COULD DIE!!

STEPS

① Make dough. Mix and sift cake flour and bread flour, cut butter into ⅓ inch (1 cm) squares, and place both into the refrigerator. Put milk, egg, and granulated sugar into a bowl and mix well, then place in refrigerator.

② Place butter into the dough bowl and use a dough scraper or pastry blender to crumble and mix it in **(A)**. Pour egg liquid ① in and use a spatula or similar tool to mix, then wrap in baking sheet or plastic wrap and let sit in the refrigerator for 30–60 minutes.

③ Place dough mixture on a parchment sheet, then place another baking sheet on top. Use a rolling pin to flatten dough until it is larger than your pie tin **(B)**.

④ Pack dough firmly into pie tin. Dust a fork with flour and use it to score the entire rim **(C)**. Cut excess dough from rim with a knife and use fork to poke about 10 holes in the bottom. Place a baking sheet on top and weigh down with pie weights **(D)**.

⑤ Preheat oven to 400°F (200°C) and bake for 10–15 minutes. Remove pie weights, lower oven to 355°F (180°C), and bake another 15 minutes. Place on cooling rack.

⑥ In a pot on medium-low heat, whisk milk, granulated sugar, cornstarch, and cake flour. Mix well. Turn on heat and stir until it begins to thicken **(E)**. Remove from heat. Add butter and lemon juice, then stir until it becomes smooth. Once it has cooled a bit, pour into pie crust.

⑦ Remove stems from Bing cherries, cut in half, and remove pits. Arrange on top of custard cream, then chill in the refrigerator.

C

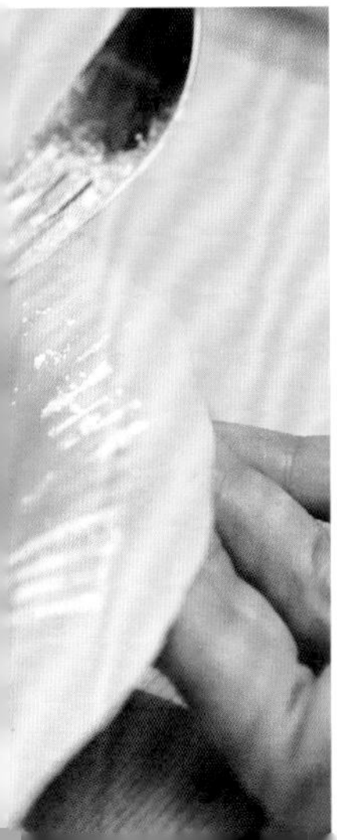

D

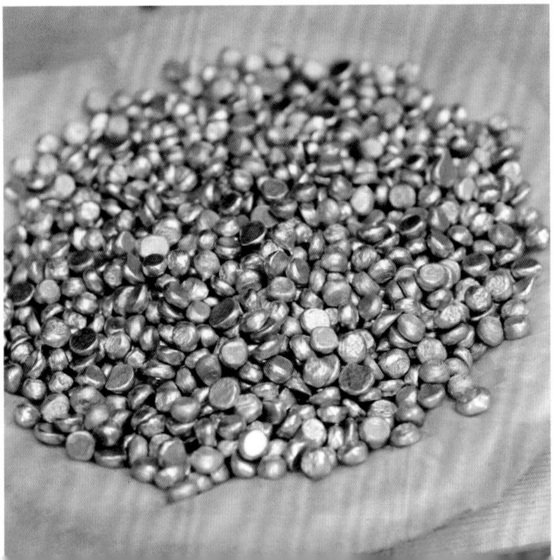

E

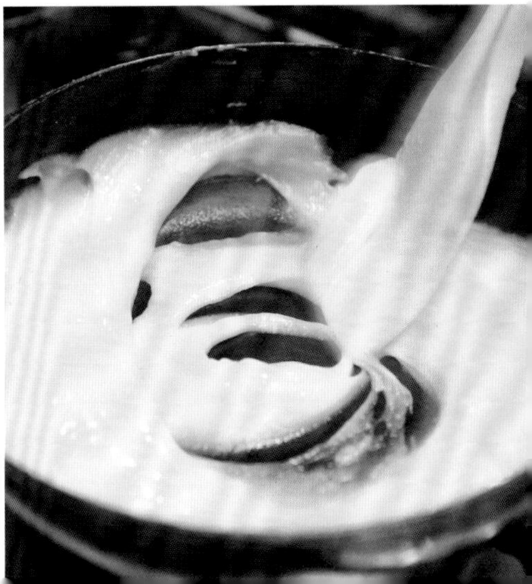

Cindry's Flan

A simple creme caramel made from just a few ingredients

INGREDIENTS

Makes 5 servings of just under ½ cup (100 ml) each

3 eggs
6 tbsp. sugar
1 ⅔ cups (390 ml) milk
⅓ vanilla bean (or vanilla essence)

Caramel sauce

3 tbsp. sugar
2 tbsp. water

STEPS

① Make caramel sauce. Place sugar and 1 tbsp. water in a pan and heat on medium. Shake the pan until it becomes caramel colored **(A)**, then add the other 1 tbsp. water. Pour into the bottom of pudding cups and chill in refrigerator.

② Use a knife to work open the vanilla bean pod and extract the seeds **(B)**. Put the milk and vanilla seeds into a small pot and heat until it reaches 120°F (50°C).

③ Crack eggs into a bowl and whisk, then mix in sugar. Pour in ②, mix, then use a sieve to filter.

④ When the caramel ① is firm, pour in egg mixture ③. Use a spoon to scoop out bubbles, then cover with aluminum foil.

⑤ Place containers ④ into a heated steam cooker and insert cooking chopsticks or another wedge to keep lid ajar **(C)**. Steam on low heat for 15-20 minutes. Test with a toothpick. If firm, allow to cool a bit before chilling in the refrigerator.

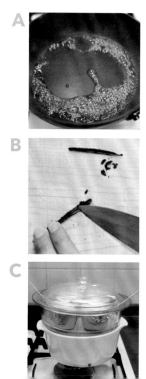

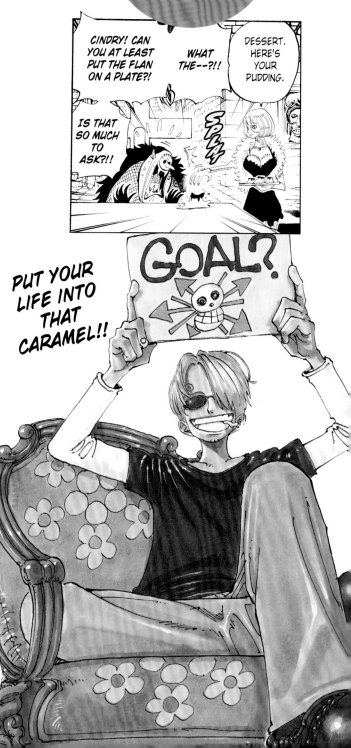

MANGA MOMENT

Nami, Usopp and Chopper visit Dr. Hogback's mansion. The mansion servant, Cindry, hates plates because of a tragic event in her past. She doesn't care, she'll slap soft flan directly onto the tablecloth!

(FROM VOL. 46, CH. 446)

DESSERT. HERE'S YOUR PUDDING.
WHAT THE--?!!
CINDRY! CAN YOU AT LEAST PUT THE FLAN ON A PLATE?!
SPLAT
IS THAT SO MUCH TO ASK?!!

GOAL?
PUT YOUR LIFE INTO THAT CARAMEL!!

A

B

C

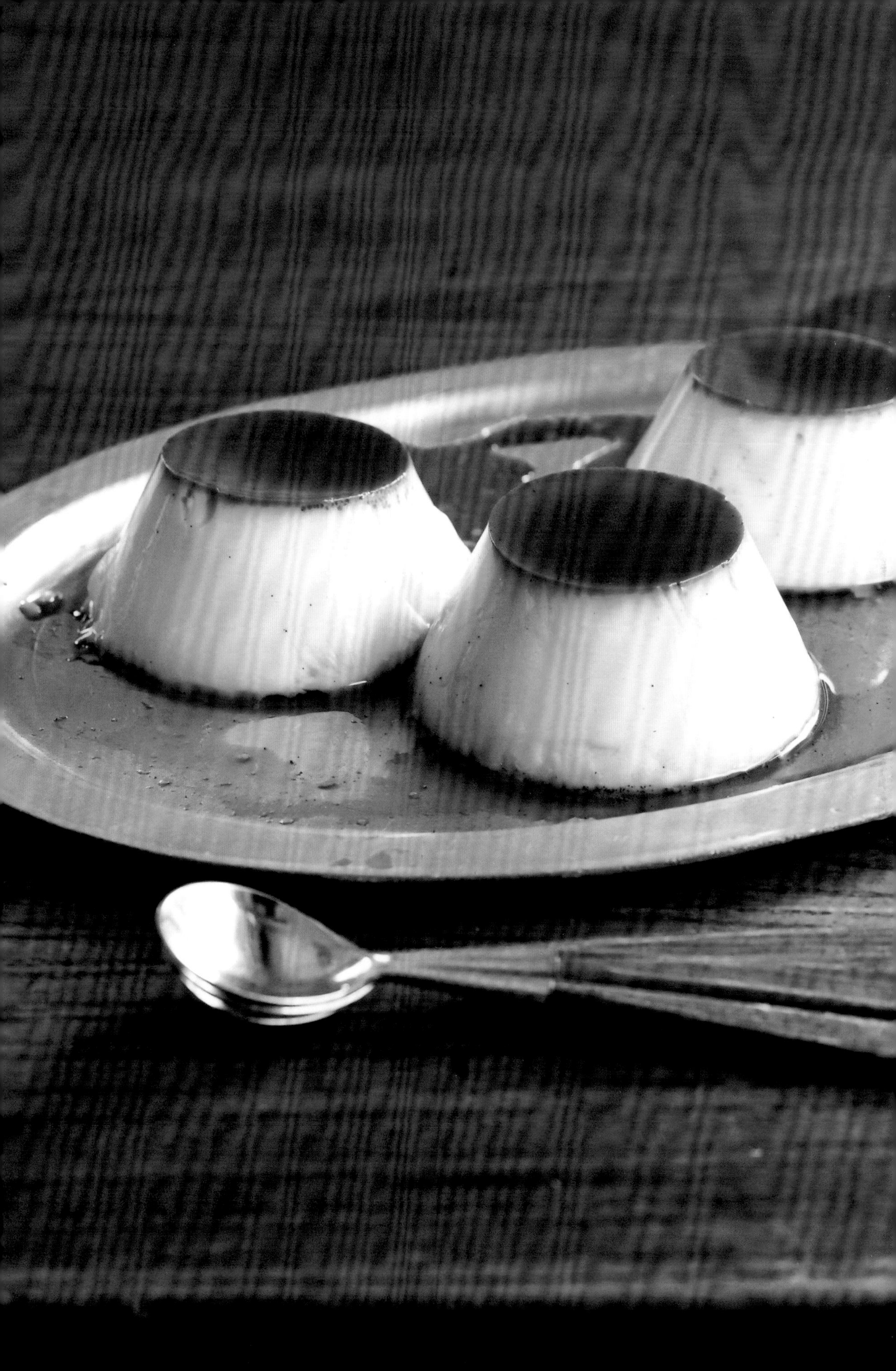

Ganfor's

Pumpkin Juice

Pumpkin au lait, with plenty of milk

FATHER! THIS PUMPKIN JUICE...
...IS SO DELICIOUS.

MANGA MOMENT

Ganfor shelters Conis at his house when she is on the run and gives her some of his fresh pumpkin juice. Pumpkins are a crop from the land, and did not originally exist in the sky island. **(FROM VOL. 27, CH. 248)**

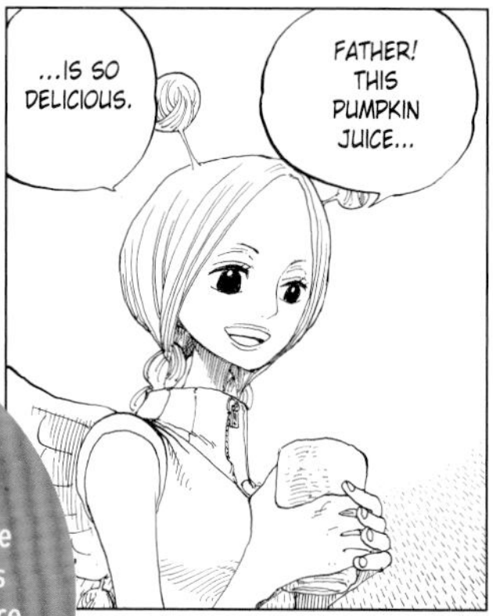

INGREDIENTS Makes 3-4 cups

about ¼ Japanese pumpkin (net weight 10–11 oz./300 g)
1 ¼ cups (300 ml) water
2 tbsp. honey
2 tbsp. (or more) granulated sugar
milk

STEPS

① Remove pumpkin seeds and shell and cut pumpkin flesh into ⅓ inch (1 cm) thick pieces. Place in a small pot, add water, cover, and simmer at medium heat. Turn off heat when pumpkin softens and let sit **(A)**.

② Pour ① into a blender, including the fluid. Add honey and granulated sugar, and blend. Chill in refrigerator.

③ Pour ② into glasses, then carefully pour milk on top and drink, stirring as desired. Tastes great heated, too.

A

B

Luffy and Zolo Love

Bread Crusts

Stylish fried bread crusts

INGREDIENTS

6 slices of bread crusts
cinnamon sugar
condensed milk
frying oil

STEPS

① Heat frying oil to 340°F (170°C). Place bread crusts in the pan, frying about 90 seconds until golden brown **(B)**. Remove and place on a drying rack over a cooking sheet lined with paper towels to remove oil.

② Dust with cinnamon sugar as desired, and dip into condensed milk to eat.

MANGA MOMENT

The Straw Hats have returned to the blue sea from the white sea 10,000 meters in the air. As they reminisce on the adventure in Skypiea, Sanji is putting together sandwiches in the kitchen. The crusts left over go to Zolo as a snack. **(FROM VOL. 32, CH. 303)**

CHOPPER, HAUL 'ER UP.
YOU'RE INCRED-IBLE, NAMI.
ALL THE DIALS STILL WORK, EXCEPT FOR THE MILKY DIAL.
I IMAGINE IT WOULD ONLY WORK IN THE ENVIRONMENT UP THERE.
THE OTHER ONES ARE PRETTY RARE TOO THOUGH. CONGRATS.
AH! LUCKY! BREAD CRUSTS! HEY, SANJI! I WANT SOME TOO!
SNIK
NOM NOM
Usopp Workshop

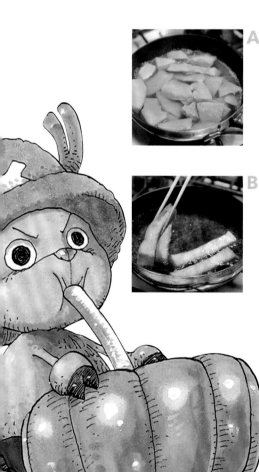

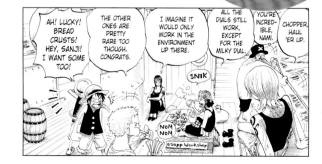

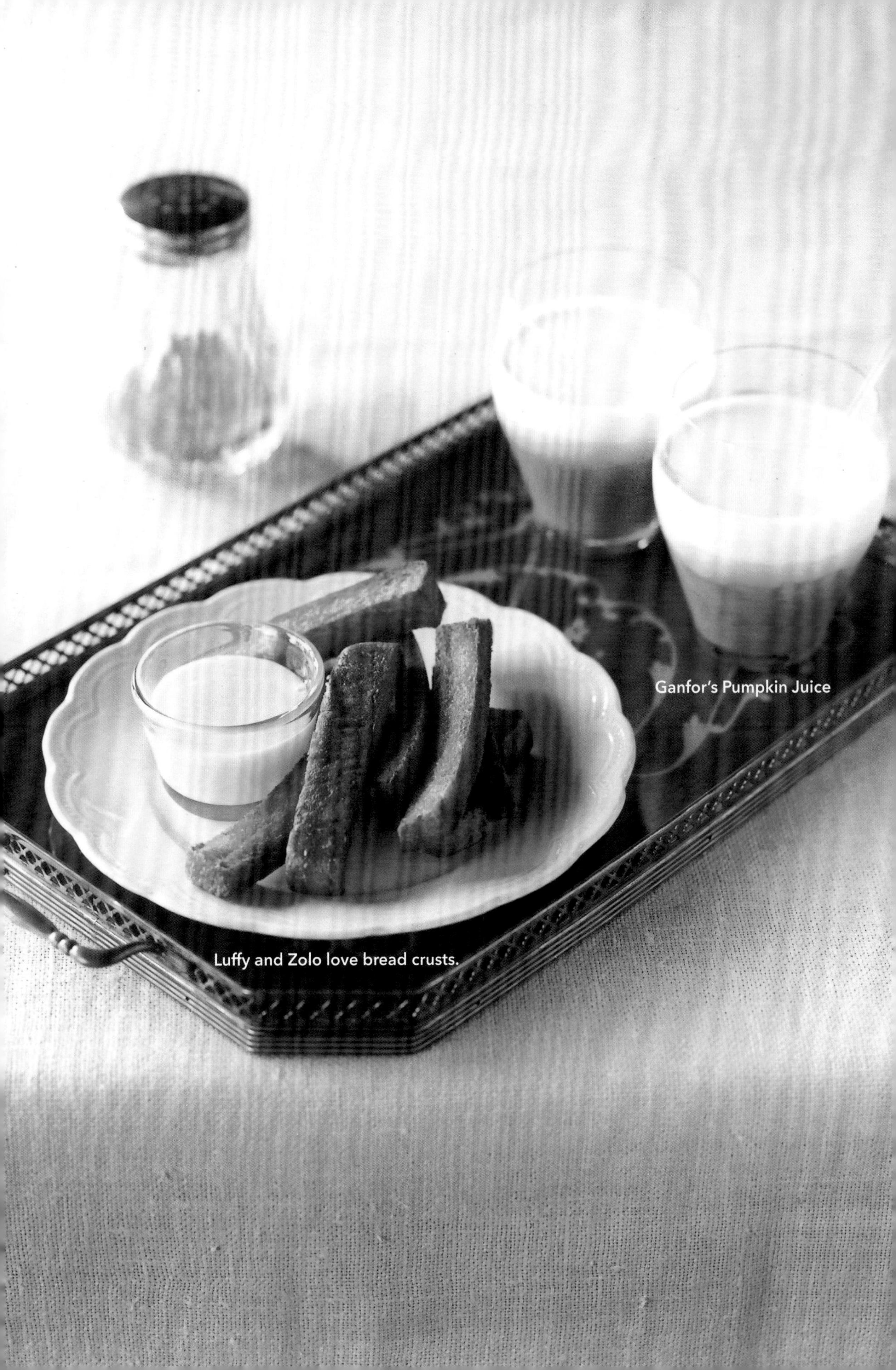
Ganfor's Pumpkin Juice
Luffy and Zolo love bread crusts.

Test Your Luck with

Exploding Apples

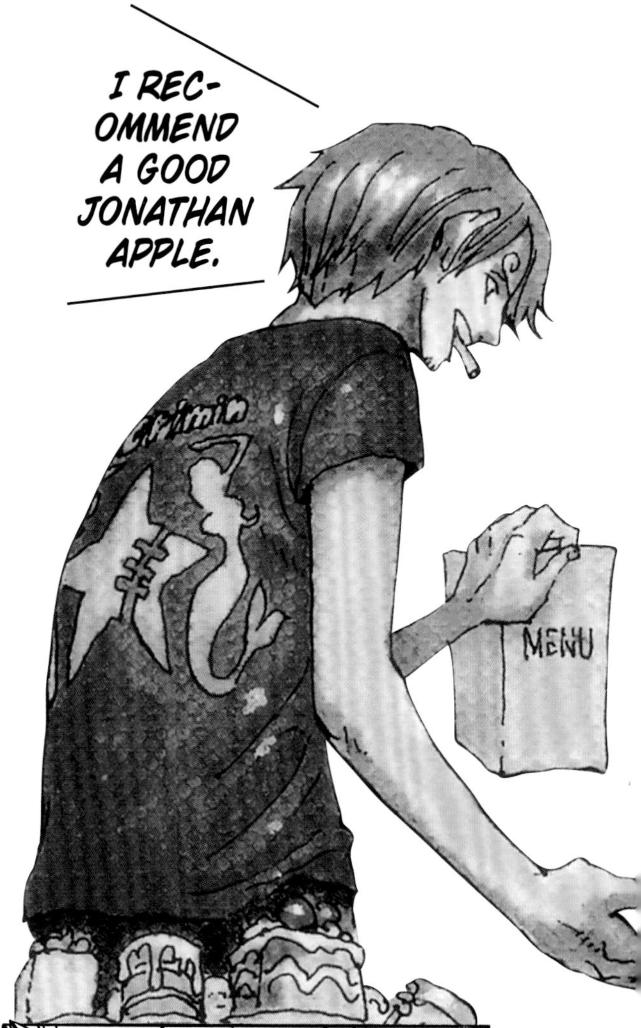

I REC-OMMEND A GOOD JONATHAN APPLE.
MENU

Baked apples you can make in the toaster oven

INGREDIENTS Serves 2

2 apples
1–2 cinnamon sticks
2 tsp. lemon juice
4 cardamom pods
1 ½ tbsp. (20 g) butter
4 tsp. granulated sugar

STEPS

① Slice apples in half lengthwise and scoop out seeds and core with a spoon **(A)**. Break cinnamon sticks into 1 inch (3 cm) pieces and dampen with water to keep from burning.

② Add lemon juice, cardamom, and butter to apple surface and stick cinnamon into center.

③ Scatter granulated sugar on surface liberally, then cover skin side of apple in foil **(B)** and bake in toaster oven with a sheet pan underneath for 20 minutes.

A

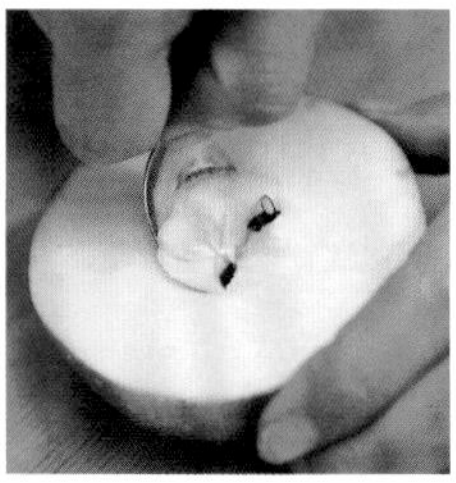

B

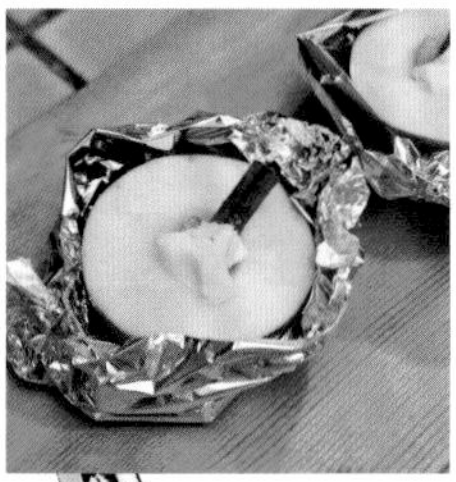

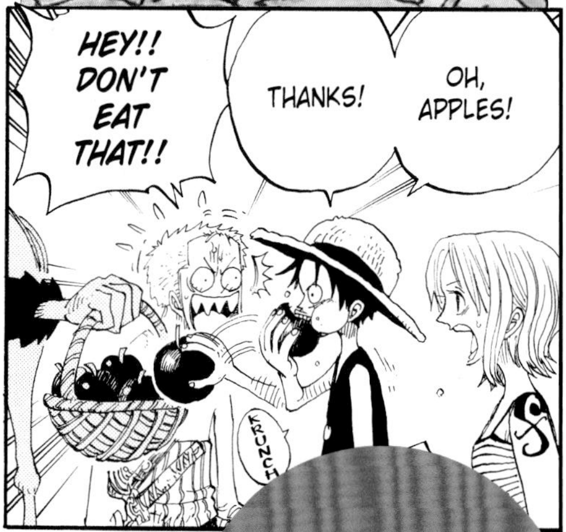

OH, APPLES!
THANKS!
HEY!! DON'T EAT THAT!!
KRUNCH

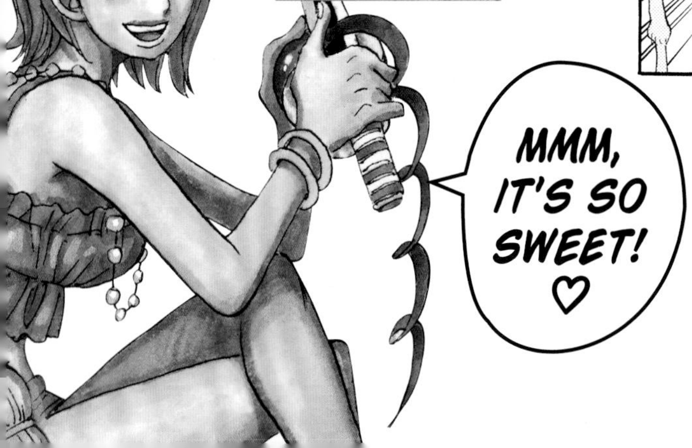

MMM, IT'S SO SWEET! ♡

MANGA MOMENT

Luffy chows down on some apples a stranger offers to him. At that very moment, an explosion happens nearby. The apples were filled with explosives meant to go off when eaten—but Luffy ate the real one and luckily escaped death. **(FROM VOL. 24, CH. 223)**

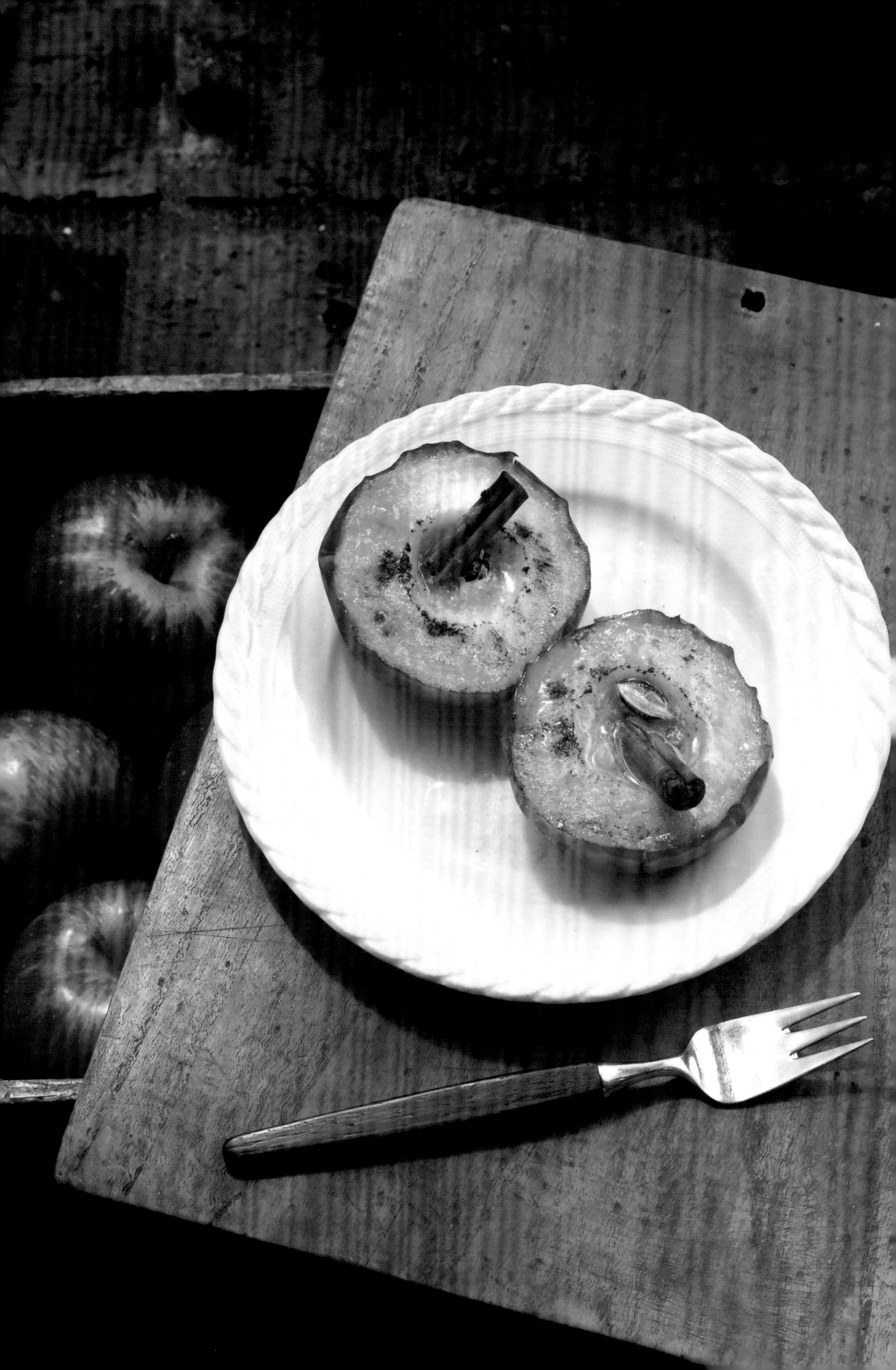

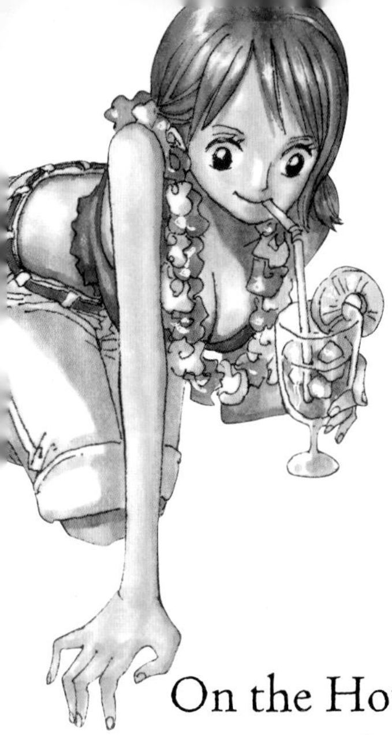

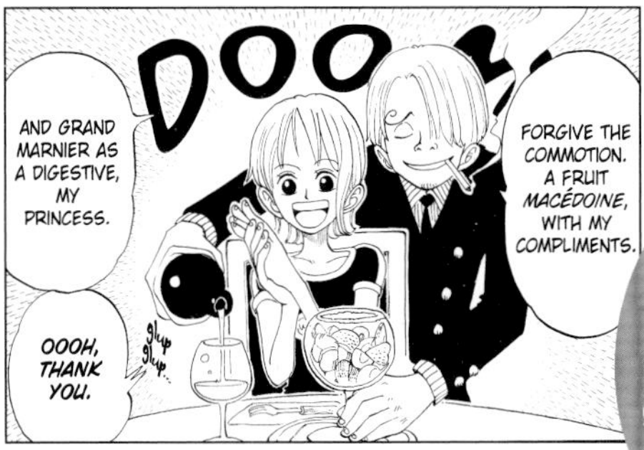
FORGIVE THE COMMOTION. A FRUIT MACÉDOINE, WITH MY COMPLIMENTS.
DOO
AND GRAND MARNIER AS A DIGESTIVE, MY PRINCESS.
OOOH, THANK YOU.

MANGA MOMENT

The crew arrives at the seafaring restaurant *Baratie* in search of a cook. This is where Luffy meets Sanji. The girl-crazy cook will get into a fight with his boss one moment and deliver a dessert to Nami in apology the next. (FROM VOL. 6, CH. 46)

On the House

Fruit Macédoine

Fruit punch with an adult twist

INGREDIENTS Serves 4

1 orange
¼ pineapple (net weight 7 oz./200 g)
6 strawberries
1 banana
1-2 tbsp. lemon juice
2 tbsp. (30 ml) liqueur (such as kirsch)
2 tbsp. granulated sugar
a few sprigs of fresh mint

STEPS

① Cut orange supremes or slices **(A)**. Squeeze juice from the rind and save. Remove pineapple peel, remove the core, and cut to bite-size pieces. Remove stems from strawberries and slice in half vertically.

② Place fruit ① into a bowl, add orange juice, lemon juice, liqueur, and granulated sugar. Mix, then chill in refrigerator for 1-2 hours.

③ Before you eat, slice banana into ⅓ inch (1 cm) pieces and mix with ② before transferring to dish. Garnish with mint.

A

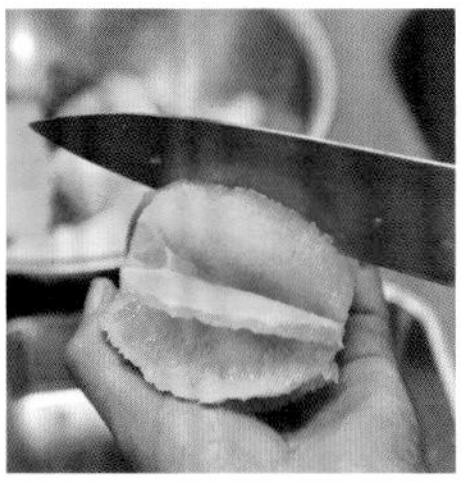

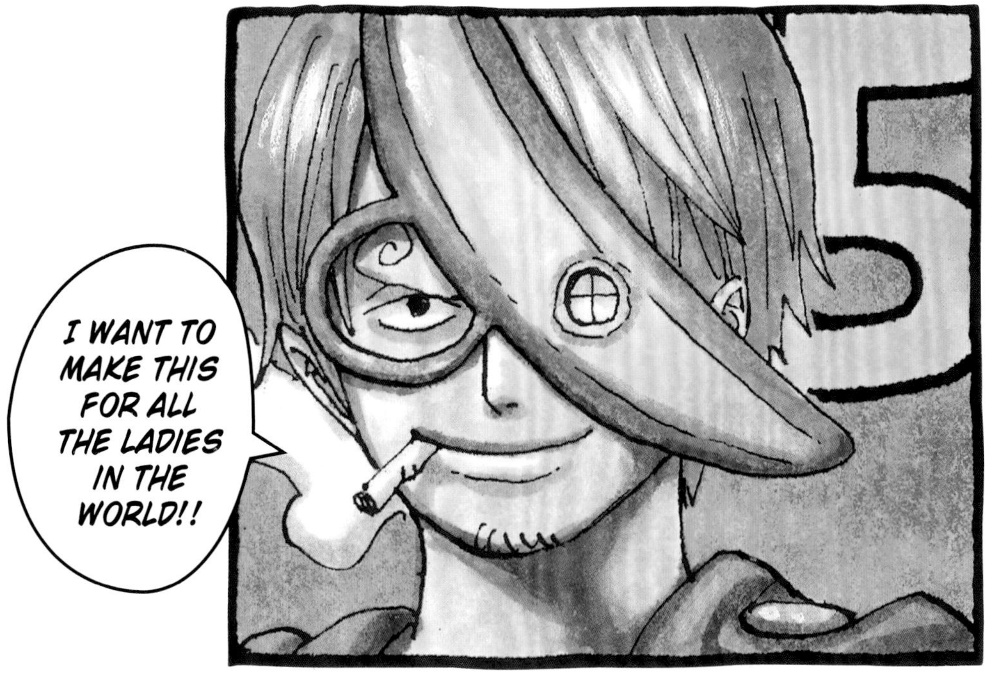
I WANT TO MAKE THIS FOR ALL THE LADIES IN THE WORLD!!

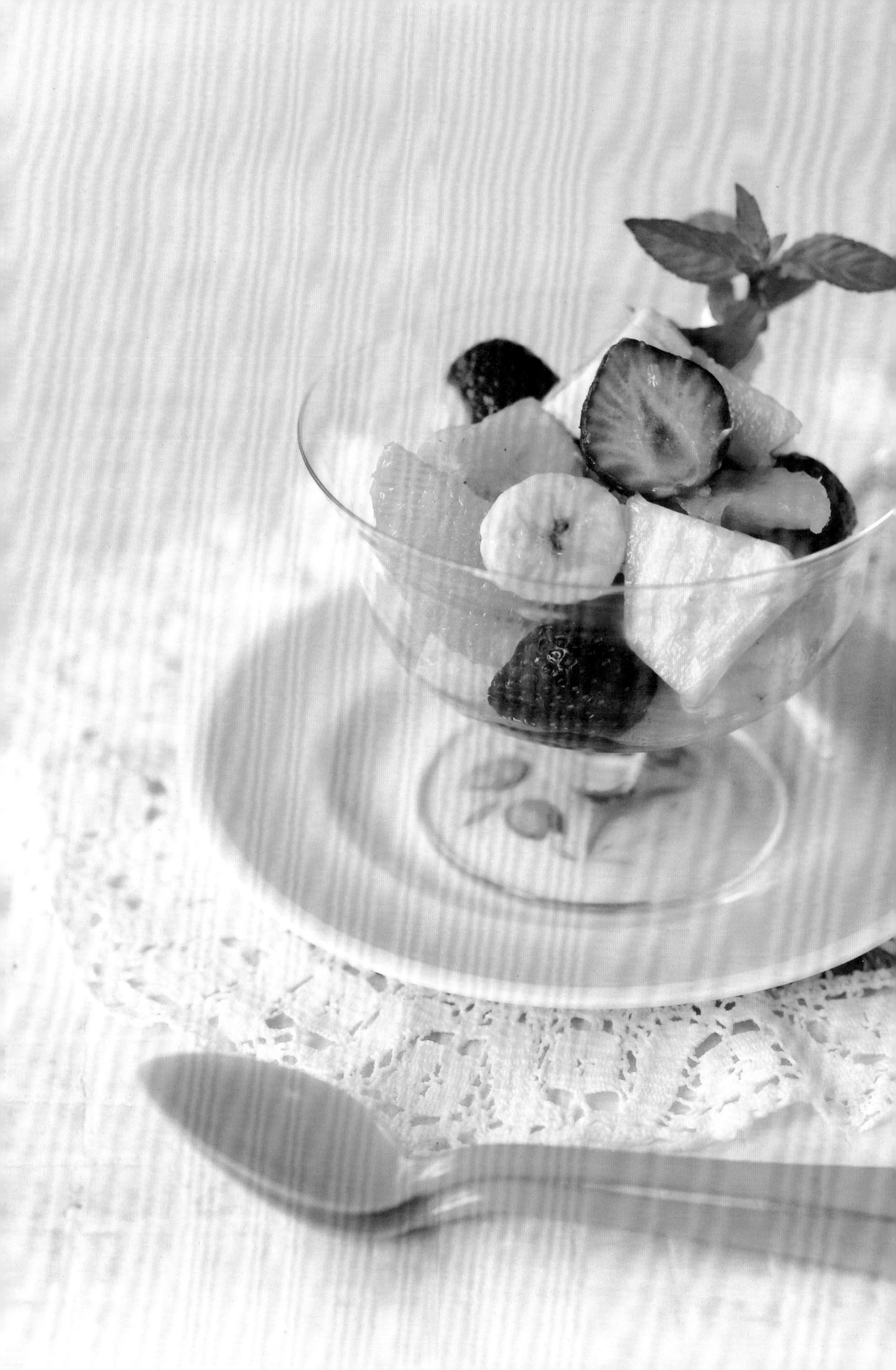

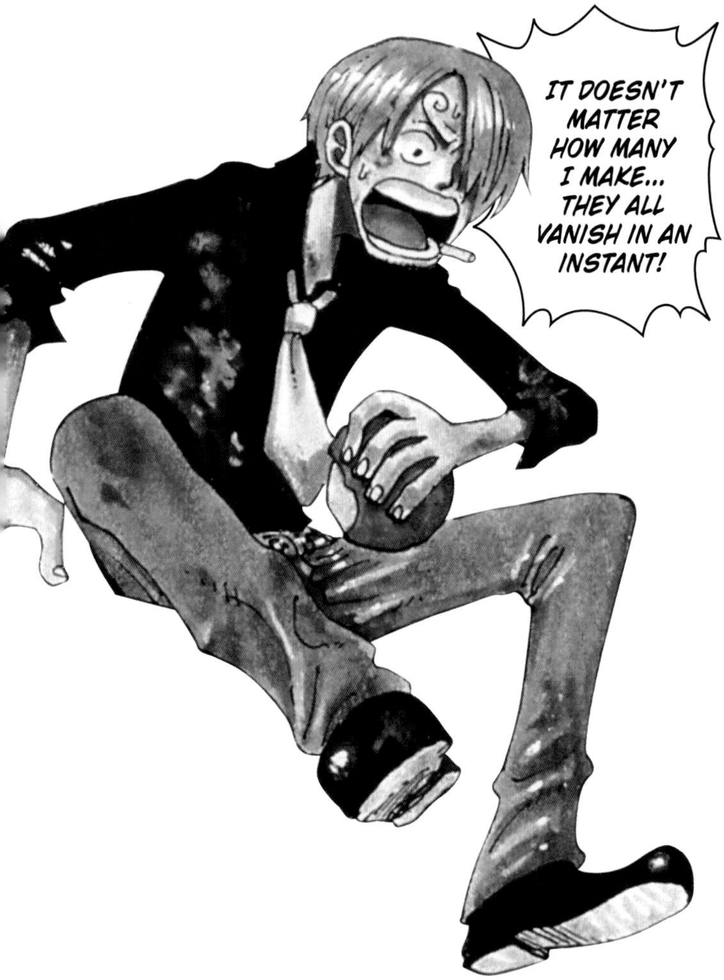
IT DOESN'T MATTER HOW MANY I MAKE... THEY ALL VANISH IN AN INSTANT!

Antonio's

Graman
(Grand Line Manju Buns)

Steamed bread filled with chestnuts and sweet beans

INGREDIENTS

Makes 8 buns in paper liners 1.2x3 in. (3x7.5 cm)

1 cup (120 g) cake flour
1 ½ tsp. baking powder
¼ cup (60 g) sugar
1 tbsp. vegetable oil
1 egg
Up to ½ cup (120 ml) milk (combined with egg)
5 ½ oz. (160 g) store-bought tsubuan (azuki bean paste)
4 candied chestnuts

STEPS

① Cut candied chestnuts in half. Crack egg and add milk to a total of ½ cup (120 ml). Add sugar and vegetable oil and mix well.

② Sift flour and baking powder, then add to egg mixture ①. Beat mixture until it is no longer powdery **(A)**.

③ Place paper trays in pudding (or cupcake) molds with two layers, then spoon batter to the halfway point. Add equal parts of azuki bean paste to each **(B)**. Divide remaining batter equally and pour on top, then add 1 piece of chestnut to each cup.

④ Heat a steam cooker and place cups in the steamer. Cover and steam on high for about 10 minutes. Test with a toothpick; if it emerges cleanly, steaming is complete.

A

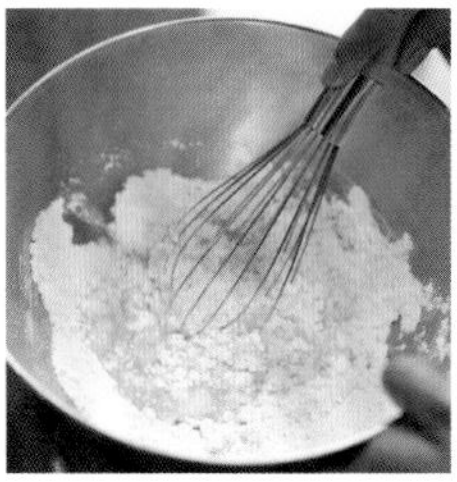

B

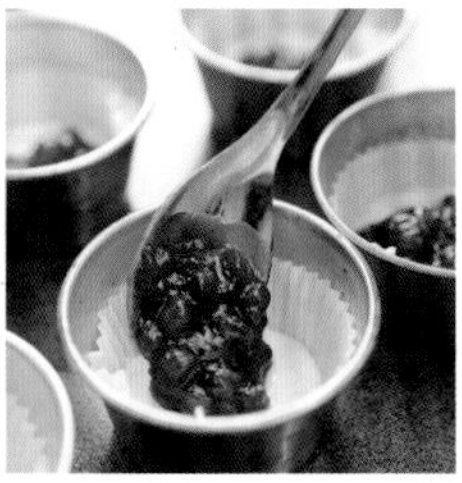

MANGA MOMENT

The crew strolls about the Sabaody Archipelago, ignoring Brook's skull jokes. Lured by a delicious scent, Luffy stops by a souvenir stand. He powers through all of the samples out front, much to the chagrin of the owner.
(FROM VOL. 51, CH. 497)

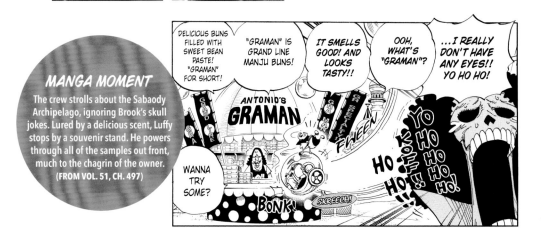

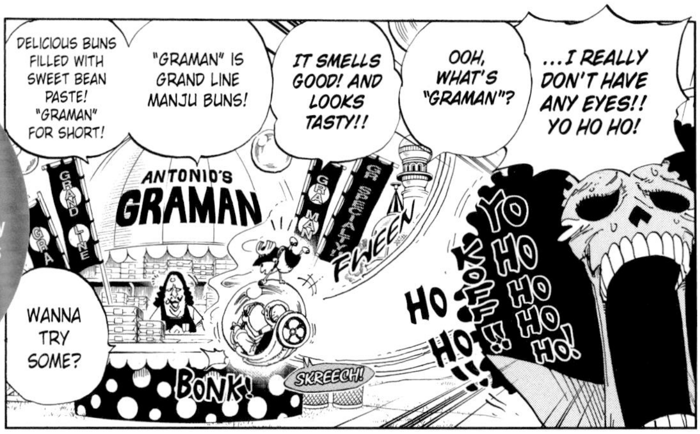
...I REALLY DON'T HAVE ANY EYES!! YO HO HO!
OOH, WHAT'S "GRAMAN"?
IT SMELLS GOOD! AND LOOKS TASTY!!
"GRAMAN" IS GRAND LINE MANJU BUNS!
DELICIOUS BUNS FILLED WITH SWEET BEAN PASTE! "GRAMAN" FOR SHORT!
YO HO HO HO HO HO!
HO HO!!
FWEEN
ANTONIO'S GRAMAN
GRAND LINE
SKREECH!
BONK!
WANNA TRY SOME?

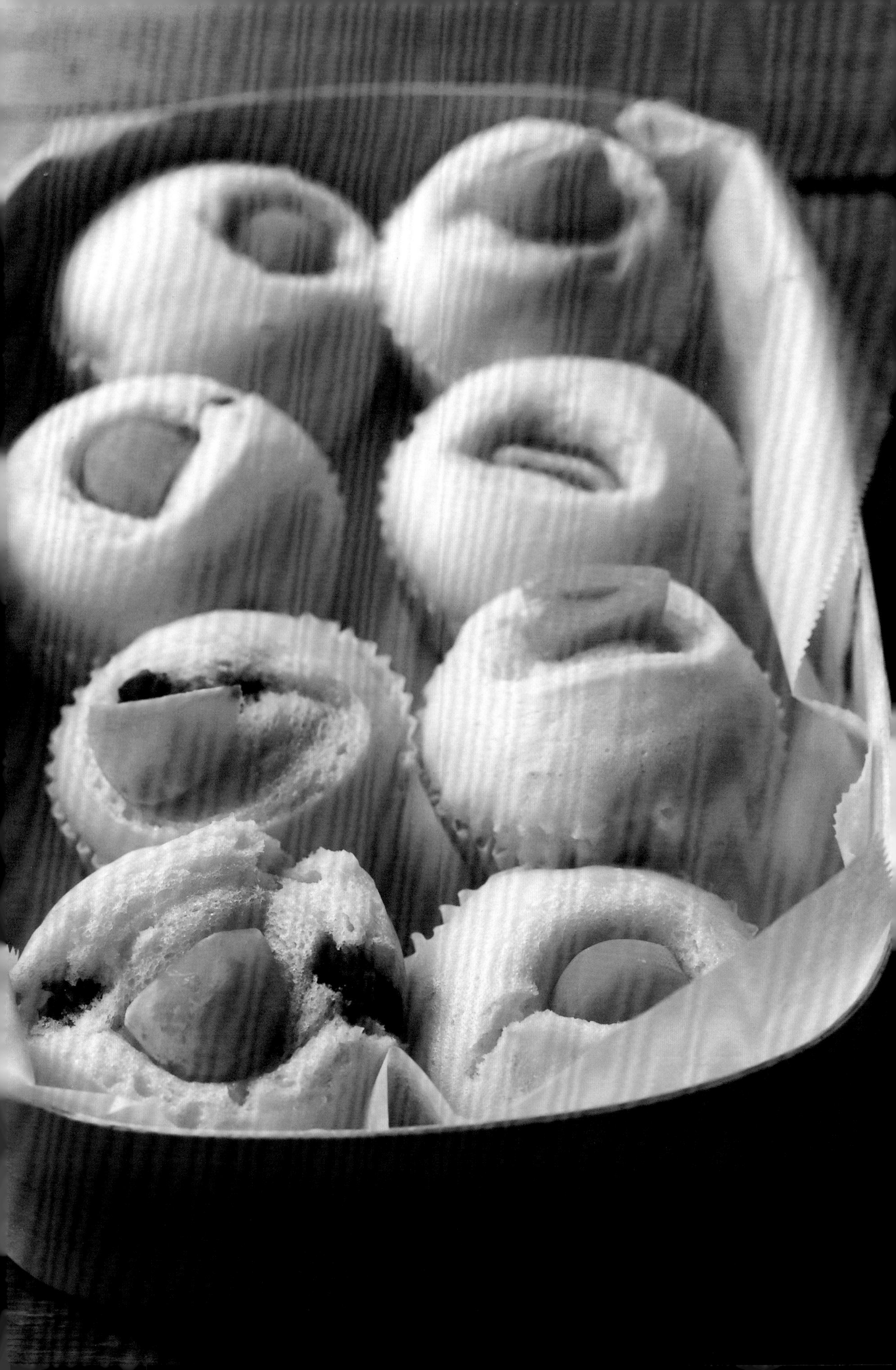

Sanji's Eye 1

Lastly, out of all the many dishes I've tackled in my life, here's some of the most special secrets and stories I've acquired. Read carefully.

Oda Sensei's Favorite

Sea Chicken® Onigiri

The secret treasure of rice balls

INGREDIENTS Makes about 6

1 ½ cups (300 g) cooked rice, kept warm
1 can (3 oz./80 g) Sea Chicken® tuna
1 tbsp. miso paste
heaping ½ tsp. sugar
2 in. (5 cm) green onion
dried seaweed sheets (nori)
salt

STEPS

① Mince green onion. Drain oil briefly from tuna can, then fry in a pan on medium heat, mixing in miso and sugar. Add green onion and mix briefly, then turn off heat **(A)**.

② Wet hands with water, sprinkle with salt, and surround a dab of ① with cooked rice **(B)** to form an onigiri. Cut nori sheet to appropriate size and wrap.

A

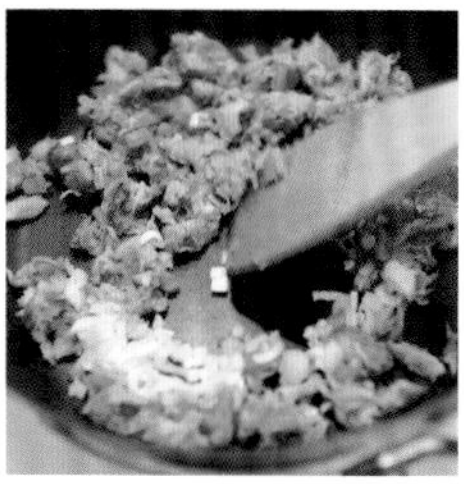

B

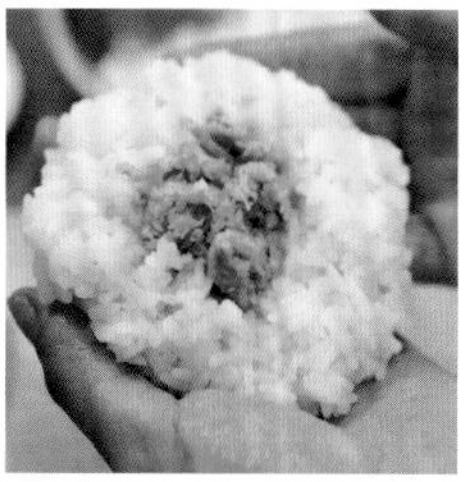

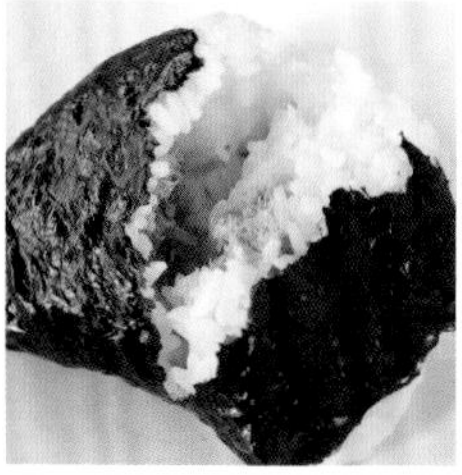

It looks like this inside!

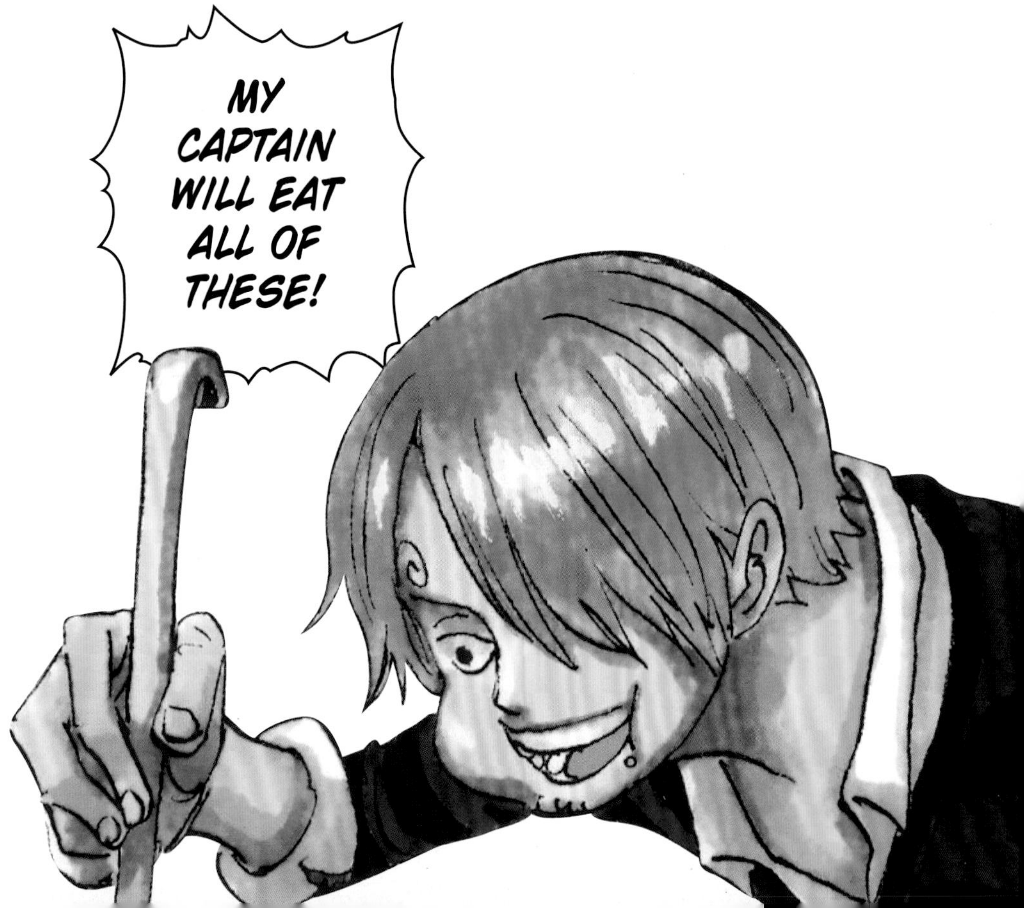
MY CAPTAIN WILL EAT ALL OF THESE!

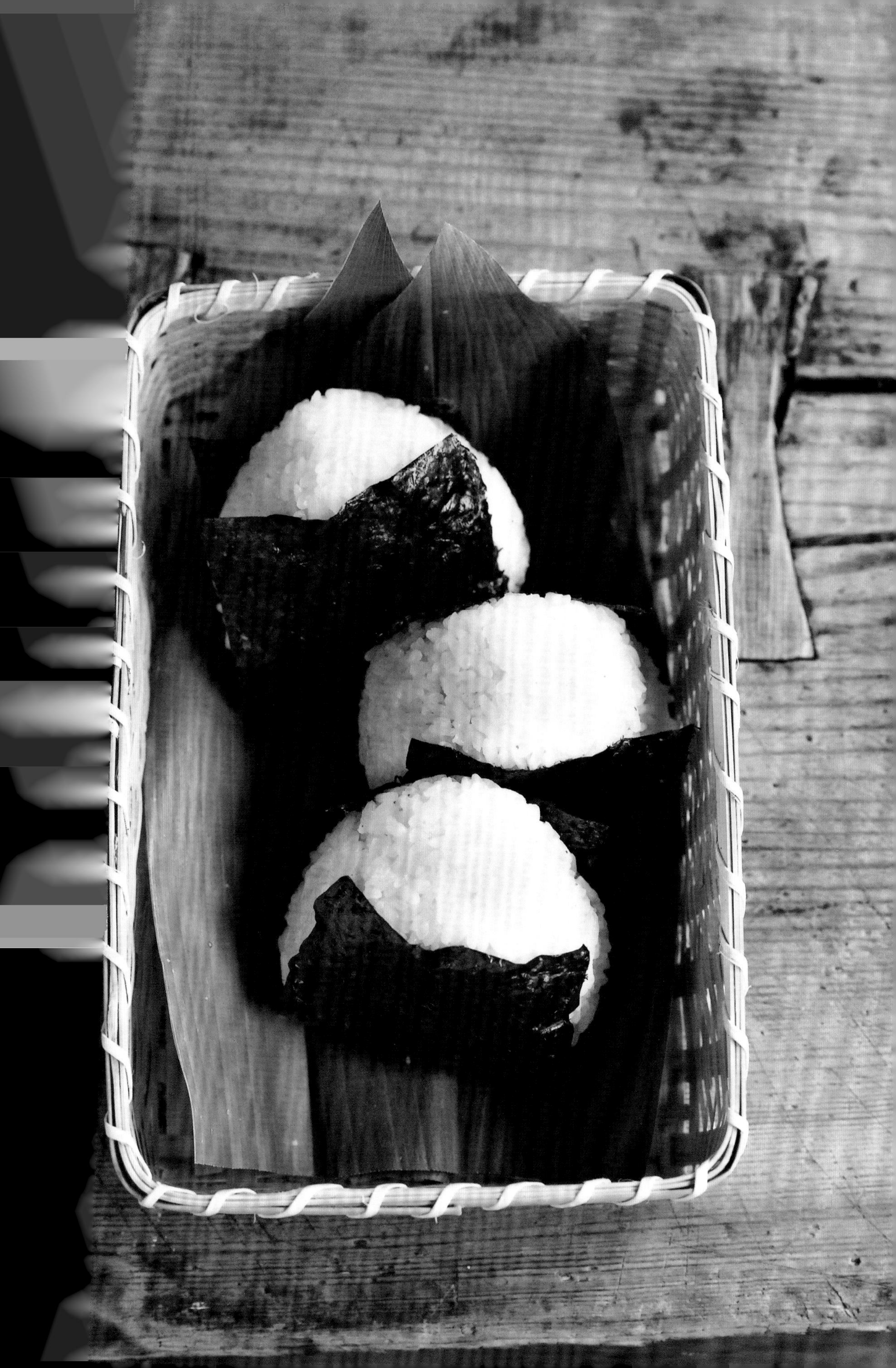

Sanji's Eye 2

One Piece Workplace Party Paparazzi!

①

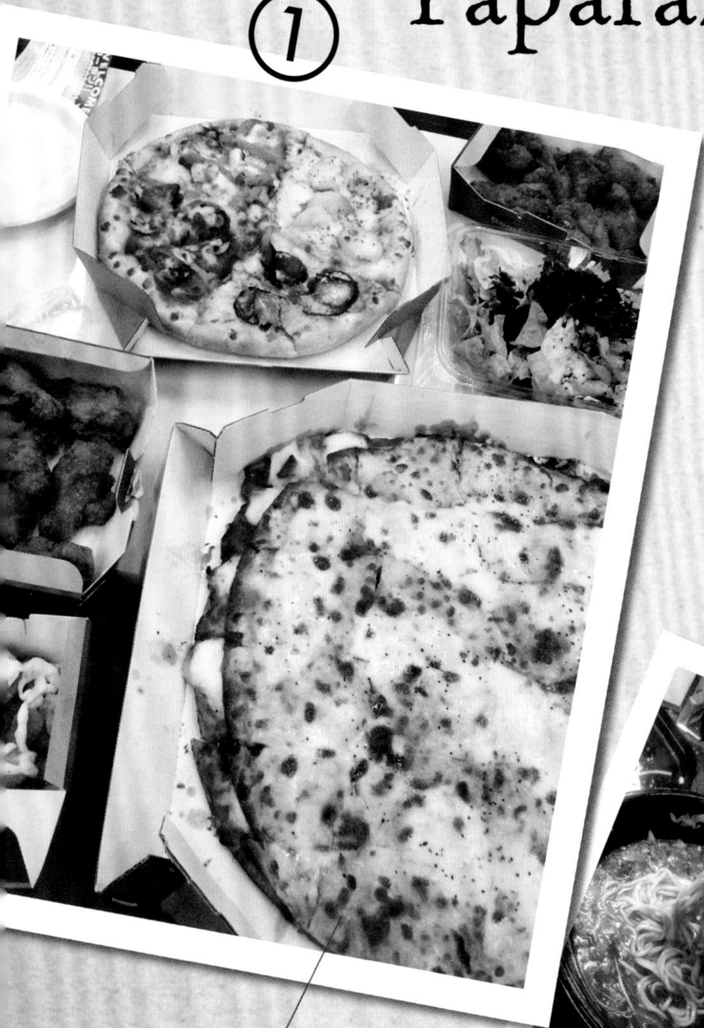

④

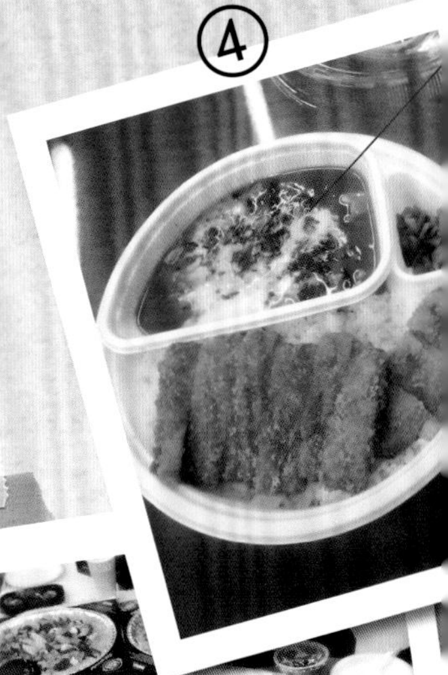

③

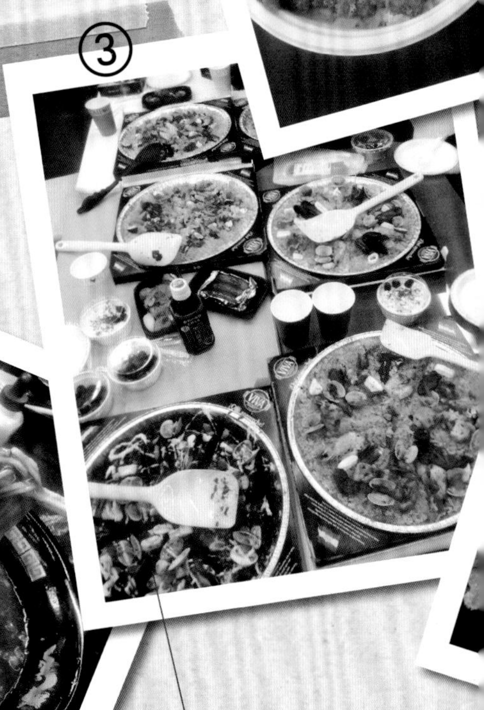

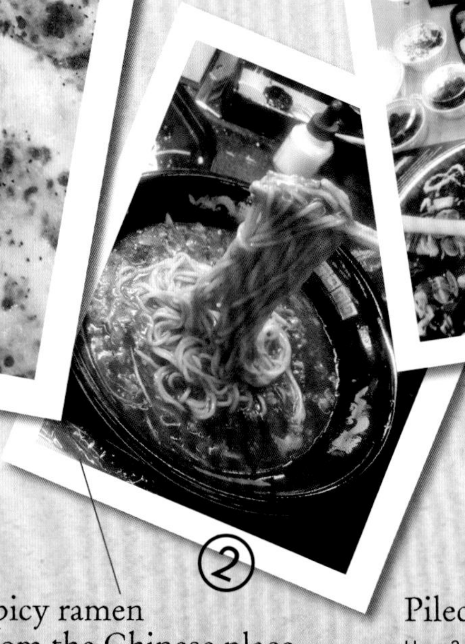

②

A big pizza party

Oooh, just look at all that heaping cheese. With packed boxes of fried chicken on the side, this is a feast any group of salty dogs can enjoy.

Spicy ramen from the Chinese place

I've got nothing against spicy food, but this one looks positively volcanic. The funny thing is that the broth's usually so good, you end up drinking it all anyway. The noodles are thick and chewy. There's nothing better to replenish your energy.

Piled plates of paella

Hmm? Is that clams and squid ink in the front, and seafood and bacon in the back? With this many options, you can keep eating without getting bored. Plus, rice sits in the stomach well, making it perfect for a workplace meal.

Curry with a variety of toppings

Katsu curry with rich breaded pork is a popular dish in Japan, but this one's got cheese and spinach resting on top too. One of the great features of curry is how versatile and customizable it is.

Pasta party with the whole studio

I love myself some spicy seafood pasta, and looking at this, it seems like Oda enjoys his pasta alla vongole and salmon roe. The tandoori chicken looks good, but it might not be enough for *my* crew.

⑥

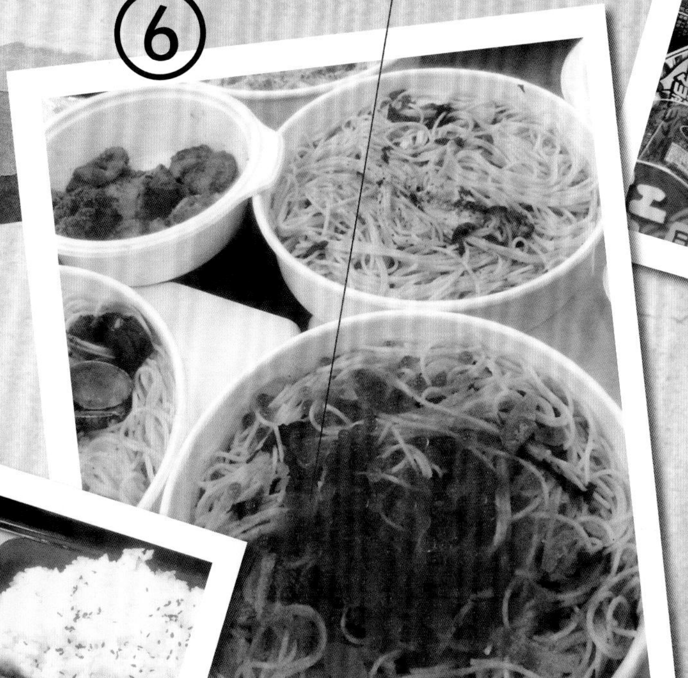

⑦

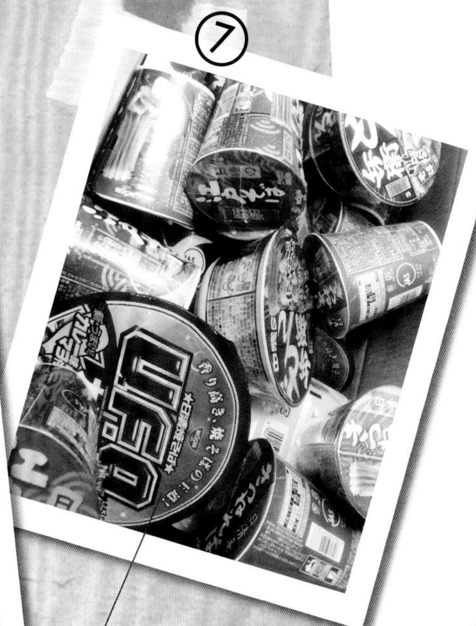

Gotta love cup noodles!

For whatever reason, sometimes you just get the craving for a cup of instant noodles. It's so quick and easy, it's perfect for a busy manga studio. But speaking as a cook...just remember to eat some fresh veggies every now and then.

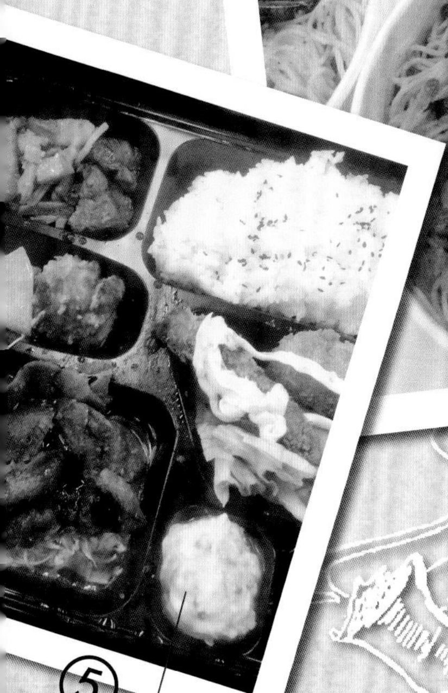

⑤

Yakiniku bento from a takeout place

Juicy yakiniku with a rich sauce on top. Plus there's fried shrimp, croquettes, deep-fried tofu, and even their famous potato salad. This is the king of stamina food.

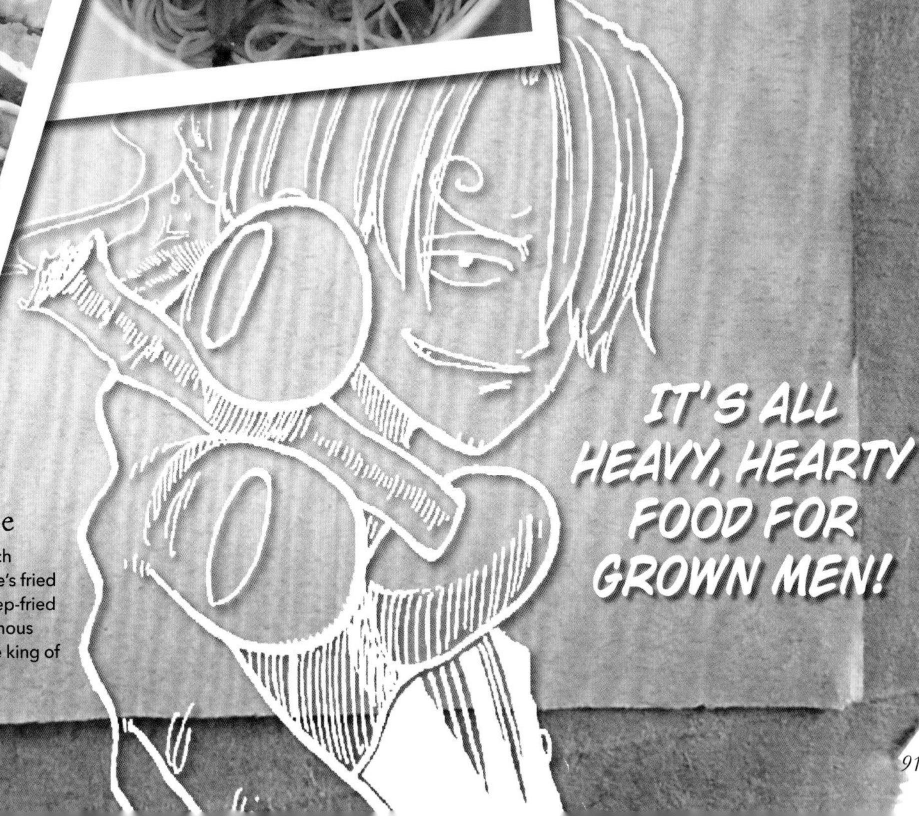
IT'S ALL HEAVY, HEARTY FOOD FOR GROWN MEN!

Sanji's Eye 3

LOOKS GREAT, AND PASSES THE NUTRITION TEST!!

Miso-style rice soup

This is a classic hot and mild soup served when you're feeling under the weather. It'll heat you right up. And with the tofu and egg added, you'll get plenty of nutrients.

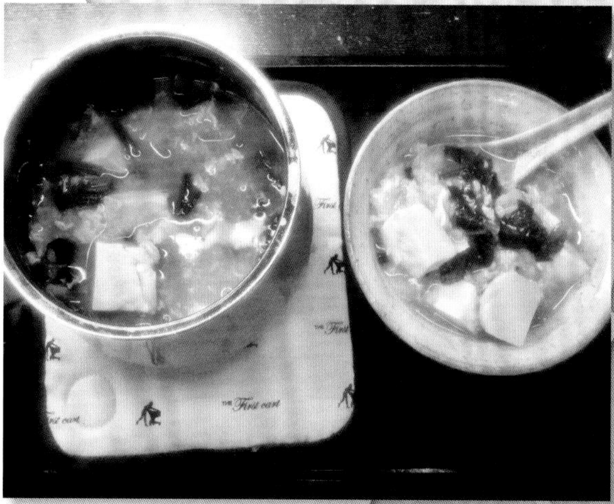

Custom bunny bath curry rice

Why, just look at that delightful arrangement. The bunny rabbit's soaking in the curry so comfortably, I almost feel bad about eating it...

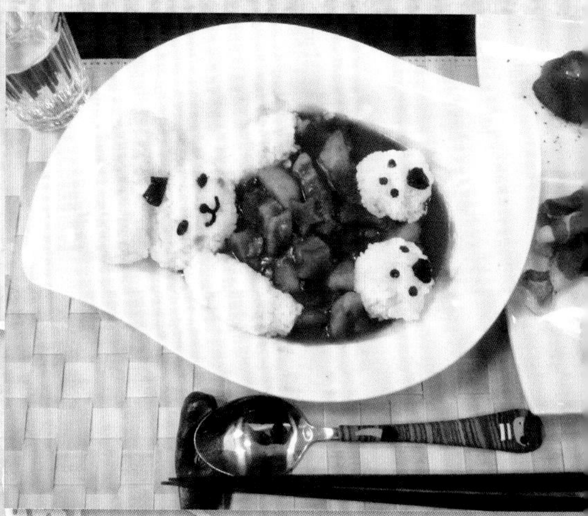

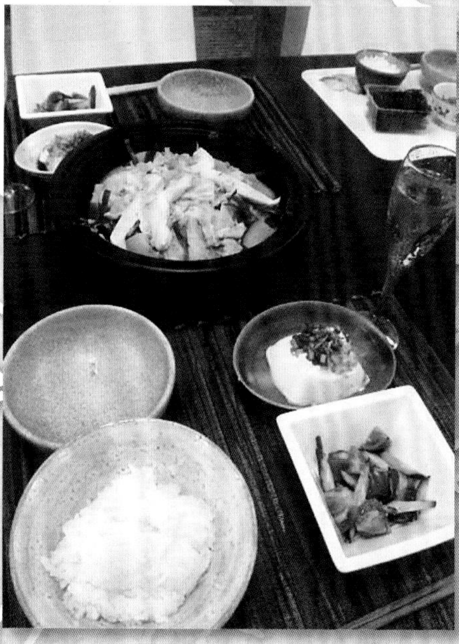

A tajine dish full of vegetables and chicken

That's a healthy-looking steamed dish. Leafy greens, squash, mushrooms—this'll give you that daily serving of vegetables. And with a soy sauce broth? Nice and low calorie.

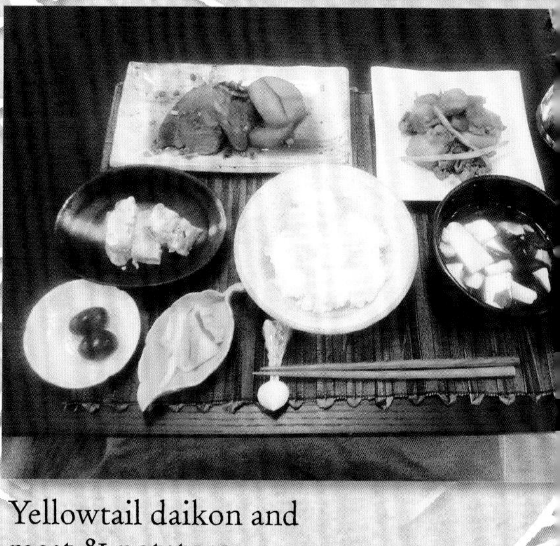

Yellowtail daikon and meat & potatoes

Just look at the beautiful color on those dishes. It's easy for them to crumble apart when you boil them, but these have good color and form. That rice is going to vanish real quick.

Home Cooking at the Oda House Paparazzi!

Lunch stew with bamboo shoots

This looks like a work lunch delivered to the studio. It's full of Oda's favorite meat and bamboo shoots. Like I always say when making food for ladies, the look of a dish is important too. This one's got great color and balance.

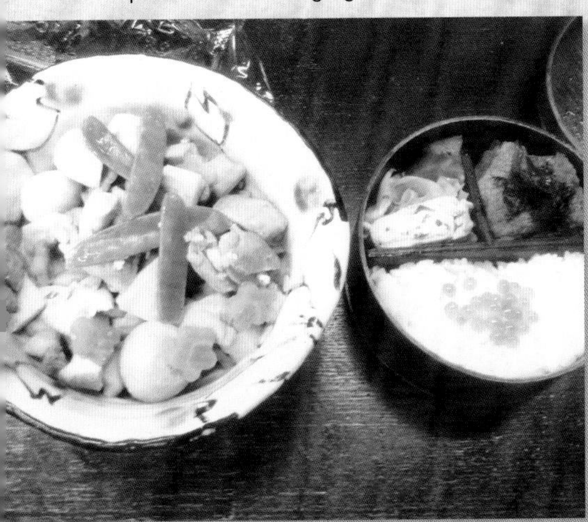

Dynamic flowing somen

What's this? Here's a fun setup. Let the noodles flow down the slide and grab them with your chopsticks! I bet our captain would love this. And there are two bowls of broth to eat them with, one hot and one cold? You're making me jealous.

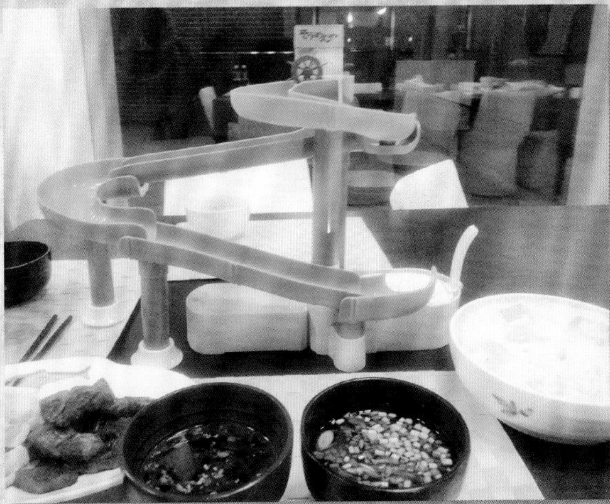

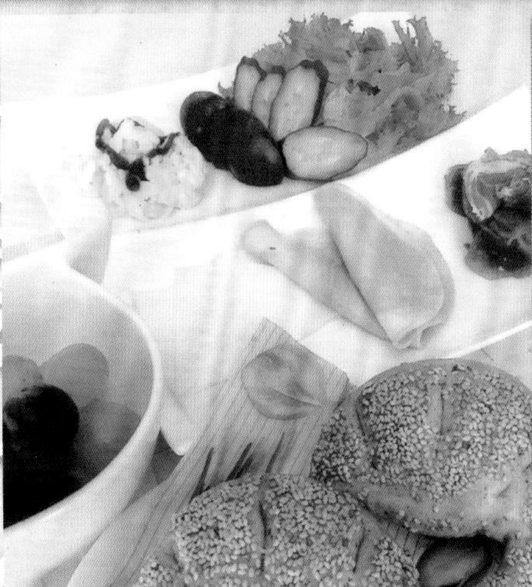

Sesame bread sandwiches

Fresh-baked bread with sesame seeds, fresh vegetables, ham, and fruit. I wish I could feed this to Nami and Robin. After a couple rich and heavy meals, there's nothing like a nice light sandwich like this.

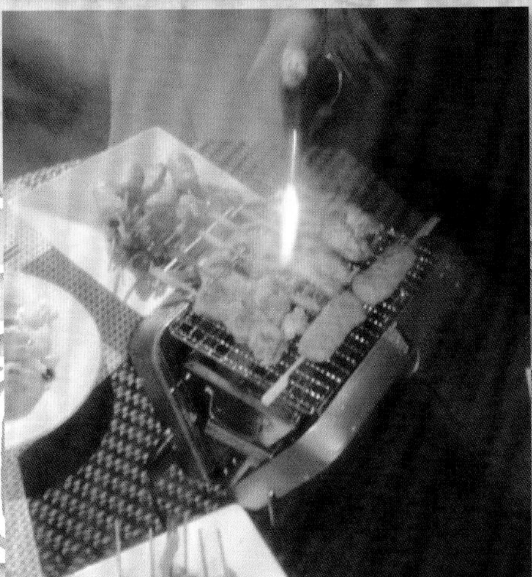

Legit! Yakitori on the grill

You gotta love yakitori cooked with charcoal. And seared from the top with a burner? That's hard-core. It's got chicken and onion skewers, chicken meatballs, and even Oda's favorite, tender tail meat. This would put any yakitori restaurant to shame.

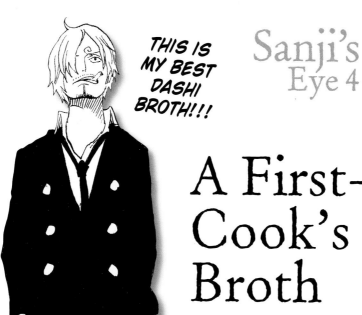

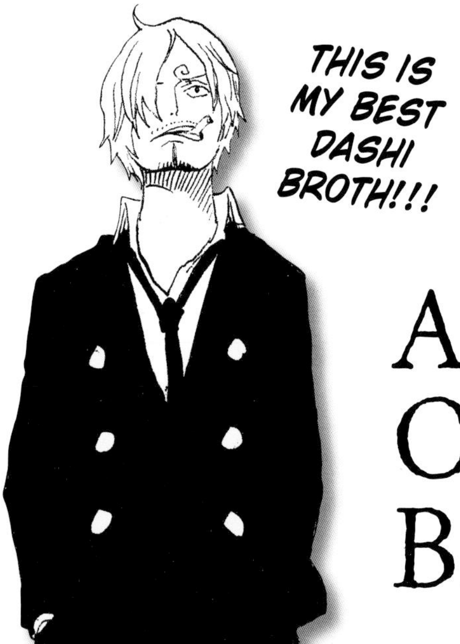
THIS IS MY BEST DASHI BROTH!!!

Sanji's Eye 4

A First-Class Cook's Basic Broth

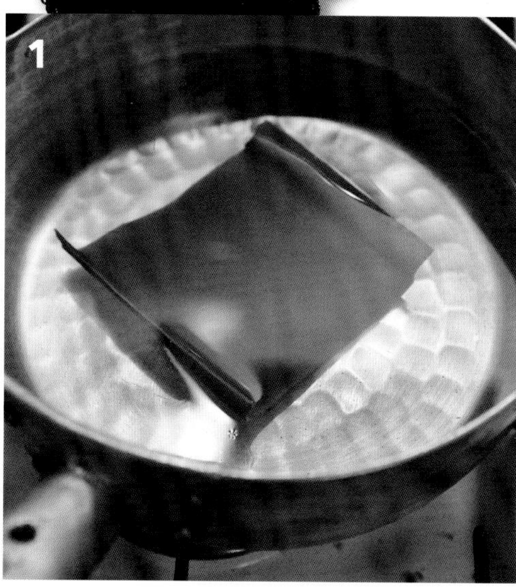
1

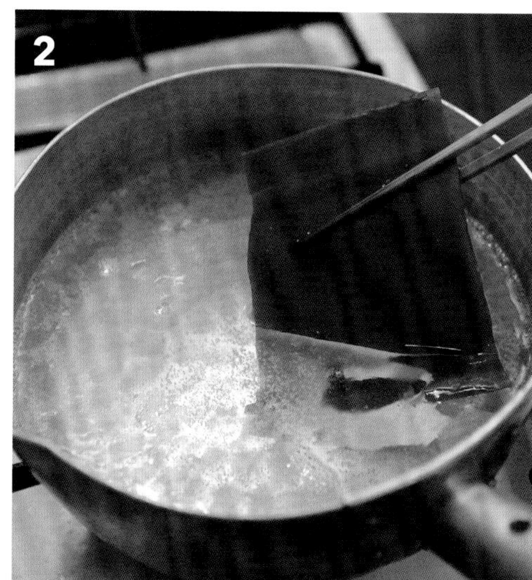
2

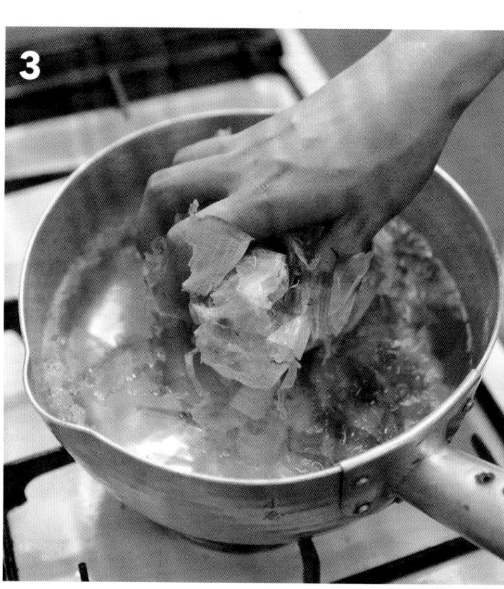
3

Kombu and Katsuobushi *Dashi* Broth

The inosinic acid from the katsuo and the glutamic acid from the kombu are major sources of rich umami flavor. This will last for two days in an airtight container in the refrigerator, and one week in the freezer.

INGREDIENTS Makes about 1 quart (1,000 ml)
5 cups (1,200 ml) water
1 sheet kombu (4x4 in./10x10 cm)
¾ oz. (20 g) katsuobushi

STEPS

① Let kombu steep in water for at least 30 minutes.

② Heat on medium. Remove kombu just before it begins to boil.

③ Toss in katsuobushi. When it has sunk to the bottom, filter liquid through a strainer.

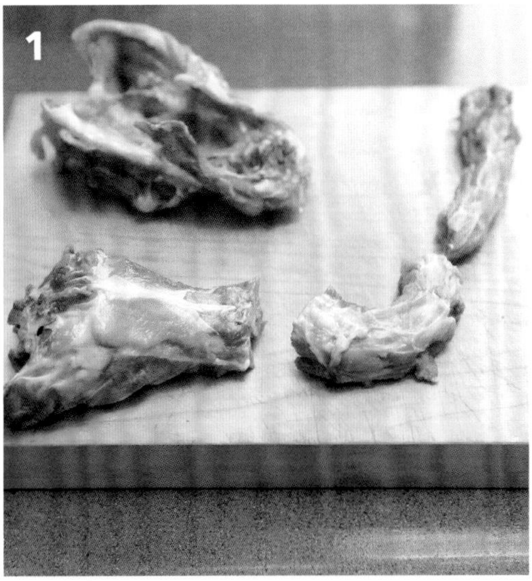
1
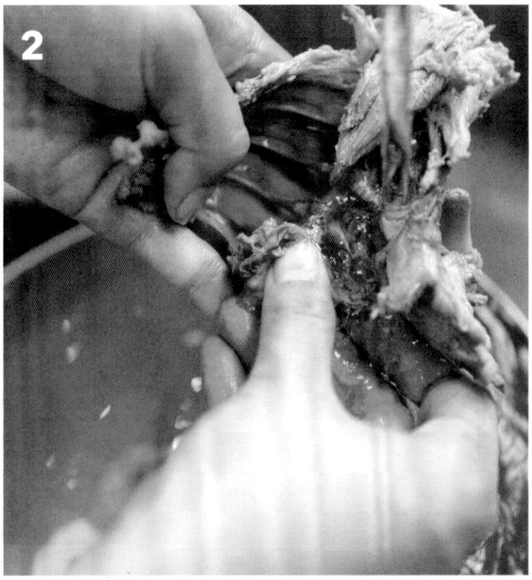
2
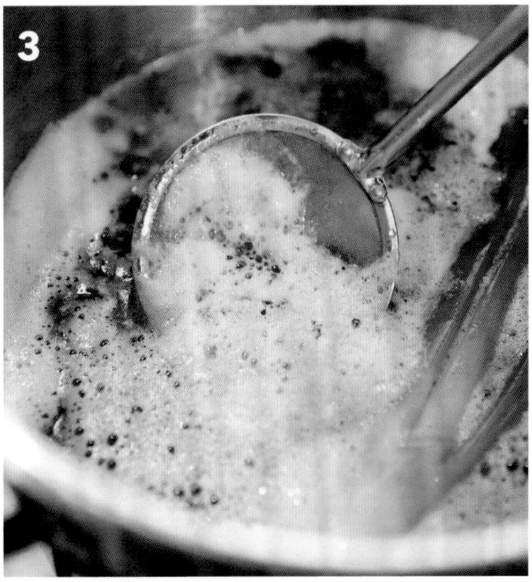
3
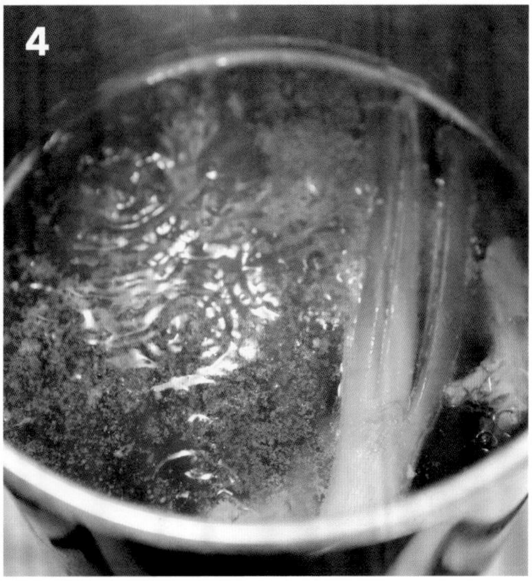
4
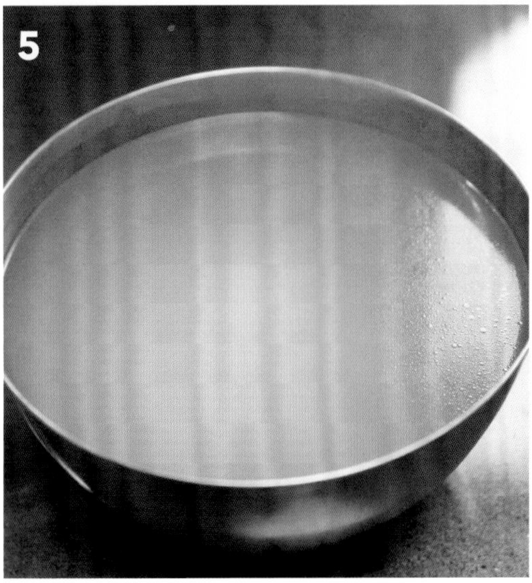
5

Chicken Stock

Use this broth as a base in curry or pot-au-feu to make it taste exponentially better. Lasts two days in the refrigerator, or one week frozen.

INGREDIENTS Makes about 2 ¾ quarts (2,600 ml)

2 chicken carcasses
12 ½ cups (3,000 ml) water, plus more for parboiling
5-6 oz. (150 g) vegetable scraps (green end of green onions, carrot peels, ginger, etc.)

STEPS

① Wash chicken frames and cut neck portion into three equal pieces.

② Boil a pot of water (not measured) and insert chicken. When surface becomes white, remove and rinse off blood and stains.

③ Place water (measured), chicken frames and vegetables into a pot on medium heat. When it boils, skim the top.

④ Simmer on low heat for 40-60 minutes.

⑤ When taste is right, strain through a sieve with cheesecloth on top.

COOKING SUPERVISOR
Nami Iijima

Nami Iijima is a food stylist from Tokyo, and handles food styling on commercials, advertisements, and movies such as *Kamome Diner*, *Midnight Diner*, and *Our Little Sister*. She is the author of several books, including *LIFE: Food for Nothing Days, Congratulations!* (Hobonichi), *Delicious Tales from the Island of Rice* (Gentosha), and *Sadako Sawamura's Menu: Dishes by Nami Iijima.*

ONE PIECE: PIRATE RECIPES

SHONEN JUMP EDITION

By Sanji

TRANSLATION: Stephen Paul

DESIGN: Alice Lewis

EDITORIAL ASSISTANCE: Luka M.

RECIPE TESTING: Jenn de la Vega

EDITOR: David Brothers

PHOTOGRAPHY: Keigo Saito

COOKING SUPERVISION & PRODUCTION/STYLING: Nami Iijima (7days kitchen)

COOKING ASSISTANCE: Umi Itai, Yuki Okamoto, Yumeka Misawa (7days kitchen)

ART DIRECTION & DESIGN: Naomi Murasawa (NAOMI DESIGN AGENCY)

LAYOUT ASSISTANT: Kyoko Miyazaki (NAOMI DESIGN AGENCY)

PROOFREADER: Mine Workshop

WRITER: Yukino Hirosawa (Recipes)

EDITORIAL ASSISTANCE: Isao Hagisawa, Genki Fujishita

ONE PIECE PIRATE RECIPES UMI NO ICHIRYU RYORININ SANJI NO MANPUKU GOHAN
© 2012 by Eiichiro Oda
All rights reserved.
First published in Japan in 2012 by SHUEISHA Inc., Tokyo.
English translation rights arranged by SHUEISHA Inc.

Library of Congress Control Number: 2021935444

Printed in China

Published by VIZ Media, LLC
P.O. Box 77010
San Francisco, CA 94107

10 9 8 7
First printing, November 2021
Seventh printing, January 2024

viz.com